POORLY
MADE IN
CHINA

POORLY MADE IN CHINA

AN INSIDER'S ACCOUNT OF THE CHINA PRODUCTION GAME

REVISED AND UPDATED

PAUL MIDLER

WILEY

John Wiley & Sons, Inc.

Published by John Wiley & Sons, Inc., Hoboken, New Jersey.
Published simultaneously in Canada.

For general information on our other products and services or for technical support, please
contact our Customer Care Department within the United States at (800) 762-2974, outside
the United States at (317) 572-3993 or fax (317) 572-4002.

Wiley also publishes its books in a variety of electronic formats. Some content that appears in
print may not be available in electronic books. For more information about Wiley products,
visit our web site at www.wiley.com.

Library of Congress Cataloging-in-Publication Data:

Midler, Paul, 1968–
   Poorly made in China : an insider's account of the China production
game / revised and updated by Paul Midler.
       p. cm.
   Includes index.
   ISBN 978-0-470-92807-3 (pbk); ISBN 978-1-118-00418-0 (ebk);
   ISBN 978-1-118-00419-7 (ebk); ISBN 978-1-118-00420-3 (ebk)
   1. Manufactures–China.   2. Work environment–China.   3. China–Economic
conditions–2000–   I. Title.
   HD9736.C62M53 2011
   338.4'7670951–dc22

                                                    2010047778

Printed in the United States of America.

10   9   8   7   6   5   4

It is better to know some of the questions than all of the answers.

—James Thurber

All war is based on deception: When able to attack, we must pretend to be incapable; When employing forces, we must seem inactive; When we are near, we must make the enemy believe we are far; Offer bait to lure him; If he appears humble, make him arrogant; If he is rested, wear him down; If his forces are united, divide them; Take action when it is unexpected.

—Sunzi (the strategist formerly known as Sun Tzu)

The first condition of right thought is right sensation—the first condition of understanding a foreign country is to smell it.

—T. S. Eliot

CONTENTS

FOREWORD

It is a long and crooked road that carries the merchandise we consume from the factory floors of China to store shelves in the United States. No maps are available for this road; there are no rules; contracts and agreements are not often honored; there are no police on the highways of commerce. The result of such system defects, not surprisingly, has been a long series of production scandals. Toxic melamine in milk products, poisonous lead paint on children's toys, and numerous other cases have made global headlines. In this vivid narrative, Paul Midler accompanies us down the twisted road of international trade, showing us what is wrong in China today by taking us through numberless, anonymous factories. He introduces us to many of the Western businessmen who have been drawn to China by the appeal of outsourcing. In the process, he reveals the perils of an economy that lacks transparency; he shows us how sharp the Chinese are, and not least, how willfully gullible Americans can be. For me, as a China specialist of more than thirty years, it is one of those rare books amid shelves filled with distorted hype or doom that elicits, "Yes! That's actually what it is like."

Midler is an agent for hire, a go-between who makes his living by connecting American importers with Chinese suppliers, and he monitors arrangements made in an attempt to be sure something like satisfaction is achieved. American executives have little, if any, appetite for the tedious and opaque transactions, and so his role as middleman, dealmaker, and inspection agent is indispensable to many. Through many years of seemingly mundane negotiations over products like ceramic pots, scaffolding, and architectural hardware (to name but a few of the goods in which he has dealt and which he describes here), he has acquired deep knowledge of China and its export economy.

His insights take us to the heart of Chinese society in a way that few accounts do; they are the real treasure in his book. Midler is at home in China. That, and not somewhere else, is where his life is. His living depends on having a working knowledge of how to get things done in that place, something even most professional China specialists lack. Such a working understanding has not been confined to limited product categories or to the obscure precincts where these certain products can be found. Rather, by its nature, such knowledge must be comprehensive. What works in business works in other areas of life as well, from friendships to politics.

So we must read Midler's book on two levels. At first, *Poorly Made in China* seems to be an engrossing, picaresque account of his endless adventures and misadventures among merchants, Chinese and foreign, each intent on getting the better of the other. The primary narrative arc here is the author's attempt to manufacture soap and shampoo for American discount store chains. That is not a compelling premise perhaps, but the story has the drama of a suspense novel. The narrative seesaws back and forth, pivoting on minor issues in manufacturing like the mysterious thinning of plastic bottles used to package cheap shampoo. The factory in this case is bemused by its customer's attempts to insist on fundamental things such as consistent product specifications. Meanwhile, the American importer in this tale goes nearly insane worrying that the importation of one faulty piece of product may cost him millions in lost contracts.

As a tour guide in China many years ago, I experienced numerous instances of unscrupulous and frustrating behavior, along the lines of what Midler describes in this book, and I even found myself reflecting on historical references, as well. Analogies can be drawn to government fiscal and monetary arrangements made between foreign countries and China, and even treaty negotiations are of a piece. If you have Midler's concrete knowledge, many mysteries of China can be cracked. If you do not, you will find yourself at sea, drifting rapidly away from the destination you had in mind.

At this second level, Midler's book is not so much a business book about China—though for any trader it is must reading—as it is a description, told through the language of commerce to be sure, of how China as a whole works, with some hard-earned insights about how to navigate its confusing currents and cross-currents.

In this swift narrative, we meet a cast of real-life characters. "Sister" Zhen is the enigmatic owner of the health and beauty care company from which Bernie, a Syrian-Jewish importer from New York, hopes to purchase shampoo and related beauty care products for the discount chains stores of America. Sister is a Chinese woman driven to achieve, and her ambition matches her cunning. She is engaging to know, yet almost impossible to know well. She exhibits tremendous savvy at cutting Bernie's already exiguous margin by introducing last-minute price increases. When her customer points to an agreement already in place, the same tough woman who has driven a brutal bargain is now seen tugging at Midler's sleeve and coquettishly appealing to the deep relationship between her factory and her client's business.

Students of Chinese history may recall the Washington Conference (1920–21), which was meant to resolve a number of security issues in the Pacific. The delegate representing the United States stayed up half the night with his Chinese counterpart, whom he counted a good friend, and tried to reach compromises on numerous issues, only to be excoriated mercilessly the following day in the general session as a blood-sucking and duplicitous imperialist. Progress was somehow made in the talks and some rather good treaties were actually signed, but it is remarkable how these two opposing approaches somehow coexisted in Chinese negotiations. Midler does an excellent job of revealing these cultural nuances, and his book provides lessons for all who deal with China.

In this book, we meet many American businessmen driven by greed but limited by their naïveté. Arriving in China, they know nothing except what they have heard, that it is the place to be, and, softened by China's red-carpet treatment, they reflect numerous hollow clichés on modern China: this is the world's fastest growing economy; this is the future; our company must expand here or else it will perish—and perhaps most importantly of all, that doing business in China is easy. There are no pesky unions or state regulations to speak of, after all; the barriers to doing business are surprisingly low. You talk directly with the boss, shake hands, and the deal is done. As if by magic, your company's catalogue is suddenly filled with new and astonishingly inexpensive merchandise.

This is fantasy, of course, and it is the sort of mirage shared not only by businessmen, but also by politicians. President Richard Nixon and his adviser Henry Kissinger knew next to nothing about China, but nevertheless assigned it a central role in their diplomatic strategy. All seemed to go well on their first visit to the Middle Kingdom: the Chinese fascinated their foreign visitors with a seeming sophistication and factual command. Rough spots were there, of course, as when Nixon presented to Chinese leader Mao Zedong his hope for a panoramic view of the world, considering not only the bilateral relationship between the two countries, but also dynamics involving India, Japan, the Soviet Union, and all powers in between. Mao slapped Nixon down, suggesting that his idea was boring and unimportant. Expectations of the two sides in these landmark talks were clearly different, and so diplomatic documents agreed upon then were necessarily kept vague, to the point almost of meaninglessness. The relationship between Beijing and Washington has been as complex and strained as the relationship between U.S. importers and their Chinese suppliers.

The Chinese display extraordinary skill at manipulating foreign perceptions and feelings, as we see in this book, and they also play on foreign apprehensiveness on the issue of raising meaningful questions. When visiting the shampoo factory for the first time, Midler is put through a rigmarole of careful hand washing, the donning of sterile scrubs and caps, and so forth, before going on to the factory floor. It is all very impressive, professional looking, and confidence inducing. Midler instinctively holds his tongue on his maiden tour, and later learns that once the contracts are signed and funds have been transferred, these rituals fall by the wayside and are no longer practiced. Midler's book is in part an awakening to the realization that so much of what goes on in China is façade. Through a business fable that entertains and educates, he allows us to see past that front.

I remember once accompanying a former speaker of the House of Representatives on a trip to China. Though I thought I had seen it all, I have never experienced such elaborate courtesy. Our chauffeured vehicles were preceded and followed by police cars complemented with flashing lights and sirens. It was an empty display, yet it did wonders for the egos of those who were in our entourage.

On the trip, specially designated gates were opened on certain streets, so as to allow us the chance to inspect immaculate precincts of a "peach blossom spring," or Chinese Eden. These were picture-perfect quarters undreamed of by ordinary Chinese citizens. They were party compounds reserved for the elite. The lawns inside the compounds were impeccable; soothing fountains played; our rooms were cool, quiet, and equal in comfort to the best that the West has to offer. Our hosts seemed to anticipate our every wish; the food was magnificent. Yet what did we really see of China?

Cocooned in such hospitality, it was not surprising that the American delegation proved docile. Questioning was softball, with all of us visitors feeling the onus not to spoil things by embarrassing our hosts. The only rough spot in the official visit came when I posed what I thought was an interesting question to the foreign minister. Mongolia, I pointed out, is a possession of the former Qing dynasty (1644–1912) that China now recognizes as an independent state. At the same time, Taiwan, which the Qing held only briefly and partially, is hotly argued as belonging absolutely to China today. How do we explain this seeming contradiction?

The foreign minister became angry and dismissed my question as being without merit. I felt a tinge of guilt for having ruffled feathers on the trip, but then I thought: What are high officials supposed to do if not answer difficult questions? The rest of the group believed that I had overstepped the bounds of good manners, but make no mistake—the minister had understood me exactly and later sent a colleague, who spent more than two hours, trying to explain the political point.

This sort of incident is typical of so many Sino-American interchanges, whether the issues be about dollar-store shampoo or national security. American delegations feel obliged to constrain questioning and to tip toe around the very issues they should be discussing. Politeness is all well and good, but what does an inherent lack of openness say about the hope of increasing economic and political ties between the United States and China?

One of the more disturbing aspects of this book is evidence of companies not delivering on the promises they make. Chinese contracts are subject to indefinite renegotiation, as anyone knows. American buyers who expect their product to be manufactured properly find that their samples are taken only as rough guides, or suggestions. Manufacturers make unilateral changes to the goods without discussion and hope that no one will notice. At one point in the story, after the shampoo factory unexpectedly alters many of the contracted fragrances to a generic almond scent and is caught, Sister offers nothing but ingenuous excuses about how to her the cheaper substitute seemed to smell all right.

I once renovated a bathroom in a rambling Edwardian house in the city of Providence, Rhode Island. I strove to reconstruct features as they would have been when the house was built. As a part of the project, I installed a complex brass bath faucet and shower nozzle, with period black-on-white enamel labels (for "hot" and "cold"). The apparatus, which was made in China, had been masterfully copied in the correct style, but I suspect it must have been the ruin of any number of American and British plumbing suppliers. All worked fine for about six months. Then the faucet assembly began to fall apart— the shower hose unraveled, the valves became loose, the whole thing just went to pieces. The product had been "poorly made in China." Its eventual replacement was a characterless, late-twentieth-century American fixture, which spoiled the effect I was seeking, but at least it delivered a good bath.

This book is not merely about faltering product quality out of China. One of its broader themes is of people who promise one thing and then deliver another. This is a book about Chinese obfuscation and subterfuge. It is about gaming, strategy, and tactics.

It reminded me of many important issues facing U.S.-China relations, and in particular it had me recalling the year 1982 and the negotiation then of U.S. arms supplies to Taiwan. The key to the talks then was the claim by the Chinese that their "fundamental" policy toward Taiwan was to remain peaceful towards the island. The American side took this as a renunciation of force and agreed to limit future arms sales. Had the U.S. side understood the Chinese language better, they would have realized that, in Mandarin, a "fundamental principle" is typically meant to suggest the preface to an exception. Like the French *en principe*, the Chinese statement that "fundamentally" something is held as a value is not so much meant to assure as to hint at what rule is about to be broken (owing to special circumstances, naturally). And just look at what China has done. Although the nation's policy is supposedly peaceful, China's arms buildup in recent years has been without precedent in scale and scope.

The prognosis for a rising China may be negative, but this is not necessarily a negative book. Midler clearly has a deep, if indirectly expressed, affection for China and its people. No one can attain an understanding of such a complex culture without an affinity for the place. Midler has lived in China for many years; he gets around easily in the language, and in fact he has no other home. Nor, it seems, does he want another. With his graduate training at an elite business school, he could have become a financier on Wall Street. His many years spent preparing himself for a career in China might have been applied toward subjects such as chemistry and biology, and with the same time spent he might have made a contribution to science instead. But he settled on a path in China, and by doing so he has made it possible for us to understand the place just a little better.

One can learn a lot about how the whole of China works by mastering one corner of it, for institutional and behavioral patterns do not change much whether your workplace is a cruise ship for tourists or a factory that makes shampoo and similar products. Knowledge and instinct are transferrable. That is why I hope this book will find an audience, not only in the business community, but also among diplomats, scholars, and others dealing with China, as well as among ordinary people who want to know what China is really like, at ground level.

Arthur Waldron
Lauder Professor of International Relations
University of Pennsylvania
Bryn Mawr, Pennsylvania

INTRODUCTION

This book started as an article written for the Wharton School of Business during the quality crisis of 2007. This was the year in which pets were found poisoned with melamine, tires made in China began falling apart, and American parents worried about lead paint in their children's toys. The piece that I wrote was in part a rebuttal to the claim made then that U.S. importers were somehow to blame for failures of products coming out of China. Having worked with Chinese manufacturers for many years, I had a slightly different understanding of the situation. The way I saw it, American companies were doing the best they could, but they were no match for savvy Chinese industrialists who often went out of their way to manipulate product specifications to widen profit margins.

Chinese factory owners played games. They delivered customers a quality product at the start of a project and over time withdrew key ingredients (or else they substituted inferior inputs for quality ones). Changes made to merchandise were never announced, and alterations were typically imperceptible to buyers. The incremental degradation was subtle and continuous, and importers had no idea what was being done until the products they represented failed. I called it "quality fade," and it was meant to be a partial explanation for why quality seemed to be heading south all at once, and across so many sectors.

Outside of China, few knew that this sort of thing went on, and much of the response from U.S. readers of the article was genuine surprise. But those who worked in the industry knew better, and insiders suggested that I hadn't gone far enough. "Your stories about quality out of China are nothing," I was told. "You should hear what happened to *us!*"

The disparate responses to the article—the confirmation from industry types on one end and the incredulity on the other—led me to believe that an expansion of the original piece might be worthwhile. I'd never written anything longer than an article before; nevertheless, I was offered a book contract. The more I wrote, the more I realized there were other things to say on the subject of China in general.

The book you hold in your hands is little more than a few stories, anecdotes collected from a career spent in a foreign country. Work episodes were chosen for their entertainment value; at the same time, I was careful to select scenes that I thought were representative of the experience.

It may be worth noting that when I first arrived in China, I had no preconceived notions. At the outset I was, in fact, something of an optimist. Over time, though, certain experiences caused me to develop other opinions, and I eventually found a framework. When I set out to write *Poorly Made in China,* my thinking went like this: If I could show some of what I had seen, perhaps others might also arrive at the same place.

When asked to summarize this book, I tend to take the easy way out by suggesting it may be simply about how culture matters. Culture can impact an economy's macroeconomic development—China's rise has undoubtedly been helped by certain cultural elements—and, on a smaller scale, culture (and the understanding of culture) can facilitate or impede success at transaction level. The book at the very least helps dispel a notion promoted by some that doing business in China is like doing business anywhere else in the world.

One complaint that I've heard voiced about this book is that while it highlights a number of problems related to China, it doesn't offer any solutions. I find it curious that some are willing to accept a book on a cultural theme only as long as it comes prepackaged with answers from the author. No matter what problems China faces, or what problems the rest of the world must now deal with, we can't arrive at solutions except through dialogue—and we can't have meaningful dialogue before we have some basic understanding of the issues. This book might be seen as little more than an introduction. It was never meant to be a final word of any kind, but a beginning.

POORLY MADE IN CHINA

CHAPTER 1

Vanishing Act

China manufactured everything in the world, and along with it, every imaginable smell. Walking through its many factories, you could catch some of those smells: the heady fumes from adhesives used to make leather shoes, the nutty scents of ceramic vases as they were baked in gas-fired kilns, the sour notes of polypropylene plastics as they melted and were injected at high temperatures. Each manufacturing process was its own olfactory experience, and if you worked in export manufacturing long enough, you might be able to guess the kind of factory you were standing in by using your nose alone.

During the years I worked in South China, I visited more types of factories than I ever imagined could exist. Oddly enough, while the impact on the senses was strong, occasionally bludgeoning, I rarely met a factory owner who was bothered in the least by the smells.

At one sinus-punishing factory, I stood at the gates with the boss, looking out over a field blanketed in a white haze. Some distance behind us, workers were dipping stainless steel tubes into a chemical bath. It was a nickel-plating process. I could actually taste the metal in my mouth, and my nose involuntarily wrinkled.

"*Hao chou,*" I said. "What a stink." As soon as the words left my mouth, I regretted making the comment, though I half expected the factory boss would agree.

He tossed away his cigarette and turned in my direction. "You foreigners," he said. "You come to China and complain about the pollution, but I don't know why." He then gestured at the blurred landscape around us. "To me, this place smells like money."

For many in China who dreamed of a better life, those winds of industry correlated with better economic opportunities, and the poorer corners of China, the ones that smelled fresh or of nothing much at all, were not envied, but pitied.

Wherever my factory work took me, I always paid attention to the various odors, mainly because of my first project. The factory made what the Chinese called *daily use chemicals*—consumer products like soap, shampoo, and hand creams.

The factory, King Chemical, was located in the countryside, at the foot of a large hill. Heading toward the plant on a bright, sunny day, with the fragrance of health and beauty care products filling the air, I thought: *so, this is what a sweatshop smells like.* The sweet and floral fragrance was immediately recognizable. You smelled it at the bank and at the grocery store, everywhere really. It was the common scent that perfumed soaps and shampoos across South China.

The factory was run by a small, attractive woman who insisted that I call her by her nickname, Zhen Jie.

It was a familiar term—*Zhen* was her last name, and *Jie* signified her as an "older sister." She said that she had the workers call her by this name because she wanted to be seen as someone that her workers might look up to and admire.

"Sister" Zhen explained that her husband could not join us on the tour because he was out of town on business. Instead, a small entourage of managers came along.

"Here. You must wear this before we go inside." She handed me a white lab coat and gave me cloth coverings for my shoes, making sure that I put them on before slipping a pair of coverings over her black, high-heeled boots.

These precautions were all about maintaining a hygienic environment, Sister explained. Chinese manufacturers did not commonly concern themselves with cleanliness, but it was a critical concern in the health and beauty care industry. Hygiene had also come up in my conversation with Bernie, who had sent me on this unusual assignment.

Before identifying this one company as a supplier, Bernie had tried to manufacture his product line in another location with disastrous results. A large shipment was contaminated with bacteria, resulting in significant losses to his company. This sort of thing, he warned, could not happen again.

The rituals of preparation created anticipation, and I was anxious to get onto the factory floor. Through a glass window, I could see most of what awaited. The place was busy, and I noticed that the workers inside were also dressed in white.

We washed our hands next. The managers who joined the tour lined up at a row of sinks. They took turns at the basins. In their white lab coats, scrubbing all the way up to their elbows, they looked like a team of doctors heading into surgery.

Scrubbed up now, I took a step toward the door, but a hand stopped me. Someone plonked a white cap on my head. In a final dash of ceremony, the doors to the plant were flung open and held wide while we passed through.

The factory was a hive of activity, and as someone not familiar with this kind of operation, I strained to grasp how things worked. The workers were busy making a hand lotion, I saw, and I watched as pink bottles moved down the assembly line. Some workers filled the bottles, while others either capped them or wiped them down. I asked if I could take a closer look at the finished product and was handed a bottle from a packed carton. The printing on the bottle was in Chinese. The company manufactured health and beauty care products for the domestic market. Bernie's company was going to be its first export customer.

As we walked down one assembly line, heads that were already bowed low bent further at our approach, the pace of work noticeably quickening. Wherever we hovered, workers seemed to hold their breath. Everyone in our small entourage was either oblivious to the fact that we were causing the workers to become anxious, or else they did not care.

I watched one young woman with short hair take a bottle off the conveyor belt. She wiped it down in an almost obsessive fashion and refused to pass it along until she had another in hand to replace it. I tried to make eye contact with the workers, but none would allow it.

Even those who were less flustered by the tour seemed conscious of being observed.

One worker, who screwed caps onto bottles, did so with an added flourish. Next to her stood a worker whose job it was to place the bottles into cardboard cartons. Instead of tossing the bottles into the box, she was cradling each with two hands—almost in the same respectful manner that the Chinese offer a business card.

The man who had asked me to make this visit was an importer who knew only that I lived in China. We had met in passing and only once; I received his phone call out of the blue, and his instructions to me had been vague.

"Have a good look around," Bernie said. He wanted me to remark on anything that seemed out of the ordinary. Not noticing anything so unusual, I pretended to have some questions.

"How many workers do you employ?" I asked.

Sister nodded as if it were the right question.

"Two hundred," she said.

I had not counted, but there seemed to be fewer than that many workers around. "When did the workers take their breaks?" I asked next. Sister said that they broke for lunch and dinner. I asked how many days off they got each month. She said that most got only one day off every other weekend.

Running out of questions, I told her that the factory was impressive. Sister complimented my Mandarin and said that Bernie was lucky to have found me. She hoped that we would work together beyond the one visit, and she went so far as to suggest that there was much she could learn from someone like me. While new to the world of manufacturing, I had already lived in China for a number of years, and this much at least I understood about the place: when you said nice things, you received unbounded compliments in return.

So much of the factory work was done by hand and, I noticed, sometimes by foot. We walked over to a station where hand cream was being pumped into bottles. The machine had been set up so that its operator could activate it by a pedal on the floor. When triggered, a pressurized squirt nozzle filled the bottle with formulation. The worker who sat at the station did not seem very good at the timing involved though, because the front of her uniform was covered in lotion—presumably from missing her mark.

I paused for a moment and watched more closely as the worker filled bottles. It seemed that she had been recently trained because there was something missing from her performance. It was more than nerves, I thought. It was as if she was doing the job for the very first time.

Just then, I felt the pressure of a hand at my elbow. It was Sister indicating it was time to leave.

This gesture of hers was a bit forward, I thought, but instead of misinterpreting the squeeze as something personal, I took it for what it was—a desire to end the visit. I had flown from another city to visit this factory, and the tour had not lasted very long at all. I had the feeling of coming off an amusement park ride that had ended too quickly. No sooner had I begun to get a sense of the factory than the exit doors were opened and we were again standing in sunlight.

"We will take you to the airport," said Sister.

She then brought me to a waiting room near her office, and I was given a cup of instant green tea. After sitting in the waiting room for a while, I wondered whether I had been forgotten. Workers came and went, and no one paid me any mind. I looked over my notes and realized that I had few impressions, none of them well formed. When someone came along to tell me that the driver was running late, I took it to mean that they were not sure where he was.

Still curious about the factory, I thought I might go back to have one last look. No one would probably even notice that I had gone, and maybe there was something to be gleaned from seeing workers when they were less self-conscious about being watched by their managers.

The factory was just behind the office and up a small incline. There was no one outside, only the sound of a slight breeze coming down the hillside. It was a peaceful and bucolic setting. I thought if this factory visit turned into some kind of regular assignment with Bernie, I wouldn't mind.

When I got to the plant, I went over to a window and pressed my face against the glass. For a moment I figured I might have been lost. *Was I at the wrong building?*

I looked through the window again. It seemed to be the right place, but the factory was deserted. Where before there had been around 50 or 60 workers, now there was only an old man with a broom in hand. He spotted me at the window and started toward the front door, as if to let me in, but then he did a rethink, turned, and hurried out a rear door instead.

What in the hell is going on?

With my forehead near the glass, I glanced down at my watch. It was just past three. Chinese factories did not have the tradition of an afternoon siesta, and Sister had already mentioned that the factory broke only for lunch and then at dinnertime.

I heard the sound of heels clicking on the pavement behind me. What at first seemed like not such a bad idea was quickly turning into a situation. I felt guilty all of a sudden, as though caught doing something illicit, putting my nose in where it didn't belong.

What excuse could I possibly offer, and how would I address the matter of what I was seeing—or, rather, what I was not seeing? Out of sheer embarrassment, someone might have to get upset about me wandering off.

The sound of fast-approaching heels grew louder until it was no longer possible to act like I could not hear them.

Clack-clack-clack-clack.

I turned around, expecting the worst. Instead of an angry expression, Sister was forcing a smile, one that widened as she approached until it appeared more like a wince. She reached me slightly out of breath.

"The workers are resting," she said.

It was a conversation stopper, like when someone in America said they were off to run an errand. You weren't meant to ask what kind. The very notion of rest was sacrosanct in China, and then saying something like that to a foreigner gave it an additional weight. Chinese have worked hard for thousands of years. If someone said they needed a breather, no further explanation was necessary.

"Let's go back," Sister said and quietly led the way.

Trying to process what had just happened, I felt as though I had been to a magic show and seen a large elephant disappear. Where the workers had gone was a mystery. They were nowhere to be seen, and there was nothing to do but rub my eyes and wonder how—or why—it had been done. *How could a factory be in full swing one moment and gone the next?*

That evening, I telephoned Bernie. I was apprehensive. Surely, nothing like such a vanishing act ever happened in America, and telling him about it would probably only succeed in making me appear foolish. At the very least, it would make me the bearer of bad news.

I decided that I would report on the factory visit—but only in a general way. There were other details to provide. I would tell him all about the visit, but I would leave out the last part since I was not supposed to have seen it anyway.

"Did they seem busy?" he asked.

It was just about the only thing that he was interested in discussing—the general busyness of the place. I decided to tell him about the very end of the trip in detail. He not only believed what happened, but he laughed about it. He had been to the factory himself several weeks earlier and suspected that a similar show had been put on for him, as well.

He was not at all worried. Quite the opposite, he said that what I was reporting was good news. I told him I didn't understand. What happened earlier that day troubled me, and I thought: *Any factory that was willing to go to such great lengths to pretend it was busy probably had a few other tricks up its sleeve.*

Bernie did not see it that way, though. He figured if business was that slow and they were trying that hard, then it would translate into favorable pricing for his company.

It was interesting to me how Bernie viewed things differently than I might have. He saw what the factory had done as somewhat flattering. If they were so motivated, he might also benefit from the company's undivided attention, which might also mean better quality.

"Tell me, was the warehouse full?"

"The warehouse?"

Bernie had not specifically asked about the warehouse before my visit, but it had been a part of the tour. I told him that I remembered it being rather empty.

He asked me to estimate the number of pallets, and I told him that there could not have been more than 50 or so.

"Fantastic," he said. "They're desperate for my business."

CHAPTER 2

Trouble Is
My Business

After graduating from business school in 2001, I returned to China, the place where I had already spent the majority of my career. One reason for feeling drawn back to the place was personal—I was at home in Asia—but there was also a business reason. The global economy was experiencing a tectonic shift, and China's economy was growing like no other. By being there, I felt that I was placing myself at the center of a unique, perhaps even historic, time and place.

I had studied Chinese history and language as an undergraduate, and while working towards an MBA at Wharton, I picked up an additional degree in East Asian business. It seemed natural that I would return to China. I had worked there for a number of years, and I even spoke the language. While my background should have prepared me for what was happening in export manufacturing, my first real glimpse of the sector suggested that I was in uncharted territory.

Exports contributed significantly to the Chinese economic miracle, and yet, none of the courses in business school or informal discussions had been about this interesting and important part of the new economy. My classmates had gone off to pursue traditional careers in investment banking, management consulting, or private equity. Coming from a finance background, I had nearly gone down a similar road myself.

I wanted to settle in South China, where manufacturing was concentrated, and I was looking for any excuse to get involved. Lucky for me, I didn't have to look all that far.

As little as I knew about the production landscape, there were many others who knew even less. Small and medium-size American importers were streaming into the marketplace, and I was recognized as someone who could help them with their businesses.

American importers contacted me, but typically, they only did so after their projects had begun to fall apart, after they had tried and exhausted other options. One reason they waited to ask for help was hubris, but also, as I would later come to understand, Chinese manufacturers were in the habit of making things look easy.

In any event, importers who contacted me were often at the end of their rope. They were desperate, and at times I felt like Philip Marlowe from one of Raymond Chandler's detective stories. I had no office with a pebbled-glass front door, but clients made their way to me in a similarly random manner. They were looking for help navigating China's "mean streets."

China was, to borrow a phrase, a world gone wrong, and the work was easy to get; it was just lying around. I had no real job description. I took care of things that needed handling. Typically called on after everything had unraveled, I was asked to put things back on track, to smooth things out, to make things right. Clients called and kept the details to themselves. "I got a job for you," was how it usually started, and without realizing it, I was soon knee deep in it. Trouble was my business.

I didn't know how long I would work these projects, but I figured it would be a while. My plan was to take whatever work came my way, and rather than deal with one or two large companies, I would assist a larger number of small and medium-size importers. The idea of diversity held some appeal because I was trying to give myself an education.

By getting involved with smaller companies, I could gain from a broader experience involving varied industries. I would have more data points, as it were, and this would offer a better sense of what was going on in this enigmatic, but important, part of the global economy. Perhaps at the end of it all, I figured, I might even draw a few conclusions.

After the soap and shampoo project kicked off, I received a call from Howard, a businessman who dealt in home furnishings.

Howard had a project that had gone swimmingly for a number of months, but then his supplier had gone incommunicado. He had never actually been to China himself, which added to his panic, but then he had never felt the need to go there. The business had been effortless. Then, one week, when he was about to place an order, the manufacturer vanished. Howard could not get anyone to return his phone calls or his email messages. This one was a missing persons case.

South China manufacturers, for whatever reason, had an aversion to the telephone. They were not particularly good with written forms of communication either. Given the incredible volumes of business these factories were doing with foreign importers of China-made goods, it was a particularly inexplicable quirk.

Howard thought the worst when his supplier could not be reached, but I told him not to worry, not just yet. It took a few tries, but eventually I found Kevin, the owner of the company. While I had succeeded in getting Kevin to the phone, he remained apprehensive and would not offer information regarding Howard's case.

At Howard's insistence, I asked Kevin if it would be all right if I stopped by his factory.

"Be my guest."

"How about Tuesday afternoon?"

"Just call me when you're in town."

"But it's a two-hour drive. Do you mind if we say Tuesday?"

"Give me a call when you arrive."

It was another one of their endearing habits: manufacturers in South China didn't like to set appointments either. They preferred to be spontaneous. They didn't like to commit to anything. Getting pinned down to a specific time and place meant that an industrialist might miss out on a more important opportunity. It meant the possibility of regret.

I hired a car on a Tuesday and traveled to the factory, which was near the city of Chaozhou in the eastern part of Guangdong Province, just a couple of hours from the shampoo factory. My driver, who was from Henan Province, had to stop several times to ask for directions, and each time he did, a big cloud of yellow dust caught up with us and covered the taxi.

China was home to a number of manufacturing clusters, and Chaozhou focused on the ceramics trade. It was said to have been a center for ceramics for thousands of years because of something to do with the soil in the area. As we drove into town, I noticed that many of the small shops had considerable amounts of fine-grained sand piled up in front of or off to the sides of their places of business.

Typically, factories in South China were built along major roads, but the way to Kevin's factory was down a narrow lane. His place was built like a fortress; instead of the standard accordion-style metal gate that fronted most plants, his had a high brick wall and a gigantic steel door at the entrance. I found the doorbell and rang it. Dogs started barking and kept at it until someone came along and hushed them.

Kevin was much friendlier in person than he had been on the phone, and he apologized to me for the long drive. He asked if I had any trouble finding the place. He introduced himself next, saying that he was from Los Angeles.

"You're American?"

"No. I'm a Chinese."

"You moved to the United States?"

"No," he said.

He enjoyed the exchange and told me about Los Angeles with a sly grin on his face. I told him that I was confused. From what he explained next, I was able to gather that he had only been abroad for pleasure—and not on many occasions either. His accent indicated that he was local Chinese, and he confirmed that he had never actually lived in Southern California.

I asked him why he called it home, and he only offered in a dreamy tone, "I love Los Angeles." It was hard for anyone who never spent much time in China to understand the extent to which intention could be mistaken for reality there.

Kevin's factory made pottery, and the kind most commonly produced was a faux Italian style that might have been vaguely antique looking, if only it had not been so vividly colored and glazed. Pieces were just coming off the production line, and Kevin showed them to me. One had the word "Italianate" incorporated into the design. Looking around at his factory, I gathered that this new style was suddenly popular in the United States.

We worked our way backwards through the processes at the plant, moving from the area where the pieces were finished to the section where workers were painting the dried pots by hand. The operation was paint by numbers. Girls who appeared too young to work sat at wooden benches and patiently dabbed away with long brushes. I took a closer look and could see that each piece of pottery had an outline. The workers kept paint in small bowls, or in some cases, shallow dishes similar to those used in Chinese calligraphy, working with no more than a few colors at a time.

The workers all sat on either side of a long table, one row of girls facing another. They worked quietly and at a leisurely pace, and I thought that the workroom had the feel of an art class.

Off in a corner—away from the girls at the long tables—was a skinny boy who held a scalpel in his hand. We stopped for a moment and watched as he used the instrument to carve up a block of yellow foam. Having cut away a small piece, he blew off the synthetic crumbs and tested his work by dipping the block into an ink tray. He then pressed the block against a large sheet of paper, revealing the outline of a floral decoration.

"This is the hardest job in the factory," Kevin said. "Not everyone is accurate."

The foam blocks were used as a stamp to outline the designs that would be painted on the pottery pieces, and the images had to be created in reverse. It was impressive, and I started to remove a small digital camera from my bag. I thought sending pictures back to Howard might be a good idea. "Sorry," Kevin said. "Pictures are not allowed."

Kevin was protective, as I would soon understand. He took me to his office and asked me to have a seat. On his desk were two computer screens from which he could see the entire factory floor. I took an interest in the system, and with the controls, he showed me how he could change the camera angles and zoom in or out.

He said it was important for him to stay on top of the workers, and he explained that his employees were not allowed to leave the premises. Many factories had such policies in place, but Kevin went even further by holding the identification cards of his employees for additional protection.

"Why all the security?" I asked.

"We have many secrets," Kevin said.

There were other things that he did to maintain control. He explained that in his factory, no more than one-fourth of the workers ever came from a single province. When too many workers came from the same place, he said, groups were more willing to conspire.

Another trick of his was to hire more workers than necessary. When there was enough work for everyone, the workers felt that they were needed and were more inclined to make demands on management. When there wasn't enough work, employees tried harder to prove their worth.

Kevin asked me to follow him to a showroom. The styles of the pottery pieces there did not match. While some of the pieces struck me as American in style, others seemed more European or possibly even Middle Eastern. The mix of styles made the factory's collection of samples look something like a rummage sale.

A delivery was in progress, and Kevin turned his attention to the arriving workers. There were three of them, and they carried in a number of samples that included vases as well as lamps. Kevin was drawn to one object, a brass-colored lamp. He inspected it immediately and then moving its tag out of the way, he took a picture of it.

I asked Kevin if the delivery workers were his employees.

He gave me a mischievous look. "No, they are my spies." As he said this, he looked at me carefully, gauging my reaction as he had done earlier when he told me that he was from Los Angeles.

Kevin explained that he had all sorts of people combing the area for samples. There were so many factories all clustered together that it made such activities possible. I imagined that workers on the inside of some factories might have snuck out samples for a small fee, or maybe the samples were taken right off the trucks before they left for export.

New designs were valuable to Kevin. If he saw a design that he liked, he took a picture and sent it off to his customers. If an order was placed, he could consider asking another factory to produce it or he could simply copy the product himself. He was not all that interested in producing electrical items, he said, so the lamp was something he would outsource.

I had never met anyone quite like Kevin. He was charming, in a devilish way, and he was of a sharper breed than most. He was defensive in keeping his workers behind a high wall—because he did not want his secrets leaked out—yet he aggressively sought to acquire the secrets of his competitors.

Copying was rampant in China, and this made manufacturers behave in strange ways. One manufacturer that I ran into produced shoes with designs "borrowed" from Europe. In China, the company worried that competitors would rob them of these newly acquired designs. Factory employees were given the chance to buy a pair of the shoes they made (at a discounted rate), but they were not allowed to take the shoes out of the factory for a full year—not until that shoe's design was more generally known to the marketplace.

In China, Kevin's behavior was understood, and most people would have said that he was wise to be cautious. And for aggressively seeking out the original designs of others, some would have called him clever.

What did his factory sell anyway but sand and water covered with paint and glaze? Any number of factories in the area could have made the same product at the same price, if not for less.

As it turned out, the problem with Howard, my frantic client, was that he had no proprietary designs of his own. Other importers from the United States were sending over interesting new samples, and Kevin was anxious to get hold of those.

Kevin said that he would like to help Howard, but that he was in a tough spot. He could not sell proprietary designs that came from American importers to others who were also from the United States. He would not say so, but I had the feeling that some of those designs might be available for sale, if only Howard had been from another market instead.

In the end, Kevin said that he could only provide Howard with product from his warehouse. Some of the designs were out of date, but they would suit Howard's product line. "What choice do I have?" Howard asked me. "I'm running out of stock."

I inspected the pottery on a later visit, and based on the amount of dust on the pieces, it looked as though they had been in the warehouse for two or three years. The items had all been made for other importers, and on the bottom of the pieces were bar codes made for specific retailers. One was for TJ Maxx, a major retail chain. If these styles were no longer in fashion, I thought, then TJ Maxx might not mind that they were being sold by their China supplier, but then what was the benefit to a customer like Howard if he purchased out-of-fashion merchandise?

The worst part about the pottery that Kevin wanted to sell was that the prices listed were high. An importer like Howard should have been paying about one-fourth of retail, but he was paying closer to 50 percent. Howard was probably paying more than what he would have paid if TJ Maxx marked the product down in an end-of-season closeout sale.

Importers that provided original designs were quoted low prices by Chinese manufacturers. They were offered a bargain in part because smaller importers paid more. Watching as some of Kevin's factory workers packed up boxes for Howard, I noticed that some of the pieces were even defective, and I had an uneasy feeling about Howard's business prospects.

Howard was disappointed, but resigned. He did not have the volume to justify hiring someone to design original pieces, and therefore, he felt at the mercy of the manufacturer. Howard also reiterated that he was in a hurry and that he needed to take whatever he could get.

We loaded Howard's product and shipped it overseas. Another few shipments later, Howard ran into trouble.

As expected, his prices were too high. An importer of ceramics couldn't purchase product for only half of its retail price and survive. Kevin knew it but pushed for the higher prices anyway.

Larger customers got discounts; smaller customers paid more. It was how business worked in China, and as I would later come to understand, this was an economically efficient business model for Chinese manufacturers. Big customers got discounts, not just because they bought in volume, but because they provided fresh designs. These were later turned out to smaller importers, who were given the squeeze on price.

CHAPTER 3

"All We Need Is Your Sample"

First-time visitors to the world of China manufacturing were often surprised by what they found. Imagining imposing, industrial structures and filth and noise, they expected to see something inspired by Charles Dickens, Charlie Chaplin's *Modern Times*, or maybe even *Charlie and the Chocolate Factory.*

In reality, the working environment was not as oppressive, and the buildings themselves were simple in their design. Missing from so many of these companies were common signs of industry; in fact, there were few smokestacks and no factory whistles. In South China, the buildings were typically multistoried boxes made of reinforced concrete, the sort of bland architecture that brought to mind housing projects.

What gave away these buildings as being industrial was that they tended to come in pairs. The factory was the plainer looking of the two, and its twin, the one with flashes of color, was the dormitory that housed the workers. Living in tight quarters, workers conserved space and kept their clothes fresh at the same time by hanging them outside their doors.

On the drive from Kevin's pottery factory near Chaozhou to Shantou, where King Chemical was located, I passed a number of such building pairs. None looked particularly inviting, but I wondered what each of them manufactured all the same. Sometimes, you could tell what a company manufactured by its name, or at least you could find some kind of clue, like the word "steel" or "plastics" on a sign by the road. With most of these factories, though, it was often a mystery what went on behind their walls.

What would happen if I randomly stopped at one of these Chinese manufacturers and just walked in? I asked my driver if he minded. He glanced at me sideways, said nothing, and then gave a delayed shrug. We were about to pass one manufacturer when I asked him to stop.

A guard who sat in a shelter box by the front gate came out to approach the car. He went to the driver's window, and I leaned down so that I could see him.

"*Shenme shi?*" he asked, wanting to know my business.

"I was just wondering. What do you make here?"

He considered me carefully and then asked whether I was a customer. It was a question that answered itself. If I were a customer, I would already know what they made. And since I did not know....

The guard picked up a phone and spoke to someone in a muffled voice. I noticed that on the wall in his small station hung a riot baton and a rifle. Putting the phone down, he said nothing and lit a cigarette.

I stood outside, while the taxi driver took the time to move his car away from the gate, pointing it toward the main road as though anticipating the need for a fast getaway. A few silent moments passed, and then a stout man in a brown work shirt emerged from the factory. He came walking toward the gate at a brisk pace, his arms swinging.

"*Huanying! Huanying!*" he said. "Welcome! Welcome!"

He grabbed my right hand with both of his, which were plump and calloused. He shook my hand for longer than was necessary or comfortable, and I felt the sudden need to make excuses.

"I was just passing by your factory," I said.

"No problem," he said.

"I was just wondering..."

"Come in and sit for a while."

"I just wanted to ask you a question."

"Sure," he said. "We'll talk all about it."

When mixed with business, Chinese hospitality could be suffocating.

I tried to explain that I was merely passing through the area on my way back to my hotel. In other words, I was curious, but I wasn't exactly up for a major detour. Going into his office would mean having a lengthy meeting, and then he would serve me tea or try to take me out to dinner, and I didn't have the time for it. Could he simply just tell me what they manufactured?

"*Aiyooooh!*" he cried, sounding like a man stuck with a sharp stick.

The look on my face must have suggested weakness or pity, because he then seized my arm and began pulling me inside. Having worried earlier that I might be chased off the property, I now wondered whether I would ever be allowed to leave.

Because the factory was located in a remote area, it was fair to assume that this factory boss didn't receive too many visitors. Still, he apologized for the state of the place and made excuses about why things were not in order. He appeared genuinely flustered by his lack of foresight, as though he should have presumed that foreigners would one day soon begin showing up at his factory unannounced. So many from abroad were coming to China to chase down merchandise; surely such random visits were the next, inevitable step.

He asked me to sit in his office, and I managed to convince him to start with the factory tour instead. This was no showcase factory. It was a rough-looking place, and I noted that the benches and stools had been banged together from wood scraps. Along one grimy wall, by a workbench, one of the workers had written the same Chinese character over and over.

Zheng, Zheng, Zheng, Zheng, Zheng, Zheng, Zheng. . . .

In Chinese, it meant "correct," and it was a character that was made up of precisely five strokes. The workers had apparently been using this ancient character as a way to keep a record of how many pieces they completed. It was a counting system comparable to the American way of drawing four vertical lines followed by a diagonal mark made at the count of five—the sort of thing you saw in the movies—scratch marks made on a wall by a prisoner who was tracking the days as they passed.

Finally, I got to find out what they manufactured. The company was in the business of making small figurines out of a synthetic polyresin. Their products were for export, though their company did not ship the items themselves, but sold them instead to a trading company, which held the contracts with buyers overseas.

In the warehouse, there were hundreds of cardboard boxes stacked along a wall. They were all marked for the same port destination: Long Beach, California.

The company was not in the middle of any production. I asked if it would be possible to open one of the boxes to see the finished product. A worker cut the tape on one of the boxes in a crude fashion, using a key. The factory boss handed me a small figurine that was inside, while watching my face for a reaction. It was a nativity scene, I saw, and at the front and along the bottom were two words: *Feliz Navidad*.

I was surprised to see the Spanish lettering. "*Xibanyawen,*" I said.

In Chinese, Spanish and Spain sounded similar, which was the result of some minor confusion. "*Bushi Xibanya.* Not Spain," he said. "This is an export for America." The factory owner apparently assumed that the lettering on the product was English.

On the bottom of the product, there was a country of origin label—MADE IN CHINA. This product was more than likely bound for Hispanic markets in the United States, and I wondered how it came to be produced so far away.

Surely the cost of labor in Mexico was low enough, and being so close to the destination market, there had to be savings in transportation costs. General coordination and communication would also have been easier, as well. This was a product, I thought, that should have been stamped on the bottom: HECHO EN MEXICO.

"It's for Christmas," I said. At this mention the factory man nodded in a vague way. He didn't seem to know what he was making, which I found strange, but then he was caught up in other details.

"Do you like it?" he asked.

"Yes, it's nice."

"Would you like to discuss the price?"

I thought it was obvious that I was just passing by, that I was not necessarily in the market for such merchandise. "We can make the product according to your requirements," he said.

Not only was I not involved in seasonal gifts, I explained, I was not even an importer. This did nothing to discourage my host, who promised that he would help. He had a manufacturer's agreement that we could use, and he knew of an export company, one that could help to get the product out of the country. Also, if I needed a freight forwarder, he would introduce me to one. Payment would be a simple matter of putting down a deposit, and then production could begin.

"We can make anything you want," he said. "All we need is your sample."

There were many people still claiming that special connections were needed in order to get anything done in China, but there were no snobs in export manufacturing. Just as a Las Vegas pit boss was happy to explain the rules of craps to a new player, Chinese manufacturers proved willing to take the time to show a newcomer how to get started. Factory owners understood that they needed first to capture a customer if they were going to realize any long-term benefits.

Getting started in export manufacturing was not difficult. There would be challenges, to be sure, but these rarely came at the beginning. Manufacturers bent over backward, if only to make it seem as though doing business with them was a breeze, and for many who were new to export manufacturing, the factory owner doubled as teacher.

After walking over to the window to see if my ride was still waiting by the gate (it was), I explained to the factory man that I needed to get going. He rounded up a number of samples. "They are free," he said. I tried to protest, but he insisted. "Maybe you can give them to a friend."

Chinese industrialists were nothing if not optimistic, and they gave out samples like so many messages in a bottle. Just as fate brought me to his doorstep, who knew in whose hands these samples of his might wind up.

Importers were coming to China in big numbers, and one of the questions many were asking was: *Why China?* Why weren't importers looking to other markets? The answer most often given was the low cost of labor, but that was only a part of it; factory labor in other economies was actually cheaper. Speed and convenience were two other important areas where China performed particularly well.

Chinese factories could take any product and move it quickly into production ("All we need is your sample"), and they showed an incredible willingness and enthusiasm for getting a relationship started. Many of those new importers streaming into China did not necessarily have prior experience in international trade. They were, in some cases, retailers and distributors who decided to disintermediate those agents who had previously sourced merchandise for them. Others were coming from completely unrelated industries. Many were leaving professional careers to jump into the trade game.

To do business in China required no special business license or certification. China manufacturing required no tests or qualifications, and traders were arriving—and often staying—on simple tourist visas that could be extended without difficulty. Thousands of newcomers were turning up at events like the Canton Fair, China's largest trade show, just to get a feel for what was happening.

Barriers to entry were lowered, and the introduction of certain technology tools was helpful. Networked computers made it easier to find factories. Web sites like Alibaba.com were providing a boost to factories that were previously unknown. Minimum order quantities were lowered, also, so that less volume was required in order to get a project started.

Infrastructure also played a role. To many who would dip a proverbial toe in the water, it mattered that they could stay at a five-star hotel in some cities for as little as $50 per night. These hotels were not to be compared with luxury accommodations in London or Hong Kong, but they were comfortable, certainly more than you could get back in the United States for several times the price. Economies that might have competed with China for business did not have their infrastructure situation under control; so while manufacturing in those countries was cheap, the cost of checking the place out could be exorbitant. Business travelers who came to China remarked that their trips cost much less than they imagined.

Chinese manufacturers gave importers every reason to get started. They kept the cost of tooling low and provided free assistance with production setup. One client I worked with, an inventor, was about to go to an American engineering company to have a prototype of her product made for $60,000 when a factory in China said that they would do the same work for close to $4,500. The lowered cost was offered as an incentive for getting started with the supplier.

Even when a product cost the same to produce in the United States on a per-unit basis, China offered significant savings in the initial phase. Start-up savings alone helped manufacturers win business, though the importers involved should have understood that such enticements were the equivalent of a no-money-down sales pitch and other too-good-to-be-true opportunities.

Everything about China was set up to get customers in the door, and importers who arrived for the first time remarked how surprised they were by the red-carpet treatment they received. "They treated me like a king," one importer told me, explaining how sweet his supplier relationship had been at the start. While these manufacturing relationships tended to become only more difficult over time, the beginning was almost always promising.

Importers responded to fawning and flattery—even if they did not realize it—but this alone did not win business. Concerns about business risk weighed heavily in the decision-making process. What importers needed to know before they moved their business to China was whether the economy was safe. One important contributing factor was a changing perception of China as a low-risk environment.

There were still economies in the world where an importer could wire transfer funds and find that the recipient and the cash had both disappeared. Importers who came to China were reporting to others that this sort of thing did not happen here. Factories delivered the goods, and outright fraud was more rare than in other corners of the world.

Compared with other economies, China came to be seen as a sanctuary. Latin America remained a place where kidnappings by professional criminals were common. In other countries, you could at least count on having your luggage stolen. Vietnam, which was just next-door to China—and which had a lower labor cost—was one of those markets where such stories of petty theft were commonplace.

Business travelers to China didn't need to worry about getting shot, mugged, or otherwise molested. China was not necessarily the safest place in the world for the Chinese, but it was for foreign business travelers, especially because locals understood that they were not to bother the country's important "foreign guests." China was on a national mission to build its economy, and it was tacitly understood that foreigners were to be treated in a manner that would encourage their return and further investment.

Mainland China, on the surface at least, seemed law-abiding in a way that other places did not. Though the city streets were full of people, there were none of the accompanying signs of social decay.

Much of it was a managed perception, perhaps, with the government doing whatever it could to make China an attractive destination.

In Shanghai, a large number of police were put on the streets to minimize such heinous public crimes as jaywalking. In Guangzhou and in other cities, the government outlawed motorcycles—if only because their presence made the place seem more chaotic or less modern. It made a difference to first-time visitors that there was no wild graffiti on the sides of buildings or outward signs of violence. Mainland China appeared peaceful, a fact that was surprising given the stories of protests and corruption.

Working closely with a number of importers over the years, I would meet many who talked about how they were drawn to the allure of doing business in China. Importers who visited other places did not manage to get the same reputational benefits. On a return from Taiwan, for example, friends and family were more apt to ask, "How was *Thailand*?" For folks back home, so much of what went on in East Asia was vague, but there was less mistaking China. It was famous.

Importers who traveled to China were considered heroes by family and friends back home; they followed in the footsteps of historic explorers. While Marco Polo spent years making his way to the Far East, now the trip could be taken in under a day. As far as adventures went, China offered a great deal of bang for the buck.

China holds a place in the collective consciousness of the West, its reputation having been established by Marco Polo in the 14th century. The country still inspires the imagination in a way that few places do, and it really did matter to those who were in business that they could go back to the United States and declare that they had gone and found success there. Importers were human, and along with money, they wanted status. They wanted to brag about their China connection.

China was exotic, but it was not bizarre. Chinese did not dress in native costumes, they wore no headdresses or long robes, they did not go around in sandals. They did not have the habit of sitting on the floor. Chinese did not bow or require that a visitor make unfamiliar hand gestures, and the people were pleasantly irreligious. Though there were holidays, meetings were not interrupted by frequent prayer times. The Chinese were traditional, but not fanatical. They did not paint their faces or tattoo or pierce their bodies. Such colorful native traditions made for interesting tourism, but people on business were not vacationers.

Some of this cultural flattening was a conscious attempt by the Chinese to appeal more easily to Westerners and appear more up to date. Seeming modern and sophisticated was a source of face, and many Chinese went to great lengths to look comfortable in a rapidly globalizing world. Factory owners dressed like their foreign business partners—slacks, collared shirts, and shoes—and they took English names for themselves.

Despite China's insistence on having a unique culture that stretched back for millennia, there is no other country in the world whose citizens have given themselves alternate English names in such numbers and with so much enthusiasm. In places like Japan, India, and Mexico, you were forced to learn how to pronounce the *real* names of the people with whom you were doing business.

Exoticism was all fine and well, but strangeness did not engender business confidence. Chinese writing looked different enough that it surprised some visitors and the food was unusual—and yes, they did eat with chopsticks. In the end, though, these differences were not shocking. Ultimately, China was as familiar as Chinatown, or nearly so.

Importers were concerned about the political environment more than anything else. "Isn't China still Communist?" clients often asked, trying to get their heads around how the environment seemed so freewheeling, and yet so carefully controlled. They worried about a regime that was totalitarian, and what it would mean for business. Chinese government officials could do whatever they wanted, whenever they wanted. The very notion of absolute political control made outsiders nervous.

George Orwell preached about the dangers of totalitarianism, warning that in such a world, there would be no loyalty, except loyalty to the Party; there would be no laughter, except laughter that came from triumph over a defeated enemy. "If you want a picture of the future," Orwell said, "imagine a boot stamping on a human face—forever."

There was a boot in China all right, but it was being made outside of Guangzhou. It came in 96 different styles and eight colors and lead time was a mere 45 days. About 3,500 pairs fit into a 40-foot container, and you didn't need to have a special relationship with the factory owner to get started.

It was a bit unfortunate that the author of *1984* had not lived long enough to see just how well totalitarianism was working out in the global economy. Placing an initial order in China was easy, anyway.

"All we need is your sample."

CHAPTER 4

Vice President of Disadvantaged Neighborhoods

"**D**id you book the suite like I asked?"

Bernie, the importer who worked in soap and shampoo, had just come to Shantou, and we were scheduled to meet Sister and her husband, A-Min, at the Regency Hotel that afternoon. To set the tone for some rather important negotiations that he had planned, Bernie asked me to find the largest suite available.

The hotel had turned its entire top floor into a single residence, I told Bernie. They called it the "Presidential Suite," and it was not commonly rented, but was instead reserved for Communist Party officials and other VIPs.

"It sounds perfect," Bernie said. "Make sure you get it."

Only after much prodding did the hotel give me a price on the suite; it rented for more than a couple thousand dollars per night. It was obviously too much, but when I told the manager why we were interested in the suite in the first place, he offered to make it available at no charge. Hotel managers in South China were often like that. If they thought you were helping the local economy, they made all kinds of concessions.

Before Sister and her husband arrived, Bernie introduced me to his company, Johnson Carter.*

The company had never been a manufacturer in the United States as I had assumed. It was a virtual company. And, as a consequence, it was not one of those companies that was directly moving American jobs offshore. Bernie had created an opportunity for himself that was based on a newly found ease in offshore manufacturing.

He handed me his company catalog while we waited downstairs. Johnson Carter manufactured a variety of health care products. Flipping through the catalog, I saw a number of items that were familiar to me, including the bubble bath, a line for which we had just begun to produce bottles and print labels.

There were three varieties of bubble bath. We had a purple, grape-scented product that was branded Galaxy Grape, another one that was red called Crazy Cherry, and a pink formulation marketed as Bursting Bubblegum. The labels for all three were decorated with cartoon bubbles filled with little smiley faces.

Turning more pages, I saw dozens of other products. Johnson Carter had a line of hair conditioners, hair gel, and body lotions. There were also many different kinds of liquid soaps. One line came in a bottle shaped like a seashell. Another in a round bottle had a pump. A banner along the top of the label for one read: "Wow! Only 99¢!" The soaps advertised "55% More—Free!"

Sister and A-Min arrived at the hotel, and we were escorted to a main room on the top floor, in the middle of which sat a white grand piano. The curtains had been opened, revealing a view of the quiet city. Sister said that she was surprised. She had been to the hotel many times before but said that she was unaware of the expansive suite.

Before we sat, Bernie asked if anyone would like to see his new catalog. Sister said that she was eager to, and she asked questions while flipping through its pages. It was the sort of brochure meant for prospective customers back in the United States, but she was taking it as a production guide.

"We can make all of these," she said.

"That's great," Bernie said.

---

*Many of the names of companies and individuals that appear throughout this book have been altered.

Sister then asked questions about a few products. On the front of some bottles were pictures of fruit. She knew what the apple product was supposed to smell like, but she had questions about the bottle that showed an apricot. Another that showed an avocado elicited additional questions.

These were fruits unfamiliar in South China. All the same, Sister said that it would not take long for her to get duplicates made and samples sent off to New York, where Johnson Carter was headquartered.

Bernie found his way to a big cream-colored sofa, and the rest of us took places on pieces of furniture spread about the large room. We sat so far apart from each other that everyone was forced to shout to be heard.

The business was about to kick off in earnest, and pricing negotiations were the main reason why Bernie was back in China. Sister said that she had received messages from Bernie regarding price targets, and that she was optimistic that the factory would be able to meet them.

It occurred to me for a moment that the idea to meet in such a luxurious suite conveyed the wrong message. Bernie was pushing for low prices. Even if we were allowed to use the suite for free, it made Bernie appear affluent. I thought it would have made Sister and A-Min reluctant to agree on low prices, but it had quite the opposite effect, and they were enthusiastic about moving things forward.

"Tell them I have *big* plans for their factory," Bernie said.

Sister and her husband heard this and smiled.

Coming downstairs from the hotel suite, Bernie carried a large case of samples to the lobby. Though he insisted that he did not need any help, Sister and her husband together lifted the case into the trunk of their car.

We passed a number of factories on the drive from Shantou to the outskirts of the city. Bernie noticed that the billboards on the side of the road did not advertise soft drinks, cigarettes, or other consumer products, but mostly heavy machinery. At an intersection on the way were several billboards cluttered together, many of which advertised plastic injection machines.

Sister and A-Min's company, King Chemical, had something to do with the plastics industry. It had once produced plastic components for toy companies in the area. Shortly after moving on to supply the cosmetics industry with plastic bottles and caps, the company went on to build a business that had them filling the bottles with care product ingredients. It was King Chemical's way of moving up the value chain.

The road to the factory was full of tractor trucks hauling 40-foot containers, those long boxes filled with manufactured goods for export. The four-door Honda that we rode in competed for space with these tractor trailers, as well as with large delivery trucks, buses, and taxis. The few other sedans that could be seen on the road were mostly high-end luxury cars. Despite all the talk of a rising middle class in China, there were relatively few private vehicles on the road. The traffic was two-tiered, much like the Chinese economy itself.

Bernie remarked on the traffic, saying that he could not believe how busy the place was. For him, it was sensory overload. We were not even halfway to the factory when he asked me, "How can you live here?" I laughed, not because I had gotten used to the traffic in South China long ago, but because it was an especially odd comment coming from someone who was asking me for help. The truth was that I called it home. I felt comfortable there.

"The place has its moments," I said.

Reaching into his jacket pocket, Bernie brought out his airplane ticket. He was going to be flying out of Guangzhou in just a couple of days. It was the city where I lived. Shantou, where the factory was located, was a 50-minute flight away.

Bernie looked at his ticket and for a second appeared puzzled by it.

"Let me ask you a question," he said, looking suddenly serious.

"Sure."

"Now, where the hell is *Canton*?"

"Canton is the old name for Guangzhou."

The city had been a major trading port for over a thousand years, and for hundreds of years the city was the only point of contact between China and the outside world. The interest that the city was seeing in trade was nothing new; in fact, it was a historic return. I wanted to tell Bernie some of this, but sensing a history lesson, he changed the subject.

Tourists had a more enlightened view of China. Business travelers saw the place as a mere backdrop to their business transactions. Bernie had little patience for information that he considered beside the point. To him, cultural lessons on the place or the people were like so much static—"red noise"—that did not illuminate as much as interfere with an otherwise clear signal.

Inside his briefcase, Bernie had a pile of orders in process, as well as a number of important potential orders. This was what he was focused on. He wanted to know what King Chemical could make and whether they could reach certain price targets. Beyond that, he wanted to know about delivery times and whether quality would be up to standard. Importers rarely wanted to know about history, just as they didn't care about macroeconomic trend data.

Close to where we would turn off the main road onto the street that led to the factory, we passed a truck that was carrying pigs. Bernie was an Orthodox Jew, and he made a fuss about the truck, pointing in its direction. At first, I thought he was offended by it, but he was, instead, amused.

"Did you see that?" he asked, laughing. "One pig was humping the other." I strained my head back to look at the truck, which we had just passed, but could only see that it was overloaded.

Sister saw how excited Bernie had become and asked if he "liked pigs." The word for the animal in Mandarin, *zhu,* was pronounced like "Jew" in English, and this caused a moment of confusion. Bernie guessed that Sister was asking about his religion and his dietary restrictions.

On his previous visit, just before I came into the picture, Bernie had turned down several offers to join the factory for dinner, explaining that there were certain things he could not eat. Given the importance of feasts and banquets in the courtship rituals of Chinese business relationships, it was a slight embarrassment, but it did nothing to slow down talks between the two companies.

This was something of a surprise to me, actually. Having spent years living in China, I was sufficiently acculturated to believe that it was impolite to decline business-related invitations. Chinese do not differentiate between business and personal relations to the same extent as Westerners, and their concept of "face" required that certain signals be delivered elliptically. Refusing an invitation could be taken the wrong way.

Some of Bernie's habits bewildered me, also. Though Jewish, as well, I was not observant, and while I understood something about Orthodox customs, Bernie had habits that were unfamiliar. Coming out of the bathroom, I had seen him throw an arm over his head while mumbling to himself. At first, I thought something was wrong, and I asked what had happened.

He explained that it had been a small prayer, one that was recited after using the toilet. It was not his arm that he meant to get above his head exactly, but any piece of cloth. He needed to cover his head when reciting the prayer. He did not typically wear a head covering—a *kippa*—like other Orthodox Jews, which was another thing that I did not get.

"It's a Syrian thing," he said. It was the first time he had indicated to me that he was a member of the famed Syrian Jewish community, and it at least explained some things. For Bernie's Chinese business partners anyway, the mumbled Hebrew prayer, the sleeve over the head, the polite refusal to eat certain foods—these were all likely rolled up with a dozen other behaviors that made him seem strange, but these did nothing to dampen their enthusiasm for the business-related opportunity.

At the end of the day spent together, Bernie wanted to tour the factory again. He had not been back to the plant since his first visit, and he reiterated an earlier concern, that workers were still labeling plastic bottles by hand. He said that he had seen a labeling machine at another factory and he wanted King Chemical to purchase one. Sister assured him that the workers could apply the labels fast enough and that hand labeling had the advantage of being more accurate as well. If the workers were not labeling fast enough, the factory would just hire more people. The machine was expensive, she explained, and labor in China was cheap.

"But tell them that our orders will be large," Bernie said.

Sister said, "Please, tell Bernie not to worry."

It was not about efficiency, though. Bernie envisioned the factory as appearing more up-to-date. He said, "I can't bring customers to a factory that looks like it's from the Dark Ages."

When Sister understood that Bernie worried only about what it would look like, about what his customers would think, she exchanged glances with her husband and they spoke for a brief moment in the local dialect. Together, they nodded slowly.

Sister said that actually they had been thinking of buying a labeling machine for some time, and that they would have one installed. The idea of the labeling machine itself had not interested the couple, nor had satisfying Bernie's random demand for a certain kind of equipment. However, the idea that such a machine would impress Bernie's customers apparently struck a chord.

■ ■ ■

In pricing negotiations with Sister and A-Min, Bernie mentioned the names of customers that he was working with. I knew the companies—they were some of the largest drugstores, supermarkets, and dollar stores in the United States. Sister and A-Min had never heard of any of them, though they would soon enough understand the significance of these retailers in the American market.

Bernie explained that he needed low prices. If certain targets in pricing were not reached, he could not close some deals, and the volumes were large.

The price target for some of the products was already too low, Sister said. On each item, there was a great deal of back-and-forth, and nearly two hours was spent discussing the pricing scheme for body wash alone. Sister and A-Min suggested that they needed higher prices, if only because they had a small factory. "We have little money," Sister said in heavily accented English.

It would be worth it, Bernie suggested, to keep prices held low. He talked up the larger business opportunity. Pricing might be a challenge in the short term, he said, but the factory would do well for itself, and the effort would be worthwhile.

"I hope so," Sister said in a way that made her appear sad.

Bernie talked about his industry associations. He said his partners were Syrian Jews who had connections at all of the major supermarkets, drugstores, and dollar stores. Once merchants in the New York area, the Syrians had long ago moved on to do international trade. The owners of some retail chains were of Syrian descent, and others had gone on to work as buyers at publicly traded retailers. It was a sales pitch that any Chinese businessperson would have made, a promise of an opportunity made possible through "personal connections."

Sister and her husband strained to understand Bernie and what he was saying. They didn't understand English, but they hung on his every word all the same. Bernie predicted that within a few short years, he would have one of the largest health and beauty care companies in America. It was a bold claim, but when the translation was offered, Sister and her husband appeared as hopeful as Bernie did.

Bernie tried to keep the meeting light. He made occasional attempts at humor, but these almost never went over well. While his jokes were not understood, when he laughed, Sister and A-Min laughed, too.

At one point, Sister had a question about some of the formulations for hair conditioner. Bernie said that he did not have an answer, and that he would have to get back to them.

"Tell them that I'm just the boss," Bernie said.

This was not a sentence that a Confucian would understand. In China, no company president would ever confess to such blatant ignorance. The boss would certainly not claim to be merely the head of the company.

When we were dropped off at the hotel in the evening, Bernie told Sister and A-Min that we would one day rent the suite at the top of the hotel for real. "There will be room enough for all of us to stay there," he said.

Bernie was in a good mood, and he was surprised by how well things had gone. In the lobby of the hotel, he impulsively threw an arm around A-Min, who was nearly swallowed inside his large, lumpy frame. Bernie laughed and in an aside to me said, "Look, he's so small. I could almost put him in my pocket."

Sister looked at me, waiting for a translation.

I asked Bernie for a rephrase.

"Tell him that he's like my little brother. Go ahead, tell him that."

A-Min heard this and grinned sheepishly. It was not the shy smile of someone deflecting a compliment, but an expression that suggested that the words had been taken out of his mouth, that he would have delivered the line if only he had thought of it first.

"Tell Bernie that I feel the same way," A-Min said.

Having released A-Min from his bear hug, Bernie next put his arm around Sister's neck. Her hair had been put up, making her appear about as tall as her husband.

"Tell her, if I wasn't already married."

Seeing Bernie laugh at his own joke, Sister asked what he had just said. It was a phrase I didn't know what to do with, and I was embarrassed to the point of speechlessness. "He said that he looks forward to working with you."

Sister spoke very little English, but took the opportunity to answer Bernie directly. "Me, too," she told him.

After the meeting was over, Bernie said that it was time for the two of us to get better acquainted. This was an odd American habit—to do business first and only later take the time to find out who you were working with. In China, they did it another way. First you met and got to know someone, and only then did you talk business.

In the hotel bar, Bernie ordered a bottle of Black Label. A cocktail waitress in a tight dress came over with the bottle and a stainless steel bucket of ice. I tonged out the ice cubes, while he poured the whiskey.

"This business is going to be huge," he said. The trip had been a success, he declared, and then he remarked how he was surprised that everything had gone so smoothly. In the end, the factory had given him nearly everything he had asked for.

"My wife isn't going to believe it," he said. Bernie told me about his family, about his children who were grown, and about one of his sons, who was also working with him in the business.

While we drank, Bernie began to scribble out numbers on a notepad that he had pulled out of a bag. He looked at his notes and adjusted his glasses. "Let me ask you something. How can they make this stuff so cheap?"

It was an interesting question because shampoo was a particularly unlikely candidate for importation from China. The formulation itself was mostly water, which made it extremely heavy and thus expensive to transport. The 40-foot containers we shipped had a weight limit, which we would always reach long before the space had been filled. For a bottle of shampoo that cost 30¢ in China, we expected to pay more than 15¢ just for the ocean freight.

Bernie was talking out loud now. "I know this business and I just can't figure it out," he said. He ticked off items from his piece of paper. "Plastic bottle . . . pump . . . label . . . formulation—they can't be making *anything* on these orders. How is it possible?"

It was just as much of a mystery to me. The factory seemed motivated to work with him, I suggested. Maybe that was reason enough. This notion, that the factory wanted desperately to work with him personally, appealed to him. He went silent while looking over his sheet some more.

Other foreigners I would work with would have a similar reaction at the start of their China projects. Everyone back in the United States had warned them about how difficult it was going to be to do business in China, but just out of the gate, they had proved these doubters wrong. Bernie was not so much mystified as he was proud of his accomplishment. Importers would arrive in China and have this feeling. They had not only found their way, but they had single-handedly managed to slay the dragon.

The whiskey and the ice disappeared quickly. The cocktail waitress came over and refilled our ice bucket. She was thin and tall, with sleek, long hair, and Bernie remarked on the tight outfit that she wore. It was a hotel uniform that was traditionally inspired yet modern, and it complemented the girl's figure well.

When she had gone, Bernie asked if I dated local girls. I told him that I was, in fact, dating a Chinese woman, Maria, back in Guangzhou. He rolled his eyes. It was, he said, something that he would like to "help me with," only he didn't know any single girls who were Jewish. He only knew Syrians, as in Syrian Jews—except he did not call them that. He referred to them as "SY," pronounced like the letters sound—*ess-why*. The expression was said as though it were a code of some kind.

It took me a while to catch on to the shorthand. He referred to Syrian Jews as SYs, and non-Syrian Jews were referred to as "jay-dubs." The notation came from the two consonants in the word Jew.

I had heard about the Syrian Jewish community before. Their association was especially tight, a freemasonry of traders. Later, I would realize the extent to which many other trading groups operating in China were bound together by ethnic ties. The Russians networked together, and the Arab traders, too. Even the Japanese traders that I would see at trade shows appeared Yakuza-like.

These groups were clubby and heavily networked. More often than not, they were wheeler-dealer types with a *souk*-sense, and they knew on instinct how to barter. These groups stuck together because they had to; it was how they gathered information on the marketplace. There were no how-to manuals or schools that offered training on working with overseas suppliers. There were tricks of the trade that had to be learned, and in order to prevent shenanigans (or to engage in them), a successful trader had to have access to a knowledge base of some kind. Learning from the experience of veterans was less expensive than learning from your own mistakes.

Bernie was proud of his SY association, and he spoke of the Syrian community with a great deal of reverence. He surprised me next by explaining that he had not always been religious. When he was a young man, he had left the community and only later in life had an awakening of sorts. It was only some time after he became religious that he found his way into international trade.

It was important to Bernie that I knew where he was coming from. Close to the end of the bottle of whiskey, he told me the story of his very first business venture. While still in school, he had an idea to sell watches. He took a train from Brooklyn, where he lived, to Manhattan and found a jeweler that was selling watches for a bargain price. He found another shop that produced boxes that were attractive ("the box cost me more than the watch"), and then he went to a man in his neighborhood called Mark the Printer ("That's what we called him") and had some certificates made up on parchment paper.

"I had business cards made and called myself the Vice President of Disadvantaged Neighborhoods," Bernie said, "and I told them that I was specially authorized to give credit. You see, no one was giving credit in those days, especially not in the neighborhoods where I was going with these watches. All they had to do was make the first payment, I told them. They could mail me the other three payments."

"The watches sold for $180, and each payment was $45. But I didn't have more than $20 in the whole deal, between the watch, the box, and the parchment."

Bernie took a sip from his glass and looked at me to see if I was paying attention.

"You see, these guys that bought my watches, they all figured that they were going to fuck me out of the three payments. But, in the end, I made my profit on just the first payment."

The story had the feel of one that had been told a million times, and I was aware that part of the point was to make a certain impression. He was playing the teacher, the savvy, streetwise guy who might teach a book-smart, business school graduate how things worked in the real world.

At the same time, though, he was making a point about business strategy, about how greed in a transaction could be used to your advantage. The story did make an impression, and it was one that would stay with me as Bernie and I continued to work together on the soap and shampoo project.

CHAPTER 5

"I Do Now"

King Chemical purchased the new labeling machine that Bernie had asked for and set it up in the room where workers had previously been producing the labels by hand. The new equipment was modern. Made of stainless steel, it came with a computer touch screen and had many dials and buttons. While it looked like it might be precise, the machine required constant fiddling. By the time its operator realized that an adjustment was needed, a large number of rejects were produced, and quite often bottles came out of the machine with the labels crooked, off-center, or badly creased.

When a label went bad, the factory had to remove it from the bottle, which was otherwise still usable. The process of removing labels required rags and solvent and was time-consuming. Because of this shiny, brand new piece of equipment, entire work teams had to be created to fix the badly labeled bottles. Sister complained often and loudly about the new machine, saying that it did nothing but increase costs for the factory.

Communication issues were a source of some early quality problems. One of the very first mess ups had to do with new labels. Johnson Carter made a lightly scented liquid soap branded "Pinky Fresh." The label was supposed to have been copied directly from a file sent over from New York. For technical reasons, the factory's art department had gone to the trouble of recreating the label, and when the labels were printed they read "Prinky" instead of "Pinky."

For the first few months, I was at the factory nearly every day, trying to get things set up. I spoke with the plant managers in Chinese, and we would sometimes talk about the body wash or the bubble bath, but after some time I realized that the workers on the line did not know these descriptions.

"Where has the bubble bath gone?" I asked a worker one morning.

My question elicited only a blank stare. It took my repeating the question for the worker to admit that he didn't know what I meant by "bubble bath." Hoping to trigger an association, I mentioned it was the one that smelled like chewing gum.

He laughed at me. "We don't make chewing gum," he said. "We make daily chemicals."

Sister and I spoke about the exchange. She suggested that I reference the code number. Every Johnson Carter product had a five-digit number associated with it. These numbers were printed on the production sheets, and they were also on the sides of the cartons.

"Do you know where I can find 23515?" I asked a warehouse worker. Without missing a beat, he pointed to the pallet stacks. I tried another one.

"What about 23528?"

He pointed in another direction, again, without hesitation.

He knew precisely where every pallet was in the warehouse, but like the other workers in the factory, he had no idea what it was we were making.

It was impossible to ask any of the workers how the shampoo was coming along, or the conditioner, or the body wash. They did not think about the products that we made in those terms.

One reason they did not know these words was that they never ran across these products in their daily lives.

Many of the workers at the factory barely had a primary school education, and most came from hundreds or thousands of miles away—from rural corners of the country where their entire families earned a fraction of what they did in manufacturing. Before they came to work at the factory, they did not know what something like "hair gel" was. Most had not grown up using things like shampoo.

Some of the challenges we faced in the manufacturing sector had to do with this gap in life experience. This point was made clear in local restaurants whose waiters were also brought in from the countryside. Workers had a hard time learning their jobs or understanding things that seemed fundamental to a restaurant experience, in part because they had never themselves been waited on—ever.

King Chemical had workers who were unfamiliar with liquid soap. The kind that we made was a dollar store item, one that you would find in discount stores across the United States. Even if it was a low-end product, consumers expected it to function properly. Chinese workers who saw such a thing as nearly a luxury could not see the big deal with a faulty pump. When pumps began to fail, they were inclined to think: *So what? You can still unscrew the cap and get to the soap that way.*

It was easy to forget that China was still a developing economy. This painful fact was made clear even in the big cities like Guangzhou. In office buildings there, you had visitors who did not understand how elevators worked. Wanting to travel up, they would push the down button because they saw that the car was on an upper floor and they wanted the car to come *down* to them. And then there were the impatient ones who pressed *both* the up and down buttons, figuring that this would double their chances of catching an elevator car.

On the mornings when I traveled from my hotel in Shantou to the factory, I caught my own ride, but as there was no taxi service in the countryside, the factory typically provided transportation for the return trip.

"There, you see?"

The driver pointed to a pair of middle-aged women who were attempting to cross the street. He shook a finger in their direction and jokingly said that they did not have the sense to get to a crosswalk.

"*Tamen de suzhi tai di la.* The education level of the people is *too* low," he said, placing emphasis on the word *tai,* as if to suggest that a certain amount of ignorance was presumed, but that folks in these parts really pushed the limits of tolerability.

He had been a driver in the military, he told me, and he took special pride in his driving ability. The other drivers on the road were not professionally trained, he pointed out; they were mere civilians. And the ones who did not drive at all were the real scourges of society.

The factory driver was a thin, amiable fellow, and he knew that I enjoyed his little commentaries on life around Shantou. One afternoon, he wagged his finger at a boy who was jaywalking. Traffic was busy, and the boy had jumped out in front of a truck and startled the truck's driver into jamming on the brakes. With cars whizzing past him, the boy stood between opposing directions of traffic, the cars but a few inches away.

"*Zhongguoren bupasi*," the driver said.

It was a terrible thing to say, but I heard the same phrase repeated many times by taxi drivers in South China—"Chinese are not afraid to die," they would say, shaking their heads, or sometimes chuckling as they said it. It seemed less a question of fear to me and more an issue with coordination.

Standing at a small drink stand near one factory, I watched one morning as a bicyclist made his way toward the factory that I was visiting. From the opposite direction, another bicyclist was heading down the same lane. As there was no one else around, they both rode freely down the middle of the quiet road.

The bicyclist who was heading toward the factory had been riding slightly left of center, and he had the idea that he probably should pass on the right. He started to move over but then changed his mind. I watched as the two bikes wobbled back and forth in a moment of indecision and second-guessing, and at the very instant when they should have been passing one another, they still had not yet sorted themselves out. It happened almost in slow motion. Even with no obstacles in the road, they—clunk!—improbably collided. It would have been amusing had it not been sad.

At the factory, we suffered from a similar kind of challenge. Where some problem might have been identified and quickly knocked out, workers did not choose to coordinate with one another. Unless someone came along and gave a *specific* set of instructions—for even the smallest task—nothing got done.

When it came to products made for foreign companies, workers didn't like to make too many assumptions. Maybe they felt that they did not have enough life experience to make judgments themselves. They worried about revealing their poor education levels. Afraid to look stupid, they inevitably did things that made them appear comically so.

While living in South China, you would hear stories about quality gaffes from other importers. One story that went around involved a Turkish importer who had placed an order for shoes with one Chinese manufacturer.

When the shoes arrived at their destination in Turkey, a nail was found driven in the bottom of each left shoe. The head of the nail stuck out of the sole about an inch.

The importer had given the factory an original sample pair and had said that he wanted the shoes made "exactly like this." The only problem was that there had been a nail in the bottom of the shoe from which it had hung on a display rack.

The workers at the factory did not think it prudent to ask anyone about the nail. They figured, "that must be how they like their shoes in Turkey—with a nail driven into the bottom of the left one," and so they filled the order just like that.

■ ■ ■

One of my primary objectives during the first few months with the shampoo factory was to get the place cleaned up. Prior to my involvement, Johnson Carter received a large shipment from a previous supplier that was contaminated with bacteria. Hundreds of thousands of dollars worth of product had to be thrown away.

Sister and I met to discuss hygiene. One concern was water contamination. The water that went into our soap and shampoo was coming in from county water lines, and China was notorious for its water pollution problem. The factory was located just a few thousand feet from waterways that were solid black with waste oil and other contaminants. Sister assured me that there would be no problem in this area, as their onsite water purification system would ensure the water was bacteria free.

With microbiology on my mind, I spotted one of the workers making his way across the factory floor. He was carrying plastic bottles—six of them, three on each hand—by placing a finger into each empty bottle.

I explained to Sister how this could be a problem. She told me that she understood and would address the situation.

"I will tell the workers not to put their fingers in the bottles when you are at the factory," she said.

"When I'm at the factory? It has nothing to do with when I'm at the factory."

Sister did not take the problem of fingers in bottles seriously in any case, though she indicated an understanding of science and germs. The factory's bottles were all sterilized before they went into production, and the plant even had ultraviolet lights placed around the factory—in the filling station area and in the packaging room—in an effort to reduce environmental bacteria.

The ultraviolet lights were really just for show, I eventually realized, just as the white coats and hats were. The plant managers never bothered to wear the white coats and hats, and after my initial visit to the factory, I was never asked to wear the outfit again either.

Bernie was disturbed by the finger-in-bottle exchange when I told him about it. "I hope they are washing their hands, at least," he said. Since the bathrooms had no soap, I told him that it was not likely.

"They should be washing their hands all the time," he said, becoming upset. "Tell them to wash especially when they are coming out of the bathroom."

Hearing this view, it was now Sister's turn to become upset. All those workers washing up so many times was going to mean supplying a great deal of surfactant.

"And just where is all of the soap going to come from?" she asked.

"I don't know," I said. "But we do work in a soap factory."

"That's what I thought. You want *us* to pay for it."

Johnson Carter would pay for the soap, I suggested, and then I took a case of our product from the warehouse and placed the bottles near every sink in the plant. The entire box of liquid soap cost Johnson Carter less than $10, but it didn't matter anyway. Two weeks after I put the soap out, the fill levels of the bottles remained unchanged. No one was using it.

A few weeks after the initial discussions on hygiene, I saw one of the plant managers spitting on the factory floor. This sort of thing was not uncommon in the streets of South China, and it was only because we talked continually about keeping the factory clean that it came as a shock.

Sister was belligerent on this one. "You can't expect me to force workers to behave a certain way," she said. She was defensive about her workers, more protective of them than she was worried about any other impact on the business. Anyway, she pointed out, spitting in the factory was not that bad when it was going on in the packaging room. At least, she said, it had not happened in the more sensitive filling station area.

While this was true, we had serious hygiene issues in the filling station also.

Johnson Carter's hand lotion was too thick to transfer with a vacuum pump system, and so workers transferred it with a large plastic scoop. When the workers moved product from a big plastic bucket to the machine that filled the bottles, they invariably made a mess of themselves in the process.

I watched as one worker transferred formulation. His upper torso disappeared into the large tub, and he came up with lotion smeared across his face. If the lotion was touching his face, then germs from his face were coming in contact with the product. I took pictures for Bernie, who responded by merely saying that he wanted me to "take care of it."

It sounded like an easy problem to knock out, but the factory resisted any instruction in this area.

The hair gel that we produced at the factory was green. One day, I noticed that the worker who filled the gel bottles had a skin condition. His hands were covered with the slick formula, and beneath the green, shimmery layer, I could see that the skin on his hands was peeling. Small, raw patches of flesh were exposed, and you didn't have to be a dermatologist to see that his skin was infected.

"We should probably do something about this one," I said to Sister, trying to sound calm, while in my head alarm bells were ringing.

Sister did not see the point. "Why?" she asked.

"It might be a health issue?"

"But the worker has done nothing wrong. It's just an allergic reaction."

Trying to press the matter, I suggested that the worker might contaminate the product.

Sister twisted around the argument. "How can he harm the product when it was the *product* that caused *him* the harm?"

She was entirely serious on this point, and she added to her argument that since the worker had been harmed, he should be *rewarded* by being kept at his post. Removing him from the filling station might be perceived as punishment, or it might translate into face loss. As she had already established, the worker had done nothing intentional to harm anyone. It was better, in other words, that we keep his infected hands at the filling station. Never mind the business or the consumer. This was, as she saw it, the "right thing to do."

The issue of consumer product safety did nothing to sway her, nor did worker safety, so I tried to emphasize how this might affect a shared business interest. Making a product that didn't suffer from quality failure made good economic sense, I suggested. After all, if anyone ever found out that the factory operated under such unsanitary conditions, it would be a public relations nightmare.

She did not like the way this sounded, and she now raised an eyebrow at me.

"How is anyone going to find out?" she asked.

She was considering me carefully, trying to determine if I was making some kind of veiled threat. The only people who knew about the worker's peeling hands were workers at the factory, management, and myself. Surely, no one at the factory was ever going to say anything to anyone. In the history of Chinese manufacturing, had any worker ever filed such a report? Whatever could I possibly be implying?

It was frustrating to see the factory not interested in improving quality for its own sake. The only thing to do was to suggest an immediate loss of business. "Bernie would be concerned," I said.

Johnson Carter was responsible for transferring millions of dollars to China. What the head of that company thought carried weight. Sister said that she would consider doing something about the worker whose hands were peeling, but only if Bernie had been told and insisted that the issue needed to be addressed.

■ ■ ■

Sister's husband, A-Min, spotted me as I was about the leave the factory. Though it was late in the afternoon, he looked as though he had just woken up. His eyelids, which were normally droopy, gave him the perpetual look of being hung over.

"*Ni xihuan hejiu.* You like to drink," he said.

It was a statement, a proposal. I had been coming to the factory for a while now, and A-Min had determined that it was time for us to go out and get drunk together.

Alcohol was an important part of factory life. It was used in part as a bonding mechanism, and in transactions, it generally helped break down facades. It helped players determine whether someone really needed the deal at a given price in order to move things forward. The best, of course, could stick to a story, no matter how blitzed they became.

Drinking games in China were a tournament in which only the most able-bodied drinkers survived. You had to understand that when you were working with a successful factory owner, you were quite likely pitting yourself against an accomplished drunk. And because these drinking outings often involved karaoke—the sort where "hostesses" were involved—you could also be assured that you were dealing with a serious philanderer, as well.

"*Ni xihuan kala-oh-kay*. You like karaoke." It was another declaration, a hint of where we were heading that night.

Most of the four- and five-star hotels in the area had a karaoke bar, the sort where you rented a room with a sofa and a wide-screen television and sexily dressed women were offered as singing companions and paid escorts.

We met two of A-Min's friends, cohorts who were also in manufacturing—die-hard locals who also spoke almost exclusively in the local dialect—and the lounge that A-Min determined we would drink in was the one located in my own hotel.

As soon as we were seated in our private room, more than a dozen girls were delivered in a lineup as if they were in a beauty contest. These were girls who would be paid by the hour. Their job was to pour drinks and sing songs. Not all of the women who worked in such a place would go home with a customer, though it was the general idea.

The government occasionally cracked down on pornography, and they had outlawed government officials from taking mistresses, but this one ritual was left untouched. Naturally, because it was an activity for men only, Sister had been left out, and I could only wonder whether she knew anything about this outing at all.

A-Min was flirting with a girl he had chosen, and I thought back to one of the first times I had ever been to karaoke. It was years ago, and the group of businessmen was mostly from Taiwan. One of the men was making overtures to the girl sitting next to him, and she resisted. She pointed to the gold band on the man's ring finger.

"You're married," she said in a protesting way.

"Who's married?"

"You are!" she said. She then pointed again to the ring on his finger.

"Who? This guy?" he said, lifting the finger that had the ring on it. "Yes, he is married," he said. Then, he raised and wiggled his other fingers one at a time. "But he's not married, and he's not married, and he's not . . ."

The girl giggled and slapped him on the shoulder, telling him that he was naughty.

Everything about karaoke was a charade, actually. The men grabbed microphones and pretended to be pop stars. They belted out tunes while their rent-a-dates clung to them and clapped enthusiastically when they were done. The room itself was a put-on, made to appear as though it were a living room in someone's home. Much of what went on in these places was about getting sex, but then the men went to so much effort at appearing to court the girls and the hostesses did their part by appearing to be reluctant. This version of karaoke was especially artificial, and when you found yourself in such a circumstance, the only thing left to do was pretend that you were having a good time.

Noticing that I was not making much of an effort to chat up my girl, A-Min asked if I was all right. I told him that I was, and then I grabbed my glass and toasted him and the little get-together that he had arranged.

It was easy to think of manufacturing as a dry science, but interpersonal relationships also played a large part. There were foreigners who, in similar circumstances, would have been glad to take a karaoke escort home—for the sake of the business, naturally. Dealing with factory owners, though, I came to understand that going along to get along was not always the best move.

On another project, I remembered how one manufacturer offered everyone at the initial meeting a cigarette. The importer I was working with accepted the offer of a cigarette, along with a light, while I took a pass. As we discussed possibilities for cooperation, I noticed that the importer was fumbling with his cigarette. He tapped at the ashtray frequently and at one point had a coughing fit.

Eventually, I asked him whether he actually smoked.

"I do now!" he said.

It was his first time doing business in China, and he was excited. Things were going well, and he seemed rather proud about having sacrificed his lungs for the sake of the deal.

This was the sort of thing that factory owners liked to see, actually. They wanted their foreign guests engaging in activities that they normally would not—smoking, drinking heavily, eating foods that they knew their guests would find strange, like insects and the internal organs of farm animals. It was all part of the acculturation process. It was a way of bringing the other side onto their own turf. If the factory owner could get a nonsmoker to pick up a nasty habit so easily, just imagine what kind of terms the importer would agree to when it came time to consider the manufacturing contract.

It was a good idea to come and have a few drinks, but I felt that I had stayed too long. A-Min was drunk and had begun pawing at his girl. When he disappeared into her lap, I took it as my cue to sneak away. Stepping past him, I realized why his head was down; he had vomited on the carpet.

One of the advantages of leaving a karaoke lounge early is not waking up with a hangover. When I walked out of the hotel the next morning, I was clearheaded and ready to deal with more issues at the factory.

On my way to flagging a taxi, I saw a car in the parking lot that I recognized. It was the four-door Honda that we had all arrived in the previous night. There was no mistaking the vehicle; I recognized the license plate number, and there was a familiar toy in the rear window. A-Min had probably crashed at the hotel and taken a room with a karaoke hostess for company.

At the factory, Sister cornered me.

"How was last night?" she asked.

"Last night?"

So, she knew that we had been out. She might have also known that her husband never returned home.

"Yes, last night. Did you have a good time?"

"It was all right."

Sister smiled and waited for me to fill the silence with details. She didn't mention karaoke or sexy hostess girls. She tried to appear innocent, but it only made it seem that she was fishing.

"Who was there with you?" she asked.

She didn't know who was there.

"There were a few people," I said.

She smiled again, and this time the silence was more awkward. She was hopeful that I might spill the beans, and, I thought, if she was a jealous wife, she didn't look the part. Maybe she was looking for something, however small, to hold against her husband.

It looked as though I was in a position to do her a favor. And favors were meant to be returned. . . .

Getting on Sister's good side might hold some value, I thought. We did have a lot of things that needed to get done at the factory, and there had been so much resistance on her part. It was a close call; in the end, my better sense told me not to get involved.

Usually Sister was the one who played thick, and now it was my turn. I told her that I hadn't stayed for very long. This was true, and showing up at the factory early gave me added credibility.

Sister dropped the subject, but she brooded. Whether she held it against me that I wouldn't talk, I never knew, but things certainly did not get any easier at King Chemical.

CHAPTER 6

Lurid Carnival of Global Commerce

With so much of my time being spent in factories, I eventually took an assistant—someone who could answer the phone, water the plants, and pay the bills while I was away. Tina was from Hunan, and while she had missed the chance to attend university, she had more than made up for it through self-study.

Many of those in South China who claimed to have a degree in English could not actually speak the language. Without much schooling or any foreign contacts, Tina had been able to teach herself to read English and to speak with surprising fluency.

She was naturally curious about the wider world, and even on the subject of China she held many frank and interesting views. It soon became our habit to go out for lunch when I was in town, and it was during some of those times that I was on the receiving end of many surprising insights.

Southern Chinese felt a natural affinity for humid environments, and while the rain kept people indoors in most places, in Guangzhou it sent them into the streets.

As we walked down the sidewalk sharing my oversized umbrella and talking about where to go, the spine of one oncoming umbrella slashed my cheek.

I muttered in pain, and Tina saw me touch my face.

"You should ask that person for compensation," she said, even before considering my physical pain. She was referring to the man or woman who was already long gone.

"I'm all right," I said, touching the spot that stung.

"But if someone causes harm, they *should* compensate."

She was making a point about principle. Tina was a country girl, someone who had not been in the city for very long, and while we both called Guangzhou home, she saw in me something of a kindred spirit, a fellow outsider.

"So, how much is a scratched face worth?" I asked out of curiosity.

"Three or four hundred renminbi," she said without the least bit of hesitation.

She knew the going rate. It was somewhere around $50. Average factory workers earned about $100 per month, and office workers were making closer to $300 per month. It was a significant sum.

"Surely they wouldn't pay. The person would just run away."

"You can hold them," Tina said. "'Don't allow them to go."

She demonstrated how this was done by grabbing at her purse strap. I could not see myself ever doing this, but I understood how such a system might work. The guilty party would be motivated to settle on the spot because getting the police involved introduced the chance of an unpredictable, possibly undesirable, outcome.

Detaining someone physically in order to force a settlement would never work in a place like the United States, I told Tina. It would result in an immediate brawl. Ironically enough, it was precisely because the Chinese were nonviolent that such rough handling could be used as a means of dispute resolution, and it also mattered that folks knew how to calculate and negotiate damages on the fly.

At lunch, I mentioned that I had seen two motorists settle the matter of a car accident by the side of the road. They did not involve the police, and they resolved their own dispute rather peaceably. Arriving at a settlement had involved taking into account allocations of responsibility, bearing in mind relative income levels and taking a guess at the amount of property damage that had been caused. I told Tina that it had been fascinating to watch and that I had been genuinely impressed with how neither of them felt the need to involve any third party.

Chinese perhaps had no choice but to work out disputes for themselves, I suggested, because they lacked access to formal remedies.

Tina said that I had it backwards, that they didn't bother with intermediaries such as insurance agents or attorneys, because they felt more
than capable of handling their own affairs.

■ ■ ■

In Guangzhou, I lived in what might have been considered a
ghetto for foreigners, though the foreign community made up a mi-
nority of the total population. Tian He, as the neighborhood was
called, was near the east train station, where the line that whisked
passengers to Hong Kong originated, and it was home to a growing
number of high-rise buildings and commercial development projects.

"We are becoming more like Shanghai," one of my neighbors
said to me one day, while pointing out that the number of foreigners
in the area was growing. She meant well by the comment, and the
association with Shanghai was an apparent reference to the number of
foreigners there.

The presence of Westerners was seen as a sign of modernization in
Guangzhou. My neighbors were in the habit of mentioning the influx
of foreigners in any conversation connected to rising real estate prices;
and related to some of these attitudes, I found myself on the receiving
end of many small kindnesses. Doors were often held open for me,
and it was not unusual for some neighbor to insist that I take the next
taxi—even though he had been waiting for some time himself. Some
chalked up such behavior to Chinese hospitality—the art of *keqi*—but
at the same time, there was something about the expatriate experience
that was nearly colonial. When China had been poor, these customs
made sense, and it was interesting to ponder how long certain attitudes
would persist.

I lived on a street called Longkou—literally, "the mouth of the
dragon." As if the name were not auspicious enough (Chinese drag-
ons, unlike their Western counterparts, are benevolent and lucky),
the housing complex was named "Eton 18," and its logo showed a
golf ball with two clubs crossing it at the center. The complex was not
associated with any famous British boarding school, nor was it near
any golf course. The number 18 was thrown in for good measure, presumably because it sounded favorable to Cantonese ears. The numbers
yao fa taken together were a homonym for "going to get rich."

More than for any lucky association, though, I lived there for the amenities. The towers of the complex were over 30 stories; there was a swimming pool; we had a pond with goldfish that swam next to a quaint, wooden bridge. It was easily one of the nicest apartment blocks in the city, and the most notable thing about the place was that a significant number of residents were employees of China's largest media organization—Xinhua News Agency. This was a news service owned and operated by the government.

The journalists in my building owned their apartments, which had been given to them by their employer. The property had come to the government through a backdoor connection. The developers needed government approval to build the complex, and so they earmarked a certain number of units for the government. Government employees—as well as the police and the military—were accustomed to getting special access to key properties. It was a perk offered in lieu of a cash payment, and while the journalists who received these apartments were supposed to live in them, many took the rent and occupied a cheaper place somewhere else. My own landlord worked for Xinhua as a journalist and lived just across the street in an apartment that rented for less than half of what I was paying him.

Such arrangements might be considered unethical business practices in other countries, but not in China, where mutual back scratching was an accepted norm.

In the United States, of course, journalists almost took a vow of poverty to pursue their careers, and their reward, perhaps, was the knowledge that they provided a meaningful check on government activities. That was one of the advantages of a free press anyway. In China, if you said the right things and kept your government's secrets, the rewards were quite sweet, and you could have a nice standard of living, if you wanted it.

I heard shouting outside my apartment one evening. At first, I thought that an international sporting event was on television and that China had scored a meaningful goal. When the racket persisted, I looked outside and saw that a small group had gathered down on the street for something else.

They were protesters who had come from another neighborhood, and they were standing in front of a building that housed a local government office. The crowd was made up of adult men and women, and some had come as couples; they were upset about a road that was going to be built near their homes. I watched for a while as they chanted slogans. They were not particularly organized, and someone in the crowd told me that they had only heard about the new road project earlier that day.

Protesters in China were typically doubly upset. They were angry over whatever issue they were up in arms about, but then they were also frustrated by the futility of their actions. By the time these protesters had learned about the road being built near their homes, it was already too late. The project was in motion, and there was no stopping it.

In a democratic country, citizens have options for channeling political energies. They can establish organizations around a common purpose, recruit members, and gather and disseminate meaningful data that might enable everyone to arrive at rational conclusions. They can discuss, debate, raise awareness, lobby politicians, bake cookies, vote—whatever.

"What happens next?" I asked one woman who stood watching.

"Nothing," she said.

"Nothing?"

I expected that at some point, someone was going to come out of the building and tell everyone to break it up and go home. The woman explained that the government office was actually closed. Of course it was. It was already late. These angry protesters had all been shouting at an empty building—and what was worse was that they all knew it.

China was documenting over 30,000 separate protests annually. All but a handful went unreported by the media. The rallies were almost invariably of a local nature, and most died right where they started. One reason for self-restraint was that protesters could not be sure what kind of attention their activities might attract. On the one hand, a fuss might bring government officers from a higher level down to help address a situation. On the other hand, it might result in local officials making things worse for the protestors in some way.

In the city's central business district, I knew of another kind of protest that was taking place. The government had announced that a power station was to be built adjacent to a residential complex. Those who had purchased their apartments thought it unfair that they had been told only after investing their money. Many homeowners in the complex hung vertical red banners from their balconies in protest. The message implied on the long signs was that certain local officials had been derelict in their duty.

It was summertime in Guangzhou, and temperatures were soaring. Some officials who had apparently felt pressure waited until it got particularly hot, and when Friday came, they cut the power to the entire complex.

For the whole weekend, residents who would have otherwise been enjoying themselves in their comfortable air-conditioned high-rise apartments were left to suffer in the heat. Such a message was clear: *Got a complaint? Sit in your sweltering apartments and meditate on it.*

Almost as if on cue, the group that had gathered near my building stopped their shouting. Having accomplished nothing, the crowd slowly dispersed. A few stomped off; most just shuffled away. These were adults, but they seemed more like teenagers who had just suffered a painful reminder of how their rights were limited, if not entirely illusory.

■ ■ ■

Guangzhou was said to be a second-tier city. It was a designation meant to cast the city as a Johnny-come-lately. In reality, though, it had been a center for international commerce long before other, better-known urban centers. China's showcase cities, Shanghai and Beijing, got most of the press, but when China began to emerge from its dark, isolationist period following the Cultural Revolution, the first steps were taken in the south. Separated from the rest of the country by mountain ranges, South China had already, for centuries, developed commercial opportunities with traders from afar. And as a result of the province's proximity to Hong Kong, whose economy remained robust, the region was poised to take off again. So it was no accident that when Deng Xiaoping announced, "to get rich is glorious," he did so from the southern province of Guangdong, where Guangzhou is located. If releasing so much pent-up entrepreneurial energy was akin to setting the economy on fire, it was near Guangzhou that the match had been struck.

In the modern era, Guangzhou was an attractive base for modern traders, if only for the diversity of manufacturers that it provided.

Most factories could be reached by car within 90 minutes from the city. Shanghai offered a similar diversity in manufactured goods, but the radius of the manufacturing area was closer to four hours. For this reason alone, Guangzhou attracted a greater number of generalists—importers who traded in "a little bit of this and a little bit of that." The Canton Fair added to the city's appeal as a base for importers.

A fast-paced city in normal times, twice each year Guangzhou hosted one of the largest trade shows in the world. The Canton Fair was an exhibition that lasted weeks and covered every major category of export manufacture. When the fair was in town, the city swelled with visitors from abroad.

So many importers from just about every country in the world attended that it was nearly impossible to find a taxi or get a table in a restaurant during fair times. For this reason, many of the foreigners who lived in town hated the fair. They planned trips so as to avoid being in town when it was on, or else they shuttered themselves indoors, as if expecting a typhoon.

I actually enjoyed the fair and attended whenever possible. It was an opportunity to get a quick overview of changes in industry, and it was also a chance to see fresh faces. The sudden influx of business travelers charged the city with energy, and these new arrivals brought with them an optimism that was palpable.

Most visitors to the show were small and medium-size importers, just as the companies operating exhibit booths were not very large. China made products for big-brand, Fortune 500 companies, but products for these sorts of corporations were not on display at the Canton Fair. This was a trade show for all of the "other" products that China manufactured.

The trade show was heavily skewed toward smaller players. It was also a great magnet for first-time importers. Instead of flying all around the country to visit dozens of prospective factories, would-be importers found that the fair was a convenient opportunity to meet with many manufacturers at once. For those who were merely curious about what was happening in China, the show provided a quick introduction.

Experienced traders had a sense of this and were largely of the opinion that the trade show was for suckers. Manufacturers tended to have the same idea and quoted higher prices at the fair than they did outside of fair times. Importing companies that spent a great deal of time and effort fighting factory price increases resented the newer, smaller players who came into the market and willingly paid higher prices for the same goods.

At the front of the exhibition hall was a large red banner, framed on either side by a long column of helium balloons. I arrived at the fair in the morning and was stopped by a man and his wife. They wanted to have their picture taken there, and I obliged. They were from Venezuela, they told me after I had taken the photo, and I didn't have to ask whether it was their first visit. Importers who were trying to negotiate for the right price while fighting to assure higher quality standards rarely looked as happy as that couple did.

The number of booths at the Canton Fair was growing fast, even as factories were said to be closing. One reason had to do with the increasing number of agents. For many of these go-betweens, the fair posed a small economic hurdle—the modest expense of a small booth space in most cases.

Many foreign visitors had no idea these were agents; their exhibition spaces appeared no different than those of the manufacturers.

Some of the largest exhibitors in certain halls belonged to trading companies, who aggregated a large number of products in a given category. I stopped by one such booth, a hardware company that carried thousands of separate products. An importer that owned a small hardware store—or perhaps a few such stores—might come and select items, as if in a warehouse. The trading company had created a small brand for itself, with attractive orange and black lettering, so that any retailer could pretend it was representing the products of a well-known company.

"Do you make any of these?" I asked a representative of the trading company, who turned out to be the company's president. Rather proudly, he said that he did—he manufactured all of the products in his booth. There were products made of plastic, and others that were made with metal. Some of the tools were precision made, but others were obviously produced using a cast-iron process. Different processes suggested different suppliers, but the factory man said that he owned 23 separate factories.

It was an amusing claim, if only because I knew factory owners who ran themselves ragged just to keep one plant operating smoothly. Maybe I even knew of one industrialist who managed to operate two factories. The idea that anyone could successfully manage 23 separate facilities was absurd, and here he was taking a full week out of his busy schedule to sit in a fair to shake hands with strangers. I understood why some made such claims anyway—it was because these trading companies wanted importers to feel as though they were going direct to the manufacturer.

Many of the smaller exhibitors at the Canton Fair—there were thousands of them—focused on products that would ensure they at least recouped their investment for the trade show. There was a heavy emphasis on products with a high impulse-buy factor, and everywhere you looked there were people selling poker chip sets, ashtrays, and gumball machines, as well as dozens of companies selling plastic cases for compact discs.

Buyers often got so excited on their very first trip that they placed an order even before they determined what they might actually do with whatever it was that they were shipping home.

The show was like an international bazaar, a lurid carnival of global commerce, and a great deal of on-the-spot haggling went on. Exhibitors would start sometimes with a high price, expecting that their customers would want to see a quick reduction.

Others liked to ask prospective buyers: "What's your market?"

Customers who came from France did not get quoted the same price as those from Russia. This business about "what's your market" incensed many importers who suspected that they might not be getting the absolute lowest price available.

Factory owners were good at sizing up their customers, and they took their cues from the vendors who sold vegetables in China's many wet markets. They tended to charge more for customers who could afford to pay extra. There was no such thing as a single "China price" for any given product. Pricing was all over the place, and manufacturers got whatever they could.

Price discrimination was nothing new in business, but it was a practice associated with marketing companies, not manufacturers. Buyers expected that a factory would make its product available to all at the same price, but this was not how it worked in China. Importers resented that they were sized up in such a crude fashion, and that they might be disadvantaged in a pricing negotiation because of their background.

I walked past a corner booth as a tall man in a checkered shirt was negotiating a price on metal posts. His English was accented, and he spoke very loudly in a brusque tone. I paused, watching, while he and the factory owner put each other through their paces.

"How much? How much?" the importer shouted. He sounded as if he were in a great hurry.

The factory owner looked down at the importer's shoes before quoting him a price: "$1.60."

"That is not price," the importer said.

The factory owner did not seem bothered by the shouting.

"I buy big quantity," the importer promised. His accent was heavy, and he pronounced it "kwan-tee-tee." Importers were always talking up their order sizes in the hope of getting a break on volume.

Neither buyer nor seller was from an English-speaking country, and yet they both spoke in English. They also both quoted prices in dollars. The supplier lowered his price by a few pennies.

"No! Big *kwan-tee-tee*! Forty-foot container!"

The supplier looked weary for a moment and glanced at his price sheets. He took out a calculator and punched in some numbers. He then gave what appeared to be his final price.

"For you, $1.39." he said.

"That's right," said the importer. "Now, I want to order 200 pieces."

"Two hundred? Only two hundred? You said you buy 40-foot container. Two hundred pieces is nothing. It does not fill even a 20-foot container."

"Yes," said the buyer. "But first I need samples, don't I?"

Walking through the housewares hall, I happened across an importer who was in an argument with one supplier. Whatever they were discussing was being made more difficult by a language barrier.

"You need any help?" I asked the importer, who looked frustrated. From his accent, I took him to be Eastern European.

At first he said that he was all right, and then he explained that he was having difficulty convincing his factory not to display his products in their booth.

He pointed to a stack of boxes on top of which was a ceramic dinnerware collection. It was decorated in a light yellow and green pattern. He explained that he was from Poland, and that he sold these items throughout Europe.

"The product is yours?"

"Yes," he said.

"You gave the factory the designs?"

"Yes, my original designs. I have customers at this show," he said. "If they see my product here, then they know where I am manufacturing."

He worried that the factory might sell his product to his customers directly. Even if the factory didn't do that, his customers might learn how much he was paying. For all kinds of reasons, he wanted to keep his supplier hidden.

The factory representative insisted that she had done nothing wrong, and that her company had the right to display examples of products that it made. If they could not show off examples of their work, then how could they get any new business?

Famous brands were not displayed at the Canton Fair for fear that trademarks might be violated through counterfeit sales. The products of smaller importers found their way onto the exhibition floor, but the same principles generally applied. Factories tended to respect the wishes of their customers on this point.

Suggesting some of this to the supplier, I managed to get the factory rep excited. Seeing her reaction, the importer panicked. "It's all right. I don't want to do anything to make them upset," he said. The man tried then to apologize to his supplier, though he had done nothing wrong, and I felt even more sorry for him.

It was something that I would see with increased frequency—importers, fearful of their suppliers, even though they were supposed to be the customer.

The worst example of this strange phenomenon was made public with the Mattel case. Chinese manufacturers had caused the company great reputational damage by delivering toys that were contaminated with lead paint. A major recall was initiated in the United States, and by the time the dust settled, Mattel executives were in Beijing issuing an apology to the Chinese government—for the damage *they* had caused the industry. It showed the true extent of Chinese savvy, that manufacturers could behave in such a reckless fashion by using toxic substances and then get those who had been victimized to issue the apology instead.

A German client of mine, a fellow named Norbert, asked me to look into heavy machinery for him. He wanted me to find a supplier of forklifts and backhoes, one that would offer him exclusive representation for Germany and Austria.

One manufacturer of two-ton forklifts asked me: "What market?" When I told him, he cut me short and said that they already had an exclusive arrangement with an agent in those territories.

I was not yet 50 feet away from his booth, having moved on, when he caught up to me and in a low voice suggested that I ring him up after the show had concluded.

"Maybe something can be arranged," he said, and I imagined that the importer who held the exclusive was either wandering around the show and the factory rep did not want to suffer the embarrassment of getting caught, or else he did not want one of his colleagues to know what he was planning.

For a different product, I helped my German client secure an exclusive for Germany and Austria. Business had been running smoothly for more than two years when I received a letter from the factory. They did not realize who they were sending the note to, apparently, and they announced that they would be exhibiting at a trade show in Hannover the following year.

When I confronted the company representative, he played innocent. My client's company still held exclusive rights to Germany and Austria, they insisted, but still my client protested. If we held the exclusive, should we not at least have been told about the plan to exhibit in Germany? The company's president explained that their attending the trade fair did not in and of itself make them guilty of any wrongdoing. They were merely planning to exhibit at the show. Yes, they would be in our territory, and yes, there would be German buyers at the show, but the supplier had not done anything improper—at least not yet.

Importers were starting to have a tough time in China, and some threatened to take their business elsewhere. Vietnam was becoming a new possible destination for manufacturing, and India seemed to be an interesting prospect. When one supplier at the Canton Fair quoted prices that were especially inflated, I protested and in a fluster suggested that foreign buyers would one day get wise and flee.

"One day soon, we will all go to India," I said.

At this mention, the industrialist brightened, and he reached for his order book. Flipping through oversize pink carbon sheets, he pointed to one.

"This is my customer. He is from India," he said. He flipped through more pages and pointed to another. "This one also—from India!"

He was proud of his Indian customers and of the fact that he had countered my suggestion so perfectly. That traders from India were beating a path to China showed the strength of the Chinese economy, he suggested; prices in China were still low.

The growing number of importers from around the world emboldened these suppliers. How could anyone ever convince them that there was something wrong with the way they operated their businesses when order sizes were on the rise and the competition itself was clamoring to come to China?

Factories were doing all that they could to draw in foreign importers. Once importers were actually in China, it was difficult to switch markets. And, anyway, where were they going to go? Talk about India was just as empty as talk about a shift of production to places around Southeast Asia. Labor costs and even currency exchange rates aside, Chinese manufacturers had figured out the system, and the convenience in manufacturing that China afforded was so significant that it forced importers to deal with a great number of drawbacks.

■ ■ ■

Foreign visitors had no trouble gaining entry to the fair, but for locals it could be tricky. Unless you were an exhibitor, you either had to have an invitation letter from a supplier, or you had to be brought in as a translator with the accompaniment of a foreign buyer. Tina was curious about the fair, and the fact that she was not allowed free permission to attend was all of the motivation I needed to work on getting her inside. We made a plan to meet the next day and enter the fair together.

The early morning sounds of the city got me out of bed without fail. The first noises to make their way to my apartment came from nearby construction projects, long before almost anyone in our complex was even considering getting out of bed. While I was still asleep, the rhythmic pounding from one project began.

Donk . . . donk . . . donk . . . donk.

Some distance away, the whirring sounds from a second construction site got started. It was a saw blade cutting into metal, a sound that told me it was still early. This was, in effect, my early morning snooze button.

Wheeeeeeeeeen. WheeeeeEEEEN!

The road in front of my building had been changed into a one-way street, and this created continual confusion for motorists who insisted on driving down the street in the wrong direction. Taxi drivers were especially ambitious in getting amateur motorists through the bottleneck. Their bleating horns encouraged others.

Bap-bap. . . . baaaaap . . .

When the horn honking climaxed at a certain pitch, it was a clear sign that it was time to get moving. And by the time the sounds from the school nearby could be heard, it already felt as though the entire city were up and on the move, though it was barely half past seven.

The sounds of the students' carefully timed calisthenics echoed through the canyon of high-rise buildings in the neighborhood, their reverberated shouts high-pitched and aggressive. The students sounded as though they were in a military exercise, and still in the hazy fog of sleep I imagined them lunging in formation with make-believe bayonets in hand.

Hyaaah! Hyaaah! Hyaaah! Hyaaah!

These were the stirrings of an economy on fast forward, the echoes of rapid progress. I never needed any kind of clock radio at my bedside. The anxious, early morning sounds served as my daily alarm.

At the Canton Fair, hundreds of Chinese stood waiting behind a crowd-control barricade. College students who were studying at the foreign trade school in the city held signs in various languages that said "interpreter," looking rather desperate—almost like political refugees or orphans hoping for a home.

To get Tina past the hordes and into the fair, I had to present identification, and we had to say that she was to be my translator. Tina presented her own ID, and she had her picture taken. The picture was sealed into a plastic badge, which she was to hang around her neck. We paid the "translator's fee" of roughly $30 and moved into the main exhibition hall.

My hope was that Tina might learn something from the show, and the only errand I had for her was to pick up a number of catalogs for a client interested in ceramic floor tiles. It would not take long, and if anything, the minor mission would lend a sense of purpose before giving her the day to explore the fair more freely.

In a nearby hall, I found my way to the pottery section, and down one of the main aisles I spotted a familiar company name. It was the factory owned by Kevin, the young industrialist who tried to convince me that he was from Los Angeles. His booth was a tall space. I stepped inside and caught him just as he was saying goodbye to a pair of trade show attendees who appeared Middle Eastern.

"Was that Arabic you were speaking to them?" I asked.

"I have many customers from Middle East," he said.

He insisted that he knew only a few words. Still, I was impressed. To hear anyone at the show communicating in anything other than English or Chinese threw me.

Chinese were actually going out of their way to learn foreign languages, which was not exactly what international relations theorists had predicted. Academics who touted "hegemonic theory" insisted that the world was speaking English if only because the United States was the predominant political and economic power. China was rising to significance, these theorists insisted—and so the world would switch to Chinese.

This was not what was happening in China, though, at least not in the world of export manufacturing. Importers, who had every reason to learn the language, were forgoing the opportunity. Instead, representatives at the manufacturers were learning the language of their customers.

Part of it was motivated by simple economics. A full-time transla-tor could be found in China for as little as $300 per month. Westerners had an opportunity cost that was much higher. And so, it made sense for the lesser-developed economies to bear the burden of bridging the linguistic chasm.

There was another reason why Chinese would learn the languages of the world before the world learned to speak its own—and this had to do with the skills required for learning Mandarin.

Chinese contained thousands of characters, which were acquired only through rote memorization. While some argued that English was just as difficult for native Chinese speakers to learn as Chinese was for Americans, the Chinese at least had a great deal of experience in cramming information. The level of skill required to achieve fluency in Mandarin turned the Chinese into language acquisition machines. Americans almost always felt more intimidated to learn Chinese than the other way around.

I had just begun to wonder what Tina might be doing with herself when she called from her cell phone. She sounded upset, like she was in some kind of trouble. She was sobbing and could not speak clearly. I asked her to tell me where in the fair she was, and when I found her she was in tears with three security guards standing nearby. Tina explained that she had been stopped, and she told me that one of the security guards had grabbed her.

"What did you do?"

"Nothing," she said.

I asked her whether she had shown them her badge, the one that gave her permission to be in the fair. She said that she had. I asked one of the guards to explain himself. He said only that he had the right to stop and hold anyone he chose, and just because Tina had permission to be at the show did not give her any special rights. The guards were unapologetic, and my arrival by itself signaled the end of the incident.

China was not a racist country, but there existed a chasm between two classes—the haves and the have-nots. It was not so much a caste system as it was a sociological divide, one based loosely on income and education. Tina was on the wrong side of the equation, but then so were the guards from the look of them. Why they stopped Tina was anyone's guess, but it was possibly because they saw in Tina something of themselves. Security guards earned some of the lowest salaries in China, and having come from modest backgrounds, they probably saw that Tina was not very well connected, that she was one of the few at the trade show who, like themselves, were left to strive for more.

Tina had not yet told me the rest of her story. Earlier in the day, she visited the tile suppliers, but few were willing to give her their catalog. It was the same sort of snubbing.

She had shown the exhibitors her business card and badge, but they were unmotivated. Tina would not say why they wouldn't give her their promotional literature, but this was also not hard to figure out. They didn't think that she was worth the effort. They figured that she was of no account and that the marketing materials would be wasted on her.

Tina was made frail from so much rejection, and it was this that the security guards had also sensed before setting upon her like a pack of wild dogs.

Hearing her tell me this story and seeing her upset, I became angry. I worked with all sorts of manufacturers, and they never treated me in such a manner. They spent small fortunes to exhibit at the trade show, and when I refused their catalogs, they pushed them onto me, even shoving them into my bag. They normally jumped at even the slightest hint of a business opportunity.

I knew these factory reps well. Just like those security guards, their problem was that they saw something of themselves in Tina. They knew that what separated them was nothing more than a bit of luck, or maybe some small personal connection. They looked at her and thought—there but for the grace of *guanxi* go I.

It was still early in the day, but Tina said that she wanted to go home. The show had been a disaster, and I felt bad. The whole idea of getting her to the fair was to expand her horizons. She had been curious and had been rewarded only with a reminder that there were limitations to her ambitions. It was unfair.

"I have an idea," I said. Tina was still in tears, and she looked down at the red carpeting. "I think you should go back to the tile exhibitors and give them a different story. This time, tell them that you are working with a foreigner, one that is really stupid."

It wasn't far from the truth; it was how I felt anyway for putting Tina in a situation that caused her embarrassment. If she simply gave up, though, that was even worse.

Tina wiped her eyes with the back of her bare forearm and looked at me to see if I was serious.

"Tell them what?" she asked.

"Tell them you work for a *really* stupid foreigner," I said. "An American, someone who can be easily cheated."

She knew what I was driving at, but it wasn't her style. It was not a very Confucian notion either. I was suggesting that she put aside any respect that she might have for me, all for the sake of a ruse. This could be done in the spirit of not giving up, I suggested, and I told Tina that she might consider it an experiment.

Her boyfriend was a marine scientist who ran experiments at sea, and so she somewhat warmed to the idea of testing a hypothesis. Maybe another approach would generate a different result. After a moment to collect herself, she agreed that she would go back and give it another try.

We met later in the afternoon. This time she was happier. When something amused Tina, her cheekbones moved high, and when she was truly amused it looked as though she were suppressing a case of the giggles.

"It wasn't a problem?" I asked.

"No," she said, bursting out in laughter. "I told them that I work for a stupid foreigner!"

Tina showed me all of the catalogs the factory reps had given her. She had two bags filled with them. Tina opened one of the bags and showed me some of the marketing materials. The company representatives that she spoke with gave them to her without hesitation after she explained her "situation" a bit more clearly.

The idea of getting hooked up with a naive foreign buyer proved a fantastic temptation for these company representatives, and it trumped whatever other prejudices they held against Tina. The line worked so well, in fact, that her phone rang for weeks after the show with follow-ups from the tile factories.

CHAPTER 7

And That's a Good Thing

American consumers grumbled about how everything was being made "over there," and what they were referring to were the products they saw in retail stores—the toys on the shelves, the clothes on the racks. It rarely occurred to them that even the shelves and the racks were being made in China.

Classic Metal was a major manufacturer of store fixtures with revenues exceeding $50 million annually. When they began losing business to competitors who were more forward thinking in pursuing cheap outsourcing opportunities, the company set its sights on China.

The head of the delegation was a Chicagoan, John, who had already identified three factories that he felt sure were capable of manufacturing the kinds of fixtures that his company designed and fabricated in the United States. He said that his company was looking for some simple, on-the-ground assistance and wanted to know if I could join his team.

We agreed to meet in Hong Kong, where I would hand him train tickets that I had purchased in advance. Just one week before the delegation's scheduled arrival, John e-mailed me and said that he had a pressing question.

"What kind of gifts should we bring?" he asked when he got me on the phone.

The question caught me off guard. Most importers I knew did not bring anything at all. It did not seem to adversely affect their business in any event, but I could appreciate the concern.

China was often painted as a mysterious place, and books on doing business in China left many newcomers walking on eggshells. Foreigners were taught to believe that a mispronounced phrase in Chinese could turn a simple sentence into an insult. These mythmakers had many people believing that the slightest misstep would ruin a deal, but it was the furthest thing from the truth.

Chinese manufacturers did not care one way or another about gifts; what they cared about were orders. Offerings could not make a bad deal look good. Importers either had orders in hand or they did not. This business of gift giving would be the least of this client's concerns anyway, as we would soon learn.

We met in Hong Kong at a hotel in Tsim Sha Tsui. John came with others—two men from the company's production department and a woman involved in logistics. Once across the border and inside Mainland China, we went to a hotel and checked in.

The hotel desk manager asked everyone to place their passports on the counter. Only one out of the four had ever been to China before, and their passports looked thin and crisp. My own had pages added to it and was swollen like a paperback left out in the rain, and from years of being jammed into various bags and pockets, the gold-colored bald eagle on the front had faded away. Placed next to theirs, mine had the look of a passport belonging to someone from another country altogether.

Since our hotel had no currency exchange service, the four of them asked to borrow some renminbi, just until we had a chance to get to a bank. One member of the group, Mike, looked at the red currency notes I gave him and chuckled. "It looks like Monopoly money," he said. After promising to pay me back the next day, John reminded me to send him receipts for expenses.

The next morning, the group from Chicago arrived in the lobby, and a factory owner, who preferred to be called Miss Lee, met us. We drove into the country past a number of tiny hamlets. It was an unusual spot for a factory, I thought. When we stopped, I noted that we were not in an industrial area at all, but near some tall grass where scrawny-looking chickens wandered about.

Miss Lee went to the side of a brick building. It was not a factory, but rather a small warehouse. John and his three colleagues walked hesitantly into the building, surveying it carefully, but there was really nothing there. No one said a word, and I was not quite sure what to think of it myself.

Along one wall there were some boxes, and in an opposite corner was a single, small sign of industry: one lone metal-stamping machine. A few chrome racks had been taken out of the boxes and set up in the middle of the small space. These were by no means custom racks; they were the sort of generic racks you might have found in a thrift shop back in the United States.

Everyone from Chicago walked over to the racks and pretended to be interested in them. They had been traveling for more than two days, and this was supposed to be the first of three factories on John's list of potential suppliers. They were expecting to see a production process, especially since Miss Lee had indicated that she owned and operated a factory.

"What do they think?" Miss Lee asked me, sounding hopeful.

John was quiet, as were the others.

"It's not exactly a factory," I said.

"Please tell them that we can make whatever they want."

John looked embarrassed when I explained what she had said. I asked how he had come to learn about Miss Lee, and he admitted that he had found her on a web site. China was full of wannabes, and there were many agents who pretended to be manufacturers. John said that he didn't understand. Miss Lee had said that her company manufactured custom store fixtures. They probably did, I offered, but at some other location. If Miss Lee was not willing to take us to that factory, it meant that her relationship with the actual supplier was a tenuous one at best—in other words, it was a bad sign.

Most importers did not want to work with agents. One reason was that agents did not always take their business to the most capable supplier, but instead directed their business to the company that provided the best commission. Often, the supplier might be a friend or a relative, which also posed a problem if there were quality issues. With a bad shipment of product, the agent was more likely to show allegiance to the factory boss than to the importer.

At least in this case, we knew from the very beginning that Miss Lee was an agent. Some importers learned only much later, after a background check or after a product went bad and there was a dispute.

It was our first day together, and I was worried for the folks at Classic Metal. Typically, whenever an American company claimed that China was the key to its future success, the chief executive flew out with the group. These four were on their own, and I wondered whether the president of the company would ever learn that his representatives had flown all the way to China only to inspect an empty warehouse.

We moved on to our second destination, and while this time there was an actual factory on the premises, the company was manufacturing a kind of exercise machine instead of store fixtures.

The factory tour itself was short, and we were led into a showroom. The collection that we were shown included a large number of random yet professional-looking retail fixtures and displays.

"This is much better," said John sounding relieved.

Attentions were turned to a copper-colored shelving system with a textured surface. One of the production team ran a finger over the surface.

"What kind of finish is this?" he asked.

"Yes, no problem," the factory owner replied. He either had not heard the question or chose not to answer it.

It did not take long to realize that this factory had not produced most of the samples in the showroom. The factory was too small for such a varied offering, and the company did not seem equipped to produce some of the items.

At the back of the sample room, I noticed a number of shipping boxes that had come in by DHL and FedEx. I glanced at a few of the addresses. They were all from the United States. The showroom products seemed to be samples that came in from American companies. It was possible that they had been samples from prospective customers, or perhaps they belonged to competitors.

Some Chinese manufacturers did this sort of thing. They set up an address in the United States and pretended they were a buyer. They then contacted competitors and requested product samples. These were then shipped back to China, where they were placed in a showroom.

A factory had to appear skilled to catch customers, and it was too expensive to make a product line before an order actually came in. Manufacturers all suffered from this chicken-and-egg problem: to kick-start their businesses, they had to fool customers into thinking they were already in motion. The easiest way to do this was by throwing samples—anyone's samples—into a showroom. If pressed for the truth, a factory owner might admit that his factory did not actually produce all of the items that were on display, but there was nothing to stop an importer from jumping to certain conclusions on its own.

Chinese factories made plenty of counterfeit products, and so it was no great surprise that they also faked entire showrooms. The purpose of these make-believe displays was to spark the imagination. It was a place for importers to dream, and this is exactly what the representatives from Classic Metal did. They oohed and aahed, and while they did so, the factory owner stood by silently and looked hopeful.

For a new factory looking to get into business, all it took was a single purchase order from a large importer. These suppliers with potential could be awakened by a meaningful client, as if by a magical kiss from a storybook prince. It didn't matter whether the factory had actually ever made any of the products in its showroom. Just one purchase order was needed, and the factory would work out the rest later.

Everyone looked at samples in the showroom, and along with the exercise equipment that was there, someone spotted an air conditioner unit that had been placed on top of one of the many racks.

"Look," someone said. "They even make air conditioners."

Everyone laughed, but not convincingly. I worried that they actually thought that the appliance had something to do with this factory. The owner had done a good job of convincing the group from Chicago that anything could be made at his plant, so it really wasn't such a far leap.

The third factory was the only one we visited that looked capable—but in the extreme.

At the front of the place, two flags were flown—the U.S. flag and the flag of the People's Republic of China—both at the same height. When we pulled in through the gate, a guard saluted, and the factory owner, Stanley, saluted back. They had hundreds of employees located among several large buildings, and they were all dressed in crisp uniforms. The place looked so impressive that if I had not known otherwise, I might have believed they were producing high-tech goods, not metal displays and racks.

The showroom was larger than the previous factory's, and this time you could believe that they made just about everything that was there.

On one side of the massive showroom were display shelves for supermarkets. In another section, there were displays for tennis rackets, athletic shoes, and other sporting goods. Depending on the angle at which you stood, you could imagine yourself in almost any kind of retail space.

The group from Chicago was dumbstruck, and they quickly revised their plans for orders at the previous factory. This one would be the factory that would produce their products, John declared, and he did not need any further convincing.

That a China manufacturing operation was efficient was not always the best sign. Quite often, it meant that the factory charged more. In China, economies of scale did not always mean a cheaper price. And more troubling was that the boss of the company, Stanley, seemed even smoother than his operation.

He told us how he got started in business. He had once been an agent, just like Miss Lee, and when one of his biggest customers placed a sizable order along with a substantial deposit, he recognized his chance and delayed shipment of the order long enough until he had found a building to rent. He then purchased some equipment and filled the bulk of the order.

In his office, Stanley delivered a small speech about all that he was doing for his employees. He had set up a karaoke lounge at the factory, he said, where workers could spend their evenings. He peppered his language with buzzwords like "corporate social responsibility" and said that he had initiated a profit-sharing plan. When we went onto the factory floor later, I buttonholed a few workers and asked them if they had anything like a profit-sharing scheme in place. Aside from the usual Chinese New Year bonus—the one that most companies gave out—the workers could not name any such arrangement.

It may have been the amount of time I had already spent working other plants that alerted me, but Stanley came off as disingenuous. My clients perceived him as sincere though, and as far as they were concerned, he was too good to be true. They remarked in front of him how happy they were with the factory, and without first discussing price they all but agreed to send Stanley their orders.

There was another problem with this factory, though. Classic Metal's competitors were using the same supplier, and their volume was more substantial. In the warehouse, John noticed the logo of a major competitor on a great number of stacked boxes.

Finding a capable supplier was important, but it was problematic to source products from the same place where your competitor got them. It was too difficult to differentiate your company's own offering in the marketplace, and in this one case there was another issue: Classic Metal's order sizes were going to be smaller than their competitor's, which meant less buying power. In an open bidding process, they would probably lose bids to their competition, and even if they did catch orders, they would have a harder time catching the factory's attention, which meant the possibility of quality failures.

When the group saw the product belonging to their competitor, hearts sank. John understood the flaw in their strategy, but he said there was no real choice. The trip had already been planned, and this was the factory that gave them the most confidence in their manufacturing capability.

The more time we spent with Stanley, the more I got concerned about doing business with him. At one point, he had claimed to own the factory outright, but then we saw a plaque in his office that suggested the factory was actually a joint venture. The American flag that flew out front was a likely indication of where the partners came from.

Stanley also mentioned that he flew to the United States often and belonged to an American industry association. There were other manufacturers that did not have such easy access to the importer's own customer base. How could Classic Metal be sure that Stanley's company would not place bids that were in direct competition?

The decision had been made to give Stanley their business, and John suggested that it was time to wrap up the visit.

"That meeting went fast," he said.

"And that's a good thing," said one of the others from Chicago. Everyone was in a hurry to get out of the factory; they had shopping on their minds. Before it was time to return to the United States, they wanted to pick up China souvenirs.

Everyone had a specific type of market in mind, the sort that sold counterfeit handbags and watches. Importers of all kinds were fans of these counterfeit products, and Stanley smiled knowingly when they said it was what they had in mind. The government was actually complicit in the maintenance of these counterfeit markets, and officials knew that while some importers complained about piracy, in general, foreign buyers liked to run out and purchase such products themselves. Like big banquets and foot massages, shopping for knock-offs was a standard stop on any manufacturing trip through China.

Stanley walked us back to the hotel from the shopping trip, and with the business relationship all sewn up, I had a final question for him. There was something about him that made me think he might not actually be from Mainland China. His act was too polished, his English too fluent, and he said he had been flying to the United States before China had really opened up in any meaningful way. I wanted to know whether he was actually from Taiwan, but the issue was too sensitive for a direct approach.

"Where did you go to school?" I asked in as casual a manner as possible.

"You don't know the place," he said. "It's about 180 kilometers away from here."

The city of Taipei was actually just so far away. I next asked whether he thought that Taiwan was a part of China. It was a big question. In Mainland China, over 99.9 percent of the general population felt that it was, but attitudes in Taiwan were more divided and there was debate on the matter.

Stanley hesitated and said, "*Most* people would say that it is."

A comment like that was considered blasphemous to people in Mainland China, and it was as close to an admission as I would get. South China was full of entrepreneurs from Taiwan. Though considered Chinese, the locals resented them. The workers accused factory bosses from Taiwan of being *xiaoqi*—cheapskates—for paying like a local company, if not worse. Taiwanese were seen as carpetbaggers, and some felt that they took away opportunities that should have gone to Mainland Chinese firms.

Taiwanese business owners were occasionally even taken hostage and held for ransom. If Stanley was from Taiwan, the threat of kidnapping was reason enough to keep quiet about his place of origin.

On the business side of things, there was another possible explanation for the hidden identity. Seasoned importers did not like to work with Taiwanese firms because they had a reputation for charging more than firms owned by Mainland Chinese. One reason that Taiwanese firms charge more for their products made in Mainland China was that their operating costs and cost of capital were often higher.

While it looked like the trip might have been considered a failure for the group—they had, after all, found only the most obvious supplier, one that also made goods for the competition—everyone from Classic Metal was satisfied. They had no option really, but they chose to see the trip as their good fortune.

After the group returned to the United States, we stayed in touch by e-mail. I submitted my invoice, which included receipts for reimbursement, but payment never came. Tiring of delays, I called the company, but no one answered the phone. There was only a voice recording where there had once been a receptionist to answer calls—the company had gone bankrupt.

I caught up with John, who insisted that he himself didn't know that it was coming. The head of the company surely must have, though. The CEO had not only stiffed his workers on their payroll, he had absconded with their retirement fund, as well.

Coming to China just months before declaring bankruptcy made their visit seem strange. Just like that, a $50-million company was out of business. It occurred to me that they might have made it if they had only come to China earlier, like their competitors had. There were many Americans who thought taking business overseas destroyed jobs in the United States, but this was one case in which coming to China at the right time might have actually saved a few.

CHAPTER 8

Grains of Toil

Maria and I continued to date, though I was out of town most of the time now. One evening, we met in Guangzhou for dinner at a Sichuan restaurant near the central business district. The restaurant, which she chose, was one of the city's more popular ones, and along a wall were many plaques of distinction, including one that marked it as a *bai nian lao dian*—a "one-hundred-year restaurant"—though it was not literally that old.

Sitting in an established restaurant of this sort, I had to remind myself that no matter how long the restaurant claimed to go back, it was almost certainly closed during the first phase of the Cultural Revolution, in the late 1960s, and most likely for many years more after that.

As hundreds of millions of Chinese were faced with starvation during the earlier part of the Cultural Revolution, the very institution of the restaurant ceased to exist. It was enough to make you wonder—how *did* all those chefs pick up where they left off? After decades of not cooking much of anything at all, did they simply dust off their cookbooks, or did they need to reinvent certain things?

In the West, restaurants were a rather recent phenomenon, having only been popularized during the French Revolution. When the aristocracy lost the household staff along with their wealth, a few cooks got the idea to establish businesses that gave their former bosses a place to reminisce. The food was the same, and the décor was designed so that patrons could feel that they were in the dining room of an estate. The only difference between dining in these new creations and at home was the check delivered to the table at the end of the meal.

Thinking about this, I asked Maria how many years of history she thought the Chinese restaurant had. Surely it had to go back further than the eighteenth century—but how far? Not missing a beat, she answered with confidence, "Five thousand years."

The Chinese government liked to promote the idea that China had a history of 5,000 years. This much I knew, but it seemed rather unlikely that restaurants appeared at the very dawn of Chinese civilization. Instead of challenging her on the notion, I asked another question.

"What about chopsticks?"

"Five thousand years."

The stern look on Maria's face told me that she was dead serious. It was as if she imagined, five millennia ago, some Chinese Abraham had arrived on the scene, chopsticks in hand, and said, "Show me to the nearest noodle shop."

No culture came about in such a fashion; a people did not spring up from nothingness and then remain static over thousands of years, and yet Chinese people held on to such notions. The Chinese of today are, of course, unlike the Chinese of the third millennium BC, and indeed, are far less like their ancestors of just a couple of centuries ago.

That the Chinese saw themselves and their history as immutable was especially ironic, given how fast the place was changing.

Maria had turned up that night in a new outfit, a yellow ensemble. Not 10 years earlier, mentioning a young woman's sharp outfit might have generated a modest response, "What, these old rags?" When I complimented Maria, though, her response had been that she knew she looked good and that she ought to because the outfit had been expensive.

Along with behavior, the language was changing, and in the most basic ways. Anyone who studied Mandarin learned quickly the difference between *ni,* the informal pronoun for "you," and the more formal *nin,* used when addressing elders and persons of distinction. It was a polite term that had once been used in daily life, but no more.

In modern China, just about the only place you ever saw the formal pronoun used was in advertising, and the only thing it had ever done for me was help me filter out e-mail messages that were obviously unwanted solicitations.

I wanted to talk more about restaurants, but Maria did not. The whole point of saying "5,000 years" was to shut down the discussion before it even began.

If any people should know how much their own history has reflected significant change, it is the Chinese, who kept meticulous records for over two thousand years. Fast forward to the twenty-first century, though, and everything is the same as it ever was. This was, in and of itself, a sign of how different things had become under Communist rule.

Modern Chinese were dogmatic when it came to the issue of history, treating the subject more like a religion—and to some extent, that is what it was to them.

The function of a religion is to supply multigenerational groups with an explanation of where they have come from and where they are going. It also provides a moral code of conduct. "Religion" comes from the Latin word *religio*, meaning to bind together, and its purpose throughout the ages has been to help groups stay tight, in part through distinguishing a distinct in-group from a separate out-group.

Chinese history provided just such a framework for its people, and, like a religion, it came with a prepackaged messianic concept. Like a prophecy that awaited fulfillment, there were preconditions. In China's case, this included the reunification of its splintered territories. It was the reason that it was almost impossible to have any kind of reasonable discussion with people from Mainland China on the subject of Taiwan or Tibet. The Chinese didn't know what exactly was going to happen when all the pieces of the geographic puzzle were conjoined; they only knew that something grand would happen—that it must happen.

Maria was not bothered by my interest in discussing touchy subjects or in expressing contrary views. Zealots are rarely ever weakened by disbelievers; in fact, they are encouraged by them. On the subject of China's history, Maria welcomed my skepticism as an opportunity to strengthen her own faith. It was, for better or worse, the primary dynamic in our relationship—the cynic and the patriot.

The attention at our table turned to a crisis unfolding. We had ordered too many dishes, and our waitress was coming in for a third attempt to clear away plates, some of which had barely been touched. It was still early on a Friday night, and so doggy bags were out of the question.

With the waitress having been chased off, Maria took her chopsticks and began moving vegetables into my rice bowl. It would have been a sign of affection at many Chinese tables, but with Maria this was desperation. The idea of letting things go to waste was an abomination to her, and she was looking for help in alleviating her guilt feelings.

As she encouraged me, so I decided to encourage her.

"*Lili jie xinku*," I said.

"That's not funny!" she said.

They were words from a Tang Dynasty poem, the last line of a classic four-liner, one that highlighted the dignity of hard labor by depicting workers in the fields:

> The sun beats down at noon
> Beads of sweat fall to the soil
> Who knew that in a single dish
> Were so many grains of toil

Grains of toil, indeed.

The poem was one that most schoolchildren in China could recite by heart, and Chairman Mao had used it to encourage savings during his rule when the country was poor—as if the tens of millions who quite literally starved to death needed to be reminded of the value that each grain held. Mao had tapped into an already strong cultural inclination, and in the more bountiful, modern era, *lili jie xinku* took on a new, ironic twist.

The waitress came around and could not have cared less about our waste, but Maria said that she was sorry. To ease any concern, she told Maria that the food was not actually going to be wasted; the restaurant's scraps were sent to feed pigs on a farm just outside the city.

Interested to see if this were true, I went back to the restaurant on another night, and I arrived in time to watch three workmen carrying plastic buckets from the kitchen to the curb. They prepared their haul first by going through the refuse with their bare hands, pulling out things that the pigs could not eat—like seashells and chopsticks. Nearly everything else was fair game: watermelon rinds, chicken bones, chili peppers, cooking oil, leafy stalks, and leftover rice.

I asked the workers about their jobs, and they told me that the restaurant paid a small amount to take away the waste. The farmers then paid another trifling sum, and between the two small sources of income, they managed to earn a living.

China was rightly seen as a major polluter, but not nearly enough credit was given to the ambitious recycling habits practiced around the country. In this case, the restaurant benefited from having its line to the sewer kept clear, and the farmers saved money on animal feed. It was an ecologically sound system. Calories thrown away one night in a restaurant could quite literally be back on the dining room table in just a matter of weeks.

Language and behavior might be changing, but one of the more enduring traits that had survived the centuries was this saving habit.

One of the first quality problems we encountered at the factory involved labeling. An error had made its way onto the list of ingredients on the back label of our shampoo. The Food and Drug Administration (FDA) in the United States concerned itself with product labeling to such an extent that Johnson Carter issued a corrected label as soon as the problem was discovered. The factory produced the new labels, but when new bottles came off the production line, we got a surprise.

"We wanted to finish up the old labels first," Sister said.

Sister knew that we were concerned about FDA compliance. Even though she understood the issue, she thought correcting the label was a lower priority than making sure the old labels didn't go to waste. The labels, which cost just a fraction of a penny each, could not be thrown out. They had to go *somewhere*.

It was easy to see how product recalls came about. Manufacturers manipulated product to save only the tiniest amounts of money. When caught at something silly, like trying to save a few dollars by knowingly using incorrect labels, Sister did not express the least bit of shame. In fact, she was glad that I learned of her secret—that we could share in her *achievement*. She wanted to be seen as clever.

The first shipments of shampoo began to arrive in the United States, and we received bad news. The cardboard that we used was apparently not up to the task of holding the product, and cartons were collapsing. A number of pallet stacks had been crushed under their own weight, causing bottles to break. As a result, the floor of one warehouse was covered in liquid soap.

Sister blamed her supplier of cardboard boxes. She also defended herself by saying that Bernie had been shown a sample, which he had approved. The original sample was brought to me for inspection. It was flat and had never been assembled. Just looking at the cardboard, I suggested, no one would be able to know if it was strong enough. But the cardboard box manufacturer would have known, and there was a very good chance that the supplier told the factory exactly what kind of risk they were facing.

Factory owners operated in an almost tournament-like environment. There was constant competition, not just among them, but also with their raw material suppliers. Someone was always trying to cut a corner somewhere, selling a product that was supposed to be high grade when it was in fact lower grade.

Because the environment was intensely competitive, operators were incredibly savvy. No factory owner that survived did so without learning the tricks of the trade, and there was no such thing as a successful and established manufacturer that was not also adept at procurement.

Sister eventually confessed that they could have used a better box. The boxes that had collapsed had a grade she called "BB." The next best box was listed as "BA." It would have done the job for sure.

"But it would have cost more," she said.

"How much more?" I asked out of curiosity.

"Three hundred dollars," she said.

Only $300? The order itself was worth more than $300,000, and never mind that the factory's relationship with Johnson Carter was already worth millions of dollars.

The factory might have invested in the better boxes, I suggested, especially given how things turned out with the other boxes. Sister disagreed with this view, insisting that while the boxes were inferior, Bernie had approved of their use. If Johnson Carter wanted anything better, it was welcome to pay a little more.

China's saving culture was so strong that it was at times detrimental to business interests.

When the company's fire extinguishers were found to be out of date, Sister ordered a full set of replacements, but the manager in charge could not bring himself to throw away the old ones. As a result, at each station, there were two extinguishers—one that was up to date and the other, which was not. They looked nearly identical; so, if a fire were to have broken out at any point, there was a 50–50 chance that someone would have grabbed the wrong one.

Johnson Carter was routinely fighting against such foolish inclinations.

Typically, the importer negotiated pricing in advance of any order. Then, throughout the production process, King Chemical would look to find savings where it could. If the supplier managed to cut a corner and it worked out, it pocketed the savings. If it did not work out, the supplier then tried to use the fiasco as a chance to raise prices in some way.

Johnson Carter assumed a great deal of risk. On all of our orders, the factory insisted on receiving full payment—in cash—before it shipped out any product. While the importer paid the manufacturer in advance, its retailers in the United States received credit terms.

As many as six months passed between the time that Johnson Carter paid the factory and when it received payment from the retailers. If at any point a problem was discovered, a retailer could stop payment, leaving the importer stuck with a loss. Worse yet, the retailer could also charge Johnson Carter for labor associated with removing products from the store shelves, as well as the cost of transportation and warehousing. Bernie explained that retailers were notorious for showing little mercy toward importers, especially if things went bad.

And sending defective product back to China was not an option. The factory would not go through the red tape associated with bringing defective goods into its country, and then there was the shipping cost. Ocean freight made up more than one-third of Johnson Carter's product cost on many items, and this expense would never be reimbursed by the factory. If the manufacturer was willing to settle a claim on a shipment, it would only be for some portion of the actual loss.

Chinese factories were loath to ever admit that they were in the wrong. "The product was fine when it left the factory," the manufacturer would say, while the importer would insist that it was not to blame. Such disagreements never went anywhere and quite often turned into cases of "he-said-*Xu*-said."

Importers were not inclined to pursue legal action when problems arose in an ongoing manufacturing relationship. An importer was not going to place its entire business on hold just to settle the matter of a few containers. Manufacturing problems tended to be small relative to the size of the overall business, and factory owners actually took this into account when they considered whether to manipulate quality levels.

In cases where a product was found to be defective and a factory did take responsibility, the manufacturer might attempt to resolve the matter by offering a discount on future orders. In other words, the only way to recoup losses created by a factory was to reward the manufacturer with further orders. And if claim losses were too substantial, the supplier could make up for it by raising prices on later orders.

Most of the initial problems we faced with King Chemical were with packaging: we had bottles that wobbled back and forth; the pumps for our liquid soap were not what we had expected; the flip-top caps for hand lotion snapped off when opened; and some caps refused to close, meaning that the product would spill out when the bottles were tilted. If the cardboard boxes were not collapsing, then the workers were packaging entire cartons upside down.

The factory had operating manuals, but it did not actually follow them. Asked to watch for a growing number of packaging defects, workers either missed them or purposely sent them down the line in order to avoid creating more work and potential losses for their company.

Johnson Carter was signing up all kinds of new accounts. Bernie was successful in getting dollar stores to pick up his company brand, and he was also entering into private label contracts with a number of drugstore and retail chains. These were some of the largest retail chains in the country, and he was even speaking with Wal-Mart.

The importer had invested a substantial amount of money as well as time into the business, and retailers wanted a risk-free experience. Anything that raised a flag was something that the factory should have also worried about because our business affected theirs. And yet, the manufacturer did not seem concerned. More than that, they felt confident in their approach to the business.

When more labeling problems were discovered, I asked where the obvious errors were being kept. The foreman was embarrassed to say that they never really set aside any defects. Most of the problems that they uncovered were typically boxed up and shipped out.

Packaging problems were a concern for us, but only because of how they reflected on the product. We didn't want retailers asking themselves: *If the packaging is so bad, what about the stuff that's inside?*

CHAPTER 9

The China Game

One of Johnson Carter's biggest accounts was a billion-dollar distributor that supplied some of the largest supermarket chains in the United States. Shop Corp wanted us to manufacture the Johnson Carter product line using its company brand in what was called a *private label* program.

The project was just getting off the ground when I received a note from Janet, a member of the buying team at Shop Corp. She reviewed different kinds of products, but was less than familiar with health and beauty care merchandise. She said that she had discovered a problem with the line that we had created for their company, and she wanted to discuss the issue with me.

"The ingredients listed on the back of your shampoo, liquid soap, and bubble bath are all identical," she said.

"That's because they are all the same formulation," I said.

"That can't be right," she said. She insisted that it must be an error, and she asked me to look into the case. I didn't need to check; I knew already that they were the same.

We were not the only company that did this sort of thing. Some successful U.S. companies in health and beauty care also marketed products under different labels, and more than one well-known brand advertised a "three-in-one" formulation right on the package.

It was an eye-opener that Janet could not imagine our products shared formulations, but then Bernie surprised me by saying that he didn't know about it either. He had a quick solution to the "problem" in any event. Rather than try to convince Janet at Shop Corp how our business worked, he suggested that we tweak the ingredient lists so that they differed slightly.

It would be easier and safer than challenging Janet, he said. Shop Corp was in the position of control. They sent us orders; they made the decision whether to buy from Johnson Carter. In the spirit of "the customer is always right," Bernie figured: If Shop Corp believed that ingredient lists ought to vary—because it *seemed* that they ought to—who were we to say otherwise?

Not that anyone at Johnson Carter knew much about the health and beauty care industry either. One day, I received a note about a baby shampoo that we were trying to create for a major drug-store chain. We were formulating what they called a *national brand equivalent*—essentially a copy of a Johnson & Johnson product, their world-famous baby shampoo. It was going to be one of those products that came in a generic package but that looked like J&J's brand. The product that we were going to make was to say "tear-free formula" instead of the more familiar, "no more tears."

Going over an analysis of the shampoo sample we created, the customer complained that pH levels were too low. Chemists use pH to measure the acidity or alkalinity of a solution. The scale runs from 1 to 14, with a measure of 7 representing neutral. The first sample had come in with a reading that was closer to 6, which suggested that the shampoo would be too acidic. In other words, it would lead to tears.

Hearing this, a Johnson Carter representative was upset, and I got a note from New York asking me why the factory was now "cheating us out of pH"—as if it were an ingredient that the factory was cutting a corner on.

Johnson Carter cared about catching orders, and retailers cared almost exclusively about not getting into any trouble. No one ever remarked on the product itself. They never asked if it was any good. I doubted that anyone at Shop Corp had ever personally tried the product. I once asked Bernie if he had ever tried our discount shampoo himself, and he shot me a look that said, *"What, are you nuts?"*

One of our products was a blue formulation called Milk & Aloe. Janet at Shop Corp noticed that the ingredient list did not include the chemical name for aloe. We had been selling the product for some time, and she was the only customer who had ever made an issue about any missing aloe ingredient. Janet said some would need to be added.

"How much?" I asked Bernie.

In a tone that suggested that the answer was obvious, he said just enough to justify putting the ingredient on the label. I asked whether Janet might later suggest that we also needed to add milk to Milk & Aloe. Bernie told me not to bring it up, that we would deal with it only if Shop Corp raised the issue. Eventually, they did.

Janet said that we needed to justify anything printed on the label. It was, she said, what the FDA was most concerned about when it came to health and beauty care products—making sure that the labels were all compliant.

"We don't expect fresh milk, of course," she said, while not indicating how we might justify the word "milk" on the packaging.

Janet sent over a large document that she had found on the FDA's web site. She remained unclear on a number of labeling issues. Reading the document myself I could not find answers to certain questions, and no one at Johnson Carter was of much help either.

Janet wanted the labels to match the ingredients exactly, but did not know the guidelines. I pointed out that we had a bubble bath called Bursting Bubblegum, which had no bubblegum in it. Our bottle labeled Galaxy Grape didn't have grapes either. Hearing these points, she became flustered. She did not know what to do or think. There wasn't anyone in the business—the manufacturer, the importer, or the retailer—that knew how to address these ingredients concerns.

■ ■ ■

One of Johnson Carter's best-selling items was a body wash that came in a tall, monster-size bottle. Several days before a truck was scheduled to pick up a large order of the body wash, I noticed many of the bottles had not been filled completely.

Sister came over and inspected them. She said that it was a common occurrence, caused by air in the formulation. When the liquid settled, the fill level dropped a little. She insisted that the bottles had all been properly full at the time they were capped.

While what she said made sense, I noted that we did not have the same settling problem with the regular-size bottles of shampoo and bubble bath.

In any case, I suggested, it did not matter how we had come to have an issue with fill levels—either way, we had a problem. It was not just a matter of aesthetics, but also an issue that involved labeling compliance. If we said that there were 850 milliliters of product in the bottle, we had to have that much in it. The shampoo formulation could be low quality; there just had to be as much of the product there as we claimed there was.

There was another reason to fix the problem: a retailer might use the fill-level issue against the importer. If the product was not selling well, for instance, the retailer could tell Johnson Carter that it needed to pull the product, using the fill issue as an excuse. Because Johnson Carter bore all of the financial risk, it had to insist that the product be made properly.

We measured the amount of body wash that was in the bottles, and it came up short of the 850 milliliters advertised on the label. Sister promised that it would never happen again, and that she wanted to ship the product anyway. I suggested that we fill only those bottles that were obviously too low.

"It is too inconvenient," she said.

She intimated that it would cause her embarrassment, and I took it to mean that she might personally suffer some kind of face loss. If she had purposefully shorted some of the bottles to save a small amount of money, maybe it was the backfiring of her plan that stung.

In any case, Sister suggested that it would be rude to reject the shipment. It was already packaged and ready to ship. It was an honest mistake, she said. It could have happened to anyone. And, anyway, it wouldn't happen again.

"For the sake of our cooperation," she said. "Please try to understand."

This sort of scenario happened all the time. Factories created a quality problem and turned it into a hot potato for importers by asking them to assume all risks. Though King Chemical had caused the problem, it suggested that Johnson Carter should be sensitive to its situation.

Manufacturers that engaged in the manipulation of quality knew that if they were caught, there was an inclination to "work things out." In this way, manufacturers came to view the idea of saving face as a get-out-of-jail-free card. Knowing that an importer was disinclined to cause loss of face for the manufacturer actually encouraged production shenanigans in the first place.

I tried to reason with Sister. "In the United States, there are rules," I said. Confucianism taught respect for guidelines, just as it placed a value on face.

"You're just saying that," she said.

We discussed the possibility of filling the bottles, and the more it looked as though I would not back down on the suggestion to fix the problem, the angrier she became. At one point, she suggested that I would have to "take responsibility for my actions." It was a threat, a suggestion that any consequence of pressing the issue would be of my own making.

When threatening me failed to produce the desired outcome, her demeanor changed, and she turned on the charm. Trying her best to appear beguiling, she flattered me. "Please speak with Bernie tonight," she said. "Tell him that it's not so bad. He listens to you."

"He will probably have the same thing to say."

"Tell him that it won't happen again."

She reached out and touched my sleeve. I told her that I would speak to Bernie, but I told her not to hold out too much hope.

The issue of filling the bottles did not seem like a big deal. It might have taken a day to fix, two at the most, but there was a sense that this issue was about something more. In export manufacturing, you didn't always get all the information you needed. All that I knew was that Sister was desperate not to rework the body wash and that the issue was serious enough that she was alternatively making threats and pleading with me.

"It's simple," Bernie said when I got him on the phone that evening. "If the bottles are not filled, you can't ship them."

"I know."

"Then what's the goddamn problem over there?"

Working as a go-between was a tricky business. Chinese have worked with intermediaries throughout their long history, and if they thought someone in the middle was an obstacle to greater profitability, they would get him out of the picture. You couldn't be at the factory, play things hard, and expect to accomplish everything you wished.

What seemed to be an easy fix—topping off a number of bottles that came in underfilled—was to Sister either a much bigger job than it seemed to be, or else it truly was a matter of personal embarrassment.

"I'm not sure what this situation is about," I told Bernie, "but for some reason, they want us to give them a break."

"Give them a break," he said sounding incredulous. "Listen to him. He wants me to give them a break!"

Bernie had a tendency, like other importers, to take the contractual view. When he placed orders, he wanted a precise result based on expectations. As a customer, he was entitled to certain things, and I understood what he was trying to do. By playing tough on this smaller issue, what he was really hoping to do was prevent the manufacturer from delivering an even bigger problem down the road.

"You don't understand something," he said. "If you give these people an inch, they'll take a mile."

At the factory the next day, I passed along the bad news. Bernie wanted the bottles filled. Sister was upset, and there was nothing to do now since Bernie had made the call.

Sister took a couple dozen workers from the plant, and a makeshift production line was set up in the warehouse. Cardboard boxes of body wash were opened, and bottles that were not full were topped off. It was a slow process, and Sister turned cool toward me.

Typically, someone at the factory drove me back to the hotel because there was no taxi service near the factory in the countryside. When it was getting close to the time for me to head back, I asked about my ride.

Sister said that her driver was indisposed.

"What about one of the delivery drivers then?" I asked.

"They have things to do," she said. "We are very busy."

I saw two delivery trucks parked in the lot out front. Even if the drivers were busy, there was usually someone coming or going who would offer to give me a lift into town. I had been to the factory many times, but this was the first time that anyone told me there was no transportation.

After waiting an hour by the lot where the cars were parked, I went to find Sister. She was in her office; she seemed to anticipate my return. Her arms were folded, and she looked smug. I asked her about the possibility of a ride.

"We have done as you asked," she said. "The bottles are all filled now."

I walked out of the factory on my own and set out down the country road that connected the remote factory to the rest of the world. Some workers standing outside the factory saw me and laughed. Walking down the quiet path alone, I probably looked to them like a down-and-out migrant worker from the provinces.

Eventually, I found a ride. I flagged down a motorcycle taxi, one of those sorry vehicles that was just a wooden-frame box attached to the back half of a motorcycle. These three-wheel deathtraps had no windows, and even the locals used them as only a last resort.

The message from the factory was clear in any case: you either work *with* us, or we can make things difficult.

An importer should have been rewarded for uncovering quality problems, but it was almost never the case. Factories did not see an attention to quality as something that would improve their business prospects, but merely as a barrier to increased profitability. Working to achieve higher levels of quality did not make me a friend of the factory, but a pariah.

Importers learned quickly that improved quality raised their costs. Every time Johnson Carter managed to find a problem and asked the factory to correct it, the factory shifted the cost back to us. Over the long run, when an importer was seen as working too hard to improve quality, it was viewed as a meddlesome customer, and other buyers by comparison appeared more attractive. Manufacturers preferred their importers to be meek and acquiescent.

There were others like me in China—foreigners who went into factories on behalf of importers to fight for quality improvements. And it was at times a comfort to know that I did not suffer these challenges alone.

I met one such individual who worked with a big network of suppliers. His company was based in Shanghai, though they had offices throughout South China as well. I asked about his quality challenge.

"We don't have any problems," he said in a flat tone.

"You don't have *any*?" I asked. It was hard to believe, especially since everyone else reported having them. I asked how it was possible.

"Easy," he said. "We have 90 quality control inspectors on the ground."

They had no quality problems; that's why they had deployed a battalion of inspectors.

What made the situation in China so bizarre was that the manufacturers themselves all had their own quality control staff. Workers who stood on the assembly lines marked products as—QC PASSED or QUALITY CONTROL OK. They were good at applying the stickers, but foreign firms still found that they needed to send in their own inspectors.

If ever there was any major indicator that there was a problem with China, Inc., this was it—huge numbers of people were hired and paid to do the job that manufacturers were either unable or unwilling to do for themselves. An entire industry of third-party inspectors was cropping up, and some of these companies had veritable armies on the ground, trained as quality control mercenaries.

Why couldn't these Chinese manufacturers do the job themselves? Why did they require so much oversight?

The day after I had been told to find my own ride back to my hotel, I expected the cold shoulder from Sister. Instead, it was as if the incident had never occurred. There was no lingering resentment; no one offered me any sort of apology, and at the same time, no one seemed to expect one from me either.

This was one of the things I found hard to understand about factory owners—how they could make such displays of emotion one moment and then put aside those feelings entirely the next.

The body wash shipped out that week, and attention was immediately turned to other orders in process. Everything seemed all right, but then the factory made a surprise announcement: they would no longer accept orders for body wash from Johnson Carter.

Sister explained that they would make all of our other products, but the body wash was too problematic—as we had all already seen.

"They can't do that to me," Bernie said. "Tell them that they *have* to make the body wash. Tell them that *I* said that."

The idea of making some of our product in one place and the rest in another was absurd. For shipping reasons alone, it would have been too inefficient. Transportation costs would go up, and then production schedules would suffer delays from coordination issues.

The factory had succeeded in making its point, and we were reduced to begging the factory to keep making the body wash. Sister eventually acquiesced, but not before emphasizing that she hoped we would never again run into the same problem of Johnson Carter making similar demands about fill levels.

This was a problem that many importers faced. The more they pushed for quality, the harder their suppliers pushed back.

Following the body wash incident, the relationship grew more difficult.

I asked Sister when I could inspect the next shipment and was told to come on a Friday. When I arrived on the appointed morning, I was informed that they had already shipped the product two days earlier.

For a moment, I thought that I was being told that the product would leave two days later.

In Mandarin, "the day before yesterday" was translated as "the day in front"—*qiantian*—and the day after tomorrow was "the day in back"—*houtian*. In Chinese, the speaker faced the past, while keeping his back to the future, and the backwards view always left me mixed up.

"You sent the product out *the day before yesterday* and did not think to mention it?"

"We didn't want to bother you," Sister said.

The factory had managed to score a twofer for itself anyway. Product that couldn't be inspected suffered no risk of rejection, and at the same time, Sister succeeded in making me look ineffective.

"How could you let them do that to you?" Bernie asked me.

The reality was that these small stunts could not be prevented and that none of the tricks that went on were enough to seriously consider switching to another supplier.

Contract manufacturing was not like buying fruit, where if you didn't like the goods at one shop, you simply walked across the street to a competitor's. Supplier relationships took a great deal of effort to set up, and it took a long time to work out the kinks. Outsourced manufacturing was a bit like marriage in some ways; even when things got rocky, it generally made more sense to work things out than to leave in the hope of finding a better partner elsewhere.

Johnson Carter's solution to some of the hide-and-seek games was to initiate surprise inspections. Bernie's feeling was that if the factory were hiding any quality problems, inspections at unexpected times would make them easier to find.

Bernie announced that, as a representative of his company, I would now be making random visits. No advance warning of my arrival would be given, and the factory was to ensure that its doors were open at all times.

It seemed demanding and a bit presumptuous, and I thought that the factory might protest the move as insulting. It was quite the opposite, however, Sister seemed surprised that it had taken so long for us to become so vigilant.

Bernie took an unusual approach to such inspections. He would randomly announce to factory reps that I would visit on a particular day—just to gauge their reaction. If the factory reps offered no protest about the visit, he would cancel the trip, figuring that there must be nothing interesting to see.

Alternatively, if anyone at the factory hinted that some days might be inconvenient, I was to rush to the factory during that time. During one of these suggested blackout periods, I flew into Shantou and arrived only to find that our product was not in process, that we had almost no finished product in the warehouse to inspect, and that Sister was out of town on business. In other words, it was a wasted trip.

■ ■ ■

Johnson Carter was shipping increasingly large volumes of product when a bad piece of news came in: a major customer complained that our bottles were being made too thin. The factory had quietly adjusted the molds so that less plastic went into making each bottle. As a result, when a bottle was given the slightest squeeze, it collapsed.

"It's a goddamn plastic bag," Bernie complained.

After an investigation, his office in New York discovered that the bottle had gone through more than one change. The factory had been making downward adjustments over a several month period. The first bottles that came off the line were sturdy, but then they came out as merely acceptable. When none of us noticed the earlier changes, the factory decided to go for it again.

Chinese factories often engaged in this sort of quality fade—the incremental degradation of a product over time. They quietly reduced the amount of materials or else manipulated the quality of raw inputs. The changes were gradual, almost imperceptible. The importer was neither asked for permission nor told.

Even more galling for Johnson Carter in the case of the plastic bottles was that it had paid for and legally owned the molds that the factory had been manipulating. Putting less plastic into the bottles generated savings, but these were not shared with the importer. The only thing passed onto the importer was an increase in product risk.

King Chemical had turned the business into a game. The terms of each deal were negotiated at the start of the project, and then the factory went on a hunt, looking for savings. Bernie's earlier question about the business—"How can the factory quote such a low price?"—was now at least partially answered.

Our job in the cat-and-mouse game that the factory had set up was to discover where the product was being manipulated. If we found the distortion, the factory might be convinced to revert to the original design. If we failed to uncover its scheme, the factory pocketed the savings. In any case, it was left to us to do the uncovering. The factory gained sometimes, but it never lost.

Johnson Carter was not purchasing a ready-made product, but a product that was made to order. The importer provided all the package designs, including bottle samples. The factory's decision to make the bottles thinner was made unilaterally.

The manufacturer issued no *if-then* conditional clause such as *if* you refuse to pay us more, *then* we will deliver an inferior product. They just went ahead with it, and far from hinting that we should expect a poor product because we were paying low prices, the factory actually guaranteed that its product would be better than what we would find at any of its competitors. That guarantee was actually met in the first order or two; but thereafter, quality went downhill.

Quality fade was an economic decision that manufacturers in China made. It was a calculated risk, and in the back of the factory owner's mind was always a "Plan B." If the importer found out that the factory owner had been manipulating quality and the shipment was rejected, just where would that product then be sold?

Even 10 years earlier, there was more risk in manipulating quality because there was nowhere for a manufacturer to dump a shipment that had been rejected. In more recent years, China found itself at a crossroads for international trade.

If we rejected a large shipment of our shampoo, there were agents who would help move the product out of the country into one of many growing export markets. And even the domestic market had developed to the point where an agent might be able to find buyers of surplus inside China.

One of the many reasons that quality problems were on the rise was because of this increase in salvage opportunities. Knowing that there was somewhere to dump product from a quality manipulation plan gone awry actually helped increase the likelihood of production shenanigans.

China manufacturing had no concept of punitive damages or penalties for bad behavior, which was another contributing factor. If (or rather, when) the factory was caught in some scheme to manipulate product quality, the only thing that the factory could be expected to do was remake the product properly. The importer would never be reimbursed for damages arising from a loss of business or reputation. The only cost to the factory for getting caught with their hand in the cookie jar was being made to put the lid back on the jar.

Because King Chemical blamed its suppliers for certain instances of quality fade, Bernie suggested that we meet with some of the companies that provided the factory with key inputs. He wanted to start with the supplier responsible for the bottles that had been made too thin.

The factory, however, did not want to set up the meeting. They did not want us gathering information from their supplier because the information might contradict what the factory claimed regarding their cost structure. A subsupplier might also possibly tip us off to another factory that was equally or more capable than King Chemical.

After repeated requests, the factory finally arranged a meeting for Bernie on one of his visits.

We were brought to the bottle factory but learned after the visit that it had only been a red herring. The supplier we met with might have been speaking with King Chemical about the prospect of supplying bottles, but they were not the actual supplier of the bottles in question.

Factory owners were often in cahoots with one another anyway— and even more so when it came to a scheme involving a foreign client. If one industrialist asked another for help, the favor was granted with the understanding that it would later be repaid.

Bernie tried to hold back orders until the bottle supplier was identified, but the pressure to get more merchandise produced became too great, and the idea was eventually dropped. Johnson Carter placed more orders, and we continued to ship more merchandise made at King Chemical.

CHAPTER 10

The Seven Steps of Problem Solving

The extreme time zone difference between the United States and China put a strain on the work schedules of those who worked in export manufacturing.

King Chemical worked a regular day, from just after breakfast until dinnertime, which kept me busy during the days that I visited. But then everyone at Johnson Carter was in the New York office when it was late in China, which often meant a long night of e-mails and telephone calls as well.

The only free time that I could count on was in the late afternoon, the few hours just before everyone in the United States was getting into work. It was during this small window of time that I would try to catch up on sleep.

While catnapping, my dreams increasingly turned to manufacturing, and sometimes I would close my eyes and find myself back in the factory—except instead of chasing after schedules, I was on the production lines myself. These were quality control nightmares. I was the one who was capping and labeling bottles, and when mistakes were discovered, fingers were pointed at me.

It was from one of these disturbing dreams that I awoke in my hotel room and went to the bathroom only to discover that the toilet was not working. The hotel had five stars. It was among the finest in the city.

Does *nothing* work here?

I thought twice before calling the front desk to complain, if only because fixing some things in China often proved too much of a hassle, and so I was pleasantly surprised when the front desk manager expressed enthusiasm about handling the problem herself.

All over South China—in the hotels and in the factories—there was a hop-to-it attitude that was disarming. Though the toilet was not what anyone would have considered a serious problem, it was comforting to see that the hotel staff was treating the matter as if it were.

The front desk manager arrived with two colleagues—a boy in a work shirt and a woman from housekeeping. The three stood in the bathroom considering the toilet, while I waited in my room. They were concentrating hard on the problem, like a group of aerospace engineers attempting to work out a design flaw on a manned space mission.

I could hear them murmuring from just outside the doorway, and I listened as they worked the lever of the toilet. After some time, they emerged from the bathroom, and the front desk manager announced that they were finished. She said that the issue had been resolved.

The front desk manager was particularly happy with the result, and she beamed with pride. I thanked her, while giving myself a little pat on the back for this one minor victory in quality control. You see, I told myself, not everything in this place was a disaster. You had to be hopeful and patient; and it didn't hurt sometimes to be lucky.

On her way out, the front desk manager smiled and gave me a knowing look. We should not forget the favor that had just been done. It was as though we now had a relationship, and the secret we shared was a crediting of accounts.

The three hotel employees were about to disappear down the hall when I felt the hairs rise up on the back of my neck. It was a sensation that I had come to associate with imminent regret, a locally developed instinct. I asked them to wait a moment.

"*Deng yixia!*"

The three of them froze, while I went into the bathroom. The front desk manager tiptoed in after me. "What's the matter?" she asked, her voice sounding meek.

I jiggled the lever of the toilet, but there was no response.

"It doesn't work," I said.

She made a face that showed disappointment and bewilderment, as though she had managed to get the toilet to work just a moment before and that it had decided by itself to stop functioning again. She pressed the lever, and focused her concentration. The toilet made a loud hissing sound.

"You see?" she said. "It does work."

The toilet made a noise, but it was not the sound of flushing water. It clearly did not work, and I told her so.

While we were both looking at the same problem, she was simply choosing not to see it. More than that, it seemed, she was hoping that I would share her view. Most of her disappointment, it seemed, was reserved for me, because I would not entertain her own version of reality.

I went through the exact same situation with Chinese manufacturers. Staring at a label that was supposed to have been printed in yellow ink, we would be looking at a brown label instead—and the factory owner would insist that it was yellow.

It was the old business about the tree in the woods—if a tree falls and there is no one to hear it, did it actually make a sound? In China, not only did it matter that someone was there, but if there were at least two people present, they could together agree on any version of events. There might not have been a tree there at all, but they could insist that there was one—a mighty, magnificent tree, one that stood tall, which was thousands of years old.

The front desk manager was sticking with her story. "But it makes a noise," she said. "You can hear it yourself."

The housekeeper looked at me in an eager way also, as if she agreed with this alternative interpretation of events and hoped that I would too. They were double-teaming me now.

We had entered into the next phase, the one where denial turned into bargaining. The four of us entered into a discussion on the definition of a working toilet. Was a toilet that made only noise considered a working toilet or a broken one? The front desk manager said that, while I had a point in suggesting that the toilet might be malfunctioning, I had to admit that it was not *completely* broken.

She had an opinion that was partially based on logic, and it was pointless to refute her view.

In order to move things forward, there was nothing to do but to concede the point. The toilet was not completely broken I admitted, and this concession seemed to satisfy her—for the moment at least.

Chinese manufacturers pulled the same move. They wanted an importer to admit that a problem was not all that bad, if only because it shored up their negotiating position. Problems that were seen as less serious required less attention and fewer resources. It was a preemptive move. If we all agreed that the problem was not so serious, then when the problem was blown off, or if it later was determined that it could not be fixed, then it could be seen as less of a failure.

Having discovered this middle ground, the hotel staff returned to the problem at hand and for the first time since they arrived, they attempted to solve the problem in earnest. This time, I could hear the clang of the ceramic lid as it was removed from the tank, and the sloshing around of water suggested that someone was investigating the workings of an internal mechanism.

After a few minutes, they emerged from the bathroom, and the front desk manager admitted now that there was no change with things. She then politely asked me if it would be possible for me to accept the situation as it was.

Accept the situation?

This was another move that I was familiar with from my work in the factories. There was hardly a mess that needed fixing that someone did not first attempt to get the importer to accept. The appeal was always an emotional one, and when it was directed at me, the suggestion was that I let it slide "for the sake of our relationship."

It made logical sense to pursue the option anyway. If someone presented you with a problem and you could convince that person to accept the situation as unresolved, did it not have the same effect as fixing the problem itself?

When it came to problem solving, Westerners often wanted answers to silly questions, such as "What is the cause of this problem exactly?" and "What are the options?"

Asked to accept the broken toilet, the ball was now in my court. The pressure was on me. Having been asked politely to withdraw my request for a repair, I was reminded of suppliers who took the same approach to basic quality problems. In a polite world, when someone asked you for a favor, the underlying expectation was that you would understand and comply.

"What's the problem exactly?" I asked. It was the sort of question meant to elicit information. It was not meant to be an accusation or an insinuation of any sort, but it was apparently the wrong button to push at the wrong time. I was not prepared for what happened next.

The front desk manager's tone changed in a sudden flash, and this time she minced no words.

"It is very strange, don't you think?"

"What's strange?"

"That *your* toilet is broken."

She raised an eyebrow at me.

"Excuse me?"

"We have many rooms in this hotel, as you know."

"And?"

"And only yours is broken."

The manager waited for me to absorb her suggestion, and I suppressed the urge to roll my eyes.

"I did not break your toilet," I said.

"Oh? Are you sure?"

She looked smug, and I found myself now on the defensive.

We had wasted the better part of an hour, and I now wondered: *How did we get here?* One moment, the manager showed up at my room, bright eyed and acting as though she would bend over backwards to help solve this problem. The next moment, claws were out, and it looked as though I might now get billed for damages.

Customer service had come a long way in China, but some instincts died hard. The Cultural Revolution ingrained certain survival skills in people, one of which had to do with defending oneself against perceived face loss. The answer when threatened was to strike back fast and hard, and not to relent until the threatening party retreated. If someone might cause you trouble, you had to get them to back off—at all costs. Face was an important concept across Asia, but in no other territory around the region was it combined so much with aggression.

That all of this was happening in a five-star hotel made no difference. We were still in China, a country that had a long cultural tradition, one that had only recently emerged from a period of political turmoil.

From other experiences, I knew that the smallest incident in China could snowball into an utter mess, and a simple apology was not necessarily going to reverse the current situation. I needed to get us back on track as quickly as possible, and making a show of weakness through an apology was not exactly the best response.

"Is this a five-star hotel?" It was a question meant to dig me out of a hole.

"Of course it is," the manager said, in a tone that suggested— *"What nerve!"*

Trying to sound as polite as possible, I asked whether the manager believed that a five-star hotel ought to have rooms with functioning toilets. It was a small piece of logic, one that could not be so easily dismissed or twisted around. Maybe she saw the point I was trying to make, or maybe she understood from my tone that I was not purposefully trying to ruin her.

The front desk manager's demeanor changed again—another switching of channels—and this time she appeared more like a little girl asking for my forgiveness. She offered me a number of excuses for why the toilet didn't work. The reasons were random and one had nothing to do with the other. The least plausible of them was that my room was located on an upper floor and so there was not enough water pressure for the toilet to function properly.

Basically, I was welcome to choose whichever explanation I liked best, and this was also no different from what happened at the factories.

When quality went bad, we were given a potpourri of excuses, a cornucopia of cop-outs: It was the supplier's fault. It was the trucking company that was responsible. It was the fault of one of the workers ("but don't worry about speaking with him directly, because that individual was just fired").

The litany of excuses was just another step in the problem-solving process. It was not meant to be taken seriously, just as pointing a finger in my direction was not about an actual shift in blame. In

China, problem solving involved a degree of zigzag. You had to do the dance, you had to have patience and faith, and you had to give those who offered to solve a problem the chance to come around on their own.

My German client complained that his suppliers never understood the value of getting straight to the point. They were perpetually beating around the bush—there was nothing *schnell* about the way they handled any situation.

China might be modernizing, it might even one day lead the world (in a peaceful rise, naturally), but the basic mechanics of getting anything done were still a challenge. Foreign companies looking to accomplish anything in this growing market had to understand the extent to which the economy remained hindered by enduring instances of cultural backwardness.

We were at the end of the road on this toilet business. The front desk manager looked disappointed, and I was disheartened in my own way. China was a place filled with promises and regrets, and I felt sad, not for the front desk manager who had tried and failed to fix a piece of plumbing, but for a broader mechanism that was broken down. In the end, none of us even knew what was wrong with the toilet. Not a single clue had been uncovered, and we were about to leave off with no plan for moving forward.

On the way out, the front desk manager asked if there was anything that she could do for me. This would be the time, she probably thought, when a customer would ask for something—some kind of consideration, like a lowered room rate. I told the manager that I was fine. She asked if I would like to change rooms. With only two days left until the weekend, I told her that it was not necessary. She apologized in a despairing way and explained that she needed to get going. It was getting late, she said. I told her that I understood.

As she was about to leave, she paused by the door, and in a voice that was barely audible said that tomorrow things might be better. The hotel had an engineer who fixed things like toilets. He was actually in charge of plumbing for the entire hotel. The engineer would have been up to my room to fix the toilet himself, except that it was his night off.

It was the last stage of the problem-solving process. For reasons that defied logic, it came closer to the end. It was that moment when the skies opened and the sun came shining through . . . *And the truth shall set you free!*

Why such a basic piece of information came only after so much wrangling was anyone's guess, but then the entire process of solving problems in China was itself an enigma.

China's economy was already larger than that of many developed nations, but this did not mean that its culture was keeping pace, and those who came to China to do business—or even diplomacy—had to know the extent to which the place was different.

CHAPTER 11

Counterfeit Culture

A-Min was stretched across the leather sofa in his office. He napped, while next to him an associate of his, a fellow industrialist, smoked a cigarette in the dark. Seeing me come in, the friend kicked the bottom of A-Min's shoe, and he snapped awake.

"Sit," he said while turning on a light.

On a small table next to the sofa was a kettle. A-Min reached for it and turned on the switch. All sorts of people came through this office—suppliers, customers, family, and friends—and they often drank tea here.

In this part of the country, factory owners were partial to a particular kind of tea set that was made of plain, white porcelain, and the cups were smaller than I had seen elsewhere. They were barely large enough for a quick, small sip.

He brought out the canister of tea and dug into it with a wooden scoop. "*Tieguanyin*," he said, indicating the type of tea.

Taking the leaves out, he filled a small bowl that had a curved lip. He then poured in hot water and placed a small lid on top, careful to position the lid at just such an angle so that when it was tilted over the cups, the tea trickled out, while the leaves remained held back.

Pouring tea in this fashion was a tricky business; the bowl itself was thin and the water scalding hot, and only the edges of the bowl could be handled. It was something of a balancing act, meant to be done with only one hand.

A-Min picked up the bowl, gripping it and the lid together, and then he poured, alternating back and forth over the small cups in a seemingly random fashion until they were all filled to the brim.

We were each given a small cup of tea to drink. A-Min slurped his tea in one go, deliberately leaving a few drops behind in the cup. He tilted the cup to show me that it contained the dregs that were too fine to be filtered by the bowl's lid.

After tossing these into the tea tray with a flick of his wrist, he showed me the cup again so that I could see that it had been properly cleaned. Just like any social ritual, there were subtleties. How someone poured tea or handled a cup might hint at background, status, or personality type.

A-Min slid the tea tray over in my direction so that I might have a turn pouring. I had been in his office enough to know that not everyone got this chance. The leaves that were already in the bowl could be used again, so all I had to do was replenish the hot water and pour.

After picking up the small bowl and holding it by its edges with my thumb and ring finger, I positioned my right pinky on the bottom to lend support, while placing a sideways-positioned forefinger on top in order to hold the lid in place. With my hand positioned just so—like a stiffened claw—I began to pour, but there was a problem. The lid was on at the wrong angle, and the leaves began to fall out. I lost the moment. Hot water came pouring down the sides, and I dropped the bowl into the tea tray.

A-Min made no comment, and I took his silence to mean that he had expected the result. He went through the process of pouring several times more, until we had about six tiny cupfuls each.

Making tea from leaves is so common across China that some historians actually believe that Marco Polo never made it to China because he failed to mention the curious practice of drinking tea. In his account, Polo went to great lengths to discuss the popularity of wine across the country, but he forgot this other, far more common beverage, which had not yet been introduced in Europe.

There were other problems with Marco Polo's account. He took the time to mention that the Chinese people ate rice, but he failed to mention *how* they ate it—with chopsticks. He described the allure of Chinese women, but made no mention of foot binding. He claimed to have arrived at China from the north, and yet, he never noticed the Great Wall.

Marco Polo claimed not only that he was a traveler to the Far East, but also that he had served the Great Khan. According to his account, he was made mayor of Yangzhou, then a pleasure city that was to imperial China what Las Vegas is to the United States. But, while official Chinese documents record other Italians who visited China during this period, there was never any mention of Marco Polo.

And he never used any Chinese place names either. Instead, he used names from Arabic and Persian. Seventeen years was a bit longer than I had lived in China, and it was certainly as long as many other expatriates I knew who were similarly rooted in the country.

Even those who went out of their way not to learn Mandarin still managed to pick up a great deal of it during their tenure. How could it be that Marco Polo never managed to pick up even a little bit of the language? Then again, he never bothered to mention the unusual-looking Chinese characters that he would have seen everywhere.

Marco Polo was an exaggerator, a teller of tall tales. He had claimed that one Chinese city had as many as 12,000 bridges, where another observer traveling through at roughly the same time claimed only 360 such structures. He said that the Chinese enjoyed eating pears that weighed 10 pounds each and that the citizens of Hangzhou lived in buildings that were eight to ten stories high when they surely lived in buildings that we not even half that height.

Whether Marco Polo actually made it to China is beside the point, really. His impact on history was to inspire generations of Western explorers. Christopher Columbus was said to have carried Polo's account with him on his journey to find a passage to the Orient, and the result of such an inspired expedition gave us both North and South America.

The notion of the Far East as an exotic place needed no exaggeration, and perhaps the real problem with Marco Polo's account was not its magnification, but that it missed the mark. It was not, as so many have claimed, China's scale that was fascinating but rather certain cultural elements, and I was most interested in those that had an impact on business.

■ ■ ■

Despite our difficulties with quality at King Chemical, Bernie had success in signing up new, larger customers, and volume kept growing.

Shop Corp was Johnson Carter's largest and most conservative customer to date, and no decision could be made on any order until a large committee had convened. When this one customer sent e-mail messages, there were no fewer than a dozen people copied, and their specification sheets were highly detailed and required the signature of Bernie himself. Nothing could be changed without prior written approval, not even the smallest change to label artwork.

Sister knew this, but decided to make changes to the label design anyway. Without notifying anyone else, King Chemical shrank the size of the labels so that they were easier to apply to the bottles. It was not a big difference, but it was a deviation from the dimensions that Shop Corp had made clear on their specifications sheets.

Once discovered, we had to inform Shop Corp of the change, however small. I told Sister that I had to notify the company.

"Don't tell them. They won't notice," she said. "*You* almost didn't notice."

In China, there was no penalty for getting caught in any production scheme. The usual consequence was being forced to make the product properly the next time around. At the very worst, the manufacturer might be asked to redo an order.

In the United States, things worked a little differently. If our customer learned that we had defied them in a way that seemed willful, they would have perceived it as a breach of trust. Johnson Carter could claim that it was innocent, but retailers cared little for the difficulties we faced in China.

Bernie won business by explaining that we were the "trouble-free" solution, and to win business, he suggested that we were involved in a joint venture with King Chemical. This had been done in order to raise the level of confidence in the operation, and so there was no way that we could tell retailers, "The factory did it to us again, sorry."

The factory staff was never forthcoming about unilateral changes it had made, and yet, oddly enough, they would answer specific questions.

If asked whether the product had been changed, generally, they would not answer in the affirmative. If asked specifically, however, whether a change had been made to label sizes, they would then admit it. It was only after I guessed that the labels had been made smaller and asked that Sister told me, yes, they had. The problem with this system was that we had to know what questions to ask in order to get at any sort of meaningful response.

American consumers were accustomed to receiving exactly what they had ordered. Chinese manufacturers had a slightly different philosophy when it came to customer relationships. They believed that the customer's exact wishes mattered only as far as they were necessary to capture the initial order. Beyond that, they figured, what an importer didn't know couldn't hurt it.

My main contact at Shop Corp, Janet, was adamant that the product match *both* the specifications sheet and the product sample set. Those who were in charge of buying at the big retailers had generously sized egos. While earning modest salaries, they understood how decisions they made directly affected an importer's economic future. If a buyer suspected that we took her for a fool, she would end the business relationship and choose another vendor.

Johnson Carter walked on eggshells, worrying how to please its customers, but King Chemical did not take the same approach with its own customers. Quite the contrary, we were eventually reduced to begging in order to have our products made properly. We had to plead in order to get the factory not to make unilateral specification changes. King Chemical felt a genuine right to make product modifications without informing us—and the scope and freedom they accorded themselves increased over time.

And the tone of the relationship changed, as well. Around the time we picked up the account for Shop Corp, whenever we sent new orders to the factory, the response was that the factory would *consider* our request. Chinese factories were turning the notion of customer service on its head.

Confucian ideology saw all human relationships as fitting within a natural hierarchy. Just as a father held a place above the son, the emperor was superior to his subjects. In China, the individuals in-volved in a relationship were not meant to be on equal footing, and in the manufacturing sector, there was a growing sense that in the natural order the factory was above and its customer somewhere below.

In ancient times, foreign emissaries traveled to China in order to pay tribute to the emperor. In return for their submission, the emperor left a visitor with gifts to carry home. King Chemical increasingly looked on Johnson Carter in a similar way. The money that the importer paid was like tribute offered, and gifts that we received in return came in the form of liquid soap and body wash.

The factory understood the notion of pleasing customers when they were just starting out, or when they were struggling along, but that was just feigned modesty, part of the stagecraft, a means of catching business. Once the manufacturer achieved a degree of success, it saw itself in the imperial role, while relegating the importer to that of a mere supplicant.

■ ■ ■

Sister and I stood in the warehouse. On one side of the long building were some of the company's counterfeit products, fake brands that they made and sold into the domestic market.

One product of theirs was called Olan and had a logo that mim-icked the famous Olay brand. Another product in the warehouse, Risoft, looked just like a Procter & Gamble product named Rejoice, which sold very well in South China. The factory even had its own knock-off version of P&G's best-selling Zest body wash. The packag-ing was identical, except that the factory's version was called Best.

It seemed at this point that the two companies had come to an understanding, and I took the opportunity to confirm that we had put some of the quality games behind us. I asked Sister if she could promise that we would not have more surprises with quality.

"Why don't you trust us?" she asked, sounding disappointed and hurt. I was inclined to give her a few reasons, but she changed the subject, asking me whether it gets cold in Chicago.

Shop Corp had a receiving warehouse not far from that city, and I thought it was a strange question.

"Yes," I said, "it does get cold in Chicago."

"Do they have snow?" Sister asked.

"In the winter, sure, they get snow."

Chinese in the south sometimes asked about snow, because they never saw any of it, but this did not seem to be about a general curiosity over weather. *What could these questions about snow in Chicago really be about?* Shop Corp was based near Chicago. Could it be that Sister was planning some kind of trip to the United States?

The mention of snow, I would understand later, was a hint, a small clue, a suggestion of where I should have been paying careful attention—and perhaps where I might have asked some specific questions.

Winter had come, not just to Chicago, but also to South China.

One evening at home, I went to a windowsill where I had placed a number of Johnson Carter products. I picked up a bottle of shampoo and noticed that the formulation seemed frozen. The temperature outside was cold, but it was nowhere near freezing.

I shook the bottle, and the shampoo came loose from the edges and bounced around a bit. It had an odd consistency, I noticed. It seemed that the cold weather had turned the formulation into jelly.

"What do you mean—*jelly?*" Bernie asked.

I told him that the formulation was acting strangely, and that it had to do with cold weather. Typically, Bernie jumped all over any bad news, but this information was too much. Instead of processing it, he blocked out what I was trying to explain. I tried again to tell him that the cold weather was making the shampoo viscous, that it had turned hard. I told him to think Jell-O.

"I don't know what that means!" he shouted.

To make it clearer, I sent him a video file that showed one of our bottles of shampoo tipped on its side. The formulation would not pour but had to be pushed out with force. It came out in clumps—plop, plop, plop—looking nothing like shampoo. The sample had come from the shipment that had already gone to Shop Corp.

There was panic in New York, and Bernie demanded to know what was going on. The factory would not provide any details on the formulation, presumably because they were afraid that we would discover something even more unsettling. Bernie asked not only for a confirmation of his ingredients list, but also for a more detailed breakdown. He had these from a previous supplier, but King Chemical would not supply data.

Desperate to learn more about the formulations, Bernie asked me to speak with anyone who might help. I met another manufacturer at a trade show months earlier. We spoke only briefly about the possibility of making them an alternate supplier, but when the prices quoted by that factory were too high, discussions had ended.

Finding a competing manufacturer who would provide meaningful details was one way of getting around a supplier who withheld information. Factory personnel were tight-lipped, except when they were dangling trade secrets as an enticement. Those who could not compete on price were especially forthcoming with such inside information. In China, where so many hid the truth, candor itself was a valuable commodity.

The factory man agreed to meet me at my home, where I handed him a bottle of our shampoo—one that was golden yellow in color. He placed a small amount of the formulation on the palm of his hand, and tapped at it with his forefinger. He showed me how his finger bounced on the surface and would not stick to the shampoo. It was, he explained, the sign of an inferior product. It was much worse than shampoos sold in China, he said.

"You couldn't sell this here, that's for sure."

"You couldn't?"

"Of course not. China has standards. This kind of shampoo would be for export only." He was surprised that we were exporting this kind of product to the United States. "I would have guessed that this would be for some market like Bolivia," he said.

It didn't sound encouraging. He then looked at the date stamped on the bottom of the bottle. We were using an expiration date that was five years out. China limited shelf life on product like this to only three years.

Bernie did not like what I told him. "What did he mean by *Bolivia*?" he asked. He also thought that was a strange comment.

It was imperative, he said, that we get the ingredient lists from the factory. As a customer, we were entitled to them, but the factory would not release the information. I had tried with persistent requests, but the factory suggested that we already had the ingredient lists. They were on the back label of each of our products, and that was enough.

Sister said that she was not compelled to provide a breakdown. The details were their trade secrets, she insisted.

This infuriated Bernie. "The product line came from *my* sample set. *What* trade secret? It's my fucking product!"

The factory insisted that it had copied Johnson Carter's original product line exactly, but the method by which they had done so was proprietary. In other words, the formulations were Johnson Carter's all right, but they could not tell us what ingredients were in them. It could happen only in China; the factory was claiming intellectual property rights over its copying methods.

■　■　■

Of all the Chinese artifacts that I have read about or seen, my favorite is a jade piece that belongs to the National Palace Museum in Taipei, where the greatest treasures of Chinese emperors are housed. As with many classic pieces, what fascinates is less the piece itself than the story that goes with it.

Emperor Qianlong, who ruled for most of the eighteenth century during the Qing Dynasty, had been admiring his collection one day when he noticed a particular item. It was a small jade cup said to have been made during the Ming Dynasty, which lasted from the fourteenth to the seventeenth centuries. While he liked the piece, there was something about it that caused him to doubt its provenance.

He called for one of his top artists to take a look and issue his professional opinion. The artist, who also served as the emperor's curator, looked at the cup and declared that he had good news and bad news. The bad news was that, while the cup had been done in the Ming Style, it was actually a fake. The good news was that he could identify the artifact's creator. It was, said the curator, the work of his own grandfather.

The curator's grandfather had been a masterful copier. He knew not just how to make the jade cup in the Ming style, but he also understood how to make it appear genuinely old, as well.

Learning that the piece was a fake did not upset the emperor at all. Quite the opposite, he was impressed, and he praised the piece. He also complimented its creator for having done such a skillful job. So many others created copies, the emperor noted, but few were as good as his work. The emperor complained that others rushed the job, and could, therefore, not be called artists.

It is hard to imagine the head of any state looking at an imitation and lavishing such unbounded praise, but that is what Qianlong had done. The emperor even had a special box commissioned for the jade cup, which he saw as a model of sorts, and on the box he had inscribed a kind of treatise on the art of counterfeiting.

American business leaders and politicians who have pushed for increased intellectual property protection in China over the years have failed to acknowledge the cultural origins of counterfeiting. It is not just that counterfeit products are tolerated in the country—they are revered.

Chinese art collections are filled with fakes, and catalogs published by the world's leading auction houses—Christie's, Sotheby's and Bonhams—all contain a prominent disclaimer to the effect that forgeries are so prevalent and of such high quality that no firm statement can be made about the authenticity of *any* of the pieces that they offer.

China's counterfeit culture runs deep, and evidence of this can be found in the great volume of counterfeit currency floating around South China, as well. In all manner of forgeries, there is a high-end market, a low-end market, and many grades in between, but these currency notes floating about were every bit like the real thing.

One morning, getting out of a taxi, I unwittingly handed the driver a counterfeit 50-renminbi note that had been fobbed off on me at some earlier point. The driver reached out to take the bill, touched it for only the briefest moment, and with his arm still outstretched, signaled for me to take it back. He had not even *looked* at it, but he could tell that it was a fake.

Counterfeiting was so common in China that average people had to learn how to identify a copy. At the factory, this ability was even more critical. Even those industrialists who did not engage in counterfeiting themselves had to know how to spot fakes that might be passed their way by competitors or suppliers.

If a manufacturer did not know how to catch a fake, then it was likely to receive raw materials that were inferior. Competition in China was intense, and manufacturers that were the most skillful at screening out fakes were the ones most likely to survive.

The ability to counterfeit products was correlated to speed in any case. One importer complained to me about how he sent a prototype to a supplier in China, and before the manufactured goods arrived by ship, a salesman had shown up at his office with samples sent by courier express. He figured that it was not his own factory in this case, but a competitor who had gotten hold of the sample and duplicated it in record time.

The speed with which China manufacturing moved was a double-edged sword. Importers could count on a manufacturer to take an initial sample and put it into production with extreme speed, but then the counterfeiters moved just as quickly—and with great skill.

Counterfeiting, as it was most commonly understood, involved the placement of a brand name on a product by a manufacturer that was not authorized to produce goods for that company. Another form involved the manufacture of a brand name product by a legitimate producer, who then moonlighted to produce excess goods in a so-called third shift operation. In some of these cases, the manufacturer produced an inferior version of the product so that the owner of the brand not only suffered sales loss, but also ran the risk of brand erosion in the marketplace.

In the worst cases—the most insidious, and perhaps the most prevalent form of counterfeiting—factories took an original product from a customer and then reinvented the product so that it looked every bit like the real thing, but was in fact a rip-off.

Johnson Carter was like that emperor who could not determine if he owned the real thing or an imitation, except that in our case, we had no curator on staff and we were considerably less thrilled by the display of talent involved in the counterfeiting of our product.

■ ■ ■

The factory's chemist was a friendly sort with the thoughtful demeanor of a scientist. He was soft-spoken and introverted, and he wore thick glasses that sat slightly crooked on his square face.

I took a chance and asked him directly if he knew what was wrong with the formulation. Looking slightly embarrassed, he said that he did, and he tipped me off about a certain chemical ingredient that was in short supply in our formulations.

In China, there was a tendency to refer to many chemicals by a numeric shorthand. He indicated the ingredient to me using a three-digit number, and he suggested that we would do all right if we argued to have more of that one ingredient added. As vague as he was, it was more information than Sister provided, and I took his discretion as concern for his job.

Factory workers traded in rumor, and it was rarely the case that only one person in any plant was privy to certain tricks. One of the things that Americans lost in taking production overseas was the ability for average workers to report consumer product safety issues. For most workers in China, the U.S. consumer was an abstraction; and even if someone at a factory was willing to make a report, where would that worker go? There was no place to leave an anonymous tip, and the media was controlled by China's central government.

In 2007, when a number of toy suppliers were found to have used toxic lead paint, there must have been hundreds of workers who knew it was happening. In addition to the boss who had green-lighted the paint, there would have been a purchasing manager as well as a receiving clerk. And then there were the hundreds of employees on the shop floor.

Lead paint was preferred in part because it dried faster. It was possible that someone noticed or at least had heard about the substitution. While factories were good at keeping secrets from foreign buyers, inside their own houses, gossip was rampant. It was used as entertainment and for survival.

In China, whistleblowers were not seen as heroes, but as social disruptors. More often than not, the whistleblower was thought to be seeking personal gain at the expense of the collective. Confucianism holds that authority must be respected, and so by definition a manufacturer gets the benefit of the doubt. Export manufacturing was a national interest, arguably the single most important interest of the ruling Communist Party. Even if a factory is actually doing something wrong, the whistleblower automatically becomes an enemy of the state.

For importers who fought for higher quality levels and clear standards, the most insulting part about input substitutions and forgeries was that the factories ended up blaming their victims. When King Chemical was caught at delivering an inferior product, their retort was like salt in a wound: *"For the price you were paying,"* Sister said, *"what did you expect?"*

Was it a legitimate defense? After having agreed to make a product at a given price, the factory responsible for manufacturing manipulated quality so that in the end, the customer received something inferior to what it had bargained for. Apologists for China manufacturing have suggested that these factories had no choice. Margins were tight, and they were not earning as much as they used to.

Arguments along these lines were specious, and Americans who allowed them for manufacturers in China would never have tolerated similarly unethical behavior from a manufacturer in their own country. In the United States, when an armed robber was caught and pled his case, the last thing a judge wanted to hear was how the accused was hard up. Poverty was no excuse.

And, anyway, how could hard times be used as an excuse when China was growing so quickly? China was hardly as poor as it was 30 years ago, or even 10 years earlier. That was doubly true of the southern region that housed so many export manufacturers. China was experiencing the greatest economic expansion in world history, and much of this was led by the export manufacturing sector, which itself was growing much faster than the overall Chinese economy.

If there was a relationship between wealth and ethics, it was more than likely a negative correlation. When China's export manufacturing miracle was just taking off, there were *fewer* quality problems, not more. Desperate manufacturers did not dare risk upsetting important new customers who were not yet beholden to them and could easily take their business elsewhere. It was only once these manufacturers achieved a degree of success and had put some money in the bank that they actually took these wild chances with manipulating quality.

The increased occurrence of quality fade had much to do with increases in skill levels and tricks of the trade. After all, it took a certain degree of ability to create a product that *looked* like the real thing but that was in fact a version that was cheaper to produce. And that skill was perfected the more it was practiced.

Because many manufacturers that engaged in quality fade had already achieved some degree of success, hard times alone could not be the only explanation. The impression that I got at some of the factories that engaged in quality manipulation schemes is that they did so after growing bored with their more conventional successes.

There was a great deal of excitement that came with getting a new business off the ground. These manufacturers were thrilled when they signed up their first major customer, and they got another kick from orders that were especially large. When deal flow leveled out, factory owners looked for others ways in which they could capture that hint of thrill.

The poverty myth was dispelled at least to some extent by one rather public example. Mattel's supplier in the lead-paint case was run by an industrialist said to be worth U.S.$1.1 billion. The manufacturer, coincidentally, had a 15-year relationship with the toy giant, which countered another argument made—that these supplier relationships necessarily improved over time and with greater familiarity.

China manufacturing was a game played on a field without referees. There was no government agency in China where an importer could go to lodge a complaint, and there were only limited opportunities for recourse through the legal system there.

In the abstract, manufacturers did not want to kill the goose that was laying their golden eggs. And, so, in practice, they focused on tactics where they might score a few quick hits. Their aim was to optimize profitability over the short term without losing the long-term customer. Striking the right balance was key.

Sister was now aware that they had gone too far in manipulating Johnson Carter's product line. She still would not explain how the product had turned into gelatin, but she said that she could "make it better." The only thing that Bernie had to do, of course, was agree to an across-the-board price increase on the Johnson Carter product line.

Sister kept us in the dark about as much as she could, and we only learned bit by bit how the factory was able to manipulate quality. No matter how long we were at it, it seemed that there was always some new and unpredictable trick. This fear of the unknown was actually what made so many importers nervous. They could not imagine what they didn't know; we had too many "unknown unknowns."

While importers claimed that they wanted to learn precisely how their products out of China were being made, at the same time they were afraid to dig too deep. Pressing for details might mean uncovering a problem that could not be ignored. It meant fixing things, and pressuring a supplier to improve quality put upward pressure on pricing.

Chinese manufacturers were good at keeping costs low—it was their true competitive advantage—but importers saw an advantage in not knowing all of their suppliers' little secrets.

■ ■ ■

Around the time that we learned that our shampoo was turning into jelly, Johnson Carter asked King Chemical if it was capable of making an underarm deodorant.

Chinese were not big on deodorant, and what was available in the local market was usually the roll-on kind anyway. What we needed for the U.S. market was a dry-stick version.

To save time, I gave the factory a stick of deodorant that I had purchased in the United States. Sister looked at it and said that, while it might take time, she was convinced that she could get it duplicated. It was a bold declaration, given that no other manufacturer in China's health and beauty care sector had managed to pull it off yet.

The prototype came in, and it looked promising. The factory had created a number of molds—five in all—and had replicated the look and feel of the casing, down to the trademark baby blue color of the original. There was even a knob on the bottom, which was turned to push the deodorant upwards.

I turned the knob and was surprised to find that the mechanism actually worked. The plastic part was not easy to make, and it required a bit of investment and time on the factory's part.

While the casing was impressive, I touched the product itself and got a surprise. The deodorant stick was not at all dry. I pressed my fingertip against the white substance and found that my finger went right into it, as if into a stick of warm butter.

The deodorant was not going to be easy to make; the factory knew this. But, rather than working on the chemical part first, they went ahead and spent probably thousands of dollars to create the casing. It was entirely backwards, but this was how manufacturers in China built their products—from the outside in.

First they made a product that looked like something that could be sold, and then they focused on the actual functioning mechanism. Outward appearances got the initial focus, and then came the product's intrinsic features. It was a production philosophy that matched the national concern for face, and in the end, it was reminiscent of

Qianlong Emperor's respect for the semblance of an art object, regardless of authenticity.

It also made good business sense. It was exorbitant to put a product into production before receiving an actual order, and the manufacturer had to convince the prospective importer that it could make the product in question. Creating the outward appearance of the thing was often just enough to get the order initiated. Once funds were transferred to China, the manufacturer could then work on the part about getting the product right.

This particular practice also contributed to quality fade. After the factory had won the initial order, and after it had expended a great deal of effort figuring out how to get the product made properly, there was often not much left to do. The factory took its surplus time and sunk it back into the product, tinkering with it to see where savings could be realized. The manufacturer looked for ways to make the product appear to be the same on the outside, while on the inside it might be a different story.

CHAPTER 12

No Animal Testing

Bernie mentioned that we would soon have visitors. Shop Corp, our largest customer, wanted to come in and conduct its own inspection. The visit would help secure more orders, Bernie explained, but he had concerns that the customer might learn too much. Bernie had claimed that Johnson Carter was a joint-venture partner in the factory, and it was precisely during an actual visit to the plant that this fiction might come to light.

When I explained to Sister that Bernie wanted the information of ownership to be kept secret, she said that she could do one better. She offered to have a sign made and hung on the front of the factory that listed Johnson Carter as an actual owner.

It was common practice in South China for manufacturers to do whatever was necessary to lock in a major piece of business. Claiming that someone was a partner was seen as only a small fudge, and at some factories in the region, you could find three, four, or even five names on a board near the entrance of the company. Manufacturers would say that these were the names of their business partners, or sometimes they indicated them as "brands." Most would reply, when asked, that they were nothing.

When the executive from Shop Corp, Donald, arrived at the factory and saw the plaque that had both Johnson Carter's and King

Chemical's names on it, he was satisfied. It proved that the two companies were, indeed, joint-venture partners.

For the first time in many months, I went through the routine of putting on a white lab coat and hat for our visiting guests. We gave the visiting executive the same kind of tour that I had been given when I first arrived at King Chemical. The questions that Donald asked were no better than the questions I asked on my very first tour of the factory. He was concerned about conditions of the workers, as many visiting Americans were.

"How many days do they get off?" he asked.

Sister gave the standard Chinese answer. "Two days," she said.

"Two days is pretty good," he said.

Donald didn't realize that she meant two days *per month*. The workers typically took off one day every other week. When told this, he was struck dumb, unable to imagine it, and all he could say was, "Oh, my."

Worker conditions concerned many foreigners, in part because they knew that Chinese workers earned less. Donald next asked me whether we had any issues with sabotage.

"What do you mean?" I asked.

"Don't you ever worry that one of the workers might intentionally harm the product?"

It was the first time that anyone had asked me this question, and it was perhaps the first time that I had even considered it. Sabotage was not a concern in China, I assured him, not like it was in the United States anyway. Factory workers saw no sense in throwing a wrench into the works. Most figured—what would be the point?

Chinese laborers earned more than their counterparts in the provinces, and they did not want to be fired from their jobs. Also, they believed deep down that they were working toward something larger than themselves. It was more than simple economics. The workers understood that they were playing a part in returning China to its former state of glory.

Donald and I walked to the production room, and then we visited the packaging station. In the warehouse, I opened a number of cardboard boxes that contained our Johnson Carter branded product. Donald looked at some examples and noticed a logo on the back label of one of the bottles.

It was a small outline of a rabbit and around the cartoon figure were the words: *No Animal Testing*.

"That's good," he said. "You don't test on animals."

It was a nice logo, and it was truthful. We didn't conduct any tests on animals. Then again, we didn't do any other testing either. King Chemical ran some basic checks to ensure the general stability of the formulation, but they were not the sort of rigorous tests that brought anyone any real comfort. We did not test for toxic chemicals or bacterial contamination, for example.

The factory had just a small laboratory located in a back room. The equipment was basic. Most high school laboratories in the United States had equipment that was more up to date. In any case, no one was checking on the factory to ensure that it produced a quality product.

Donald wanted to know what kind of tests we ran, and I answered by suggesting that we could run whatever tests Shop Corp wanted. This was Johnson Carter's standard line on testing.

Retailers that wanted additional tests had to pay a third-party testing laboratory. For health and beauty care products, such testing could be expensive, and so we put the ball in the retailer's court. No retailer that we worked with was ever interested in paying these costs, just as Johnson Carter also avoided the expense of additional testing.

One problem with testing was that the laboratory had to be told what tests to run. Retailers did not know what they should be looking for, and to a similar extent, neither did Johnson Carter. It was not possible to ask a third-party testing laboratory such as SGS or Bureau Veritas to "make sure there is no bad stuff" in the product. They charged a fee based on a specific screen. If you wanted to know whether a harmful substance was present, you had to name that substance before sending the sample off to the lab.

Even before China delivered a number of headline-creating product recalls, there had been concerns about quality. Importers scratched their heads when it came to determining which factories were the most reliable. China had such a short history when it came to manufacturing, and most suppliers had track records of only a few years. The new companies, in order to make themselves seem more professional, obtained industry certifications. Companies that were not directly involved in manufacturing latched onto the distinction. Airports, shops, and even restaurants could be certified by the International Organization for Standardization (ISO).

But certification was no guarantee of anything. Once the certifiers went back to their offices, there was no assurance about how the factory operated. The shampoo factory was certified, but the workers still walked around with dirty hands and spit on the floors. And no certification process would prevent quality shortcuts. A factory could obtain a certification and then start playing games. It could replace quality ingredients with junk. Large multinational companies that suffered product recalls certified their own factories, and what good did that do in preventing those recalls?

Bernie didn't care about certifications. He instead preferred to come to his own conclusions. He knew certificates could not solve any problems at a factory. If anything, they only created them.

A factory that obtained an official designation was more likely to attract customers that would compete with Johnson Carter for attention at King Chemical. There was nothing all that special about an ISO designation. And it wasn't as if the folks at ISO went from one factory to another, threatening to pull a factory's certificate if things didn't look right.

By now, it was clear to me that such inspections were pointless anyway. Whatever could go wrong with a manufacturing process was not going to be seen on a walk-through. If there was something that would raise a serious alarm—a worker's peeling hands, for example—the factory owner could easily make sure that it was hidden for a few short hours while inspectors were in the plant.

ISO certifies procedures, not products; and so, it was no surprise that the third-party inspector later sent by Shop Corp didn't check a single bottle of our product in the warehouse. These visits were entirely cursory, and nothing that the inspector remarked on was of any real value. There was no official report generated either, and I was told that we would be given a green light if we just fixed a few things.

The strangest request of all was that we cut down a small tree next to the warehouse—because of the possibility of insects.

Never mind that the tree was merely a sapling; the warehouse was not anywhere near where we filled the bottles with product. For a bug to get into a bottle of our shampoo in the warehouse, it would have had to find its way into a cardboard box and then unscrew a cap. While keeping cardboard boxes insect-free was a reasonable goal, what should have been a bigger concern was the soap and shampoo itself.

Like importers who visited to perform their own cursory inspections before committing to a supplier, these investigators also focused on outward appearances. They did not seem to understand the extent to which the things that were not on the surface were really the most troubling. It was the production process and the actual formulation we were selling that we worried about.

■ ■ ■

The factory, having passed inspection, went about making antibacterial soap. We sent samples to the laboratory in Hong Kong, and we got immediate bad news—the lab said that there was almost no antibacterial agent in the samples.

A second attempt was made with almost the same result.

Bernie was upset about this, and he worked to stall Shop Corp while we tried for a third time. The factory did not know what went wrong, only that they had a failed result. To get around the problem, the factory created 10 different samples with varying levels of the active ingredient.

This time, nine of the results came back as failed, and *one* passed. The factory sent the successful result to Johnson Carter, who sent it to the retailer. When the retailer received the positive test result, it issued the purchase order.

There were many problems with third-party testing. One problem was that the factory itself was commonly responsible for choosing the sample that was sent to be tested. The testing laboratories did not go to the factories to pull random samples. The factory could thus be in the habit of making a substandard product while sending over acceptable samples for testing. The testing companies that gave approval did not themselves insist that samples be randomly chosen, and neither did Johnson Carter's own customers.

Testing companies were in competition with one another; and over time, we learned that one laboratory was more lenient in its testing practices than the others. These laboratories were businesses, and they knew the benefits of providing favorable laboratory results. This did not mean that they falsified data, but that they offered *clues*.

For example, one laboratory might not provide the criteria by which a pass or fail was issued while another one did. The more information that was provided about what caused a fail meant more scope to provide a workaround, at least for the purposes of a testing sample.

The testing that we did focused primarily on external factors. For example, we tested for pH levels and viscosity, but you could create a product of mud that matched pH and viscosity. These measures alone did not make a product a quality shampoo.

In time, we also came to discover that the Hong Kong office of one testing company was more helpful than its North American office. Retailers that relied on these tests did not often know about such variations within the testing sector, but many manufacturers did—and they used it to their advantage.

Statistically speaking, third-party testing did work—but for reasons that few understood. A factory that knew its product would not pass was not likely to send its product to a testing laboratory in the first place—so yes, products that were tested usually had a higher chance of passing. But third-party laboratories had actually tested many of the products that were recalled in the United States, so the limitations of the system were clear.

In the end, the quality problems that the factory caused were not immediately life threatening, but they caused us to wonder. We were put in a constant state of never being quite sure of just what it was that we were receiving. And as the importer, we *should* have known. We should have been in a position to know *everything* about our product—but we didn't.

CHAPTER 13

Joint Venture Panacea

When my newest client mentioned that he had an interest in cigars, I took him to the China Hotel where they had a bar that sold them.

Darren explained that he was not interested in cigars exactly, but some colleagues in his company's San Francisco headquarters insisted that he bring some back because they had heard that Cuban cigars were legal and available in China.

Cuban cigars were of course popular with Americans to some degree as a result of their being prohibited due to the embargo placed on Fidel Castro's "Communist regime."

A hostess led us into the humidor, and Darren looked at prices. "Jesus," he said. " How can the Chinese afford these?"

Seeing his reaction, the hostess asked me what Darren had just said. When I told her, she said, "*Xianzai, Zhongguoren youqian.*" The Chinese now have money.

She made it sound as if a great switch had been thrown. One day, the country was broke; and the very next, everyone was smoking $37 cigars.

Darren chose two wide-gage sticks—Partagas Serie D No. 4—and the hostess placed them onto a velvet-lined wood tray. "They are also good tippers," she added.

In the lounge, we were shown to a semicircular sofa with a high back that faced a trio of Filipina performers. The Philippines sent large numbers of singers to work in Chinese hotels on short-term contracts. The nation also happened to send many artists to South China, where they worked as designers for furniture manufacturers. Despite China's vast population and low labor rate, some talent was more efficiently sourced from abroad.

A hostess clipped and lit a cigar, waving it high above her head, fanning the smoke in a manner that suggested an improvised or local convention.

"How do you say thank you in Chinese?" Darren asked. "Wait, don't tell me.... *Shay-shay*!"

"Close enough," I said. Seeing me wince made him laugh, and he repeated the phrase as the hostess went away.

Darren and I were classmates from business school, and neither of us was in the habit of smoking cigars. He explained that his colleagues enjoyed them—the pricier the better—and that they also had a taste for other extravagances, including sports cars, boats, and exotic travel.

His employer, Build Corp, was a privately held, billion-dollar construction company on the West Coast. It had built luxury hotels and commercial towers and had more recently purchased the patents related to an aluminum system that was used in making concrete buildings.

It was a kind of scaffolding system, Darren explained, into which concrete was poured. The unit was modular and lightweight, and though it could be used to build skyscrapers, it took only two workers to set up the system and take it down. The product was an industry innovation, and the opportunity led Build Corp to sell and rent it out to other large construction companies.

The equipment was produced in China, and there were a number of issues that needed to be resolved.

One problem was that the manufacturer had been manipulating quality. Build Corp's product was made up of components that were carefully designed. Engineers knew precisely what each part should look like, and there was a small surprise when the supplier was found to be taking metal out of certain components. One key part that weighed about 48 kilograms was coming in at less than 90 percent of its intended weight. The factory had taken the weight reduction as a cost savings for itself and had passed only the resulting product risk on to Build Corp.

There had already been one instance of a collapse, resulting in a fatality, and there was concern that there would be more.

"This joint venture is going to fix a lot of problems," Darren said. "I'm going to need your help in getting the project on track."

At the factory, we met Robert, the boss. Darren wanted to cover quality issues first. He had earlier rejected a large shipment of high-end plywood, and the factory was quietly slipping portions of the bad shipment in with later product that was good.

Darren wanted to discuss one other issue, as well. He had requested samples on his last visit, and the factory would not supply them. He wanted to have the metal tested in China to ensure that quality levels were acceptable, but the factory worried that he would take the samples and send them to a competing company.

"The products are for export only," said Nancy, a feisty assistant who worked for Robert.

Nancy suggested that the only way to get the samples was to have them exported to the United States and then sent all the way back to China.

It was our first day of a visit meant to last four days, and I was already tired. Darren said that he wanted to table a number of issues so that we could all discuss the joint venture proposal. In the car on the way to the factory, Darren had already told me that he expected the joint venture to solve most of Build Corp's problems with the supplier.

"How's that?" I asked.

"You see, right now," he said, "the factory is screwing us. But if we become joint venture partners, it would be like they were screwing themselves. They wouldn't do that."

There was another reason that Build Corp wanted to do the joint venture. Robert's motivation was dwindling rapidly. While Build Corp's order sizes were growing, the factory's overall business was growing at an even faster rate.

At one time, the San Francisco company had accounted for almost all of the factory's business. Two years earlier, it made up 75 percent of the factory's book of business; now, the rate had fallen to below

45 percent. Smaller importers had come along and were paying higher prices than Build Corp, which meant also that Build Corp was contributing even less in profitability.

Darren's company wanted to sink $2 million into Robert's factory, but the valuation presented another problem. The factory was growing so quickly, the amount of equity that Robert was willing to give Build Corp was shrinking by the week.

"I want to show you something," Darren said.

He took me to a piece of land at the back of the property. Robert's factory had added a number of new buildings. While Build Corp and its supplier were discussing the possibility of a joint venture, Robert had quietly been expanding the business. By the time they got around to calculating the factory's assets, the value of new buildings had to be placed on the balance sheet.

"You see what they've done?" Darren asked, pointing to the new construction. "Our money created all of this in the first place, and now it's being used to shrink our stake in the factory."

Darren wanted to enter into an agreement with the factory before it was too late. There was a sense that an opportunity was slipping. "If we don't get Robert to sign this deal right away, I'm telling you, we're fucked." He was desperate, but was trying to push for things that he thought Build Corp should have as a part of the deal, like guarantees related to how the business would be operated.

Robert had been dragging his feet for months, but he said that he was interested in doing the deal. The problem was that he did not want to agree to some of the things that Darren was looking for in a joint venture. Robert didn't want to share any of his financial information in the course of due diligence. And when the joint venture was done, he didn't want to share control either.

In other words, Build Corp was free to invest its money, but all it was ever going to get was a piece of paper that said that it owned a stake. No information would be shared with its partners, and Build Corp would not have any say in what went on. Everything had to be taken on faith.

I had met factory owners like Robert before. They understood the part about how foreigners wanted to give them cash, and they looked at these infusions as a kind of reward. This attitude of theirs was just as well because most foreign investors couldn't justify their inflated valuations anyway. Foreign companies focused on the dollar figure that they needed to contribute, and they took these amounts as the price of admission to a game in which they wanted to join.

I asked Darren how his company would know if it had gotten a good deal out of the investment, especially if Robert was not going to allow anyone to look at his books. And wasn't Build Corp worried about its exit strategy?

"It's fine," Darren insisted in a nonchalant way.

More bad news then followed.

The factory, which had revenues in excess of $8 million, was not paying taxes and was running all of its finances through the personal bank accounts of Robert's relatives. Strong government connections had enabled him to avoid paying taxes and fees, and it had been one of his advantages in business.

Foreign ventures were not nearly as lucky in this regard, and a joint venture was almost surely going to be more carefully scrutinized by officials. Robert knew this, and it was one reason why he kept putting off a commitment to the joint venture.

"The JV will end up having to pay taxes," I said.

"I know," Darren said in an ironic tone. "It's going to suck."

"I mean your costs are going to go up," I said, connecting the dots for him.

"No, they won't," he said defensively.

Darren sounded quite sure on this one point, and he explained why. Build Corp was going to invest $2 million with Robert, but then it was going to write $10 million in new orders that it had waiting. For the cash investment and the guarantee of more orders, the factory was going to provide Build Corp with a 9 percent discount on all future purchases.

"The equity is really just icing on the cake," Darren said, and then giving me a self-satisfied look, he added, "It's all in the agreement. You'll see."

For the rest of the afternoon, Darren played tough guy. The deal was either going to be done on his terms, or Build Corp was going to look for another partner. Darren had asked me to assemble a list of alternative suppliers, and he had this list with him. He placed the data on the table, and the names of some competitors must have jumped right off the page because Robert went bug-eyed.

The next morning, Darren woke me early.

"Bad news," he said. "Robert sent a note to my guys in San Francisco. He announced a price increase."

The factory was going to increase prices by 11 percent. In other words, Build Corp would invest its $2 million, and in return its net costs were going to go up by 2 percent.

Having invested a couple million dollars, Build Corp was going to be unable to leave for another supplier, which meant an even greater likelihood of further price increases.

When I caught up with Darren a few minutes later, he was in the hotel restaurant, cutting into a pair of fried eggs.

"You guys going to cancel the deal?" I asked.

"No way," he said with his mouth full. "My guys back in San Francisco told me not to come back until I get the deal signed."

Given what we knew about the deal now, it seemed absurd, and I told him so. Darren stopped eating and pointed his fork in my direction.

"Look," he said. "These guys want the deal to happen. There's nothing I can do about it. I've got the CEO of my company talking to everyone about how 'China is the future,' and there are all these other guys in the office who are counting on this deal."

Darren explained that some of his colleagues had end-of-year bonuses tied to the joint venture. They had to be seen as moving the business forward, and they wanted to create something that at year's end might look like some kind of accomplishment. These were executives who would never have much to do with Robert's factory; they were never going to visit China. These executives at Build Corp who wanted to be seen as progressive were a mystery to me. I told Darren that I didn't get it.

"This is how American companies work," he said. "You don't understand because you spend all your time here."

He was right to an extent; I didn't understand, because I worked in China. Even the largest Chinese companies that I knew operated as if they were small. They were more nimble, and they could be counted on to turn on a dime if a deal started to look bad.

"If everyone wants the deal, it's fine by me," I said. What else was there to say? The deal stank; they all knew that there was a problem, and yet they wanted to move forward anyway.

"Now, you're thinking the right way," Darren said. He picked up his computer bag and handed me an orange. "We have to get back to the factory, and we have to get Robert to sign that paperwork on the joint venture—today."

Darren said that he also planned to fix Robert's wagon for going around him to address his colleagues. It was a sore spot with him, primarily because the move had worked. Robert knew just enough about office politics in the United States to understand which individuals at Build Corp were making key decisions.

On the way to the factory, I scratched some ideas into a notebook, *Chinese companies don't allow foreigners to break their ranks, and yet they divide foreign teams without difficulty.*

At the factory, Robert acted as though he knew nothing about the e-mails he had sent, though they had a clear impact back at Build Corp. The San Francisco office was buzzing about what was happening in China. Darren was not even there, and he was feeling the pressure of office politics.

Later that day, Darren said that he wanted to get back to Guangzhou, which was four hours away. He had called his airline to confirm his seat and had found that they could not get him into business class.

Another day or two at the factory, I thought, and we might actually make headway on a number of issues, like the joint venture deal or some of the quality issues. In the end, Darren would pass these on to me, while he went to take care of his flight. He grumbled about Robert, complained about his colleagues back in San Francisco, and made a point of how he was not about to go back to the office and tell everyone that he had to fly coach.

Build Corp continued to purchase its China-made products from Robert's factory.

Even with all of his conditions met, Robert found other reasons for not getting into the joint venture. Meanwhile, politics back in San Francisco turned into something else. There had been a coup of sorts, which resulted in some of the original founders getting tossed out of the company they had built.

Darren reported that things had ended well for him personally— he had been handed a nice severance package before leaving—but after he stopped working on the business, margins for the aluminum product shrank to nil. The division had gone from being one of the company's highest margin businesses to one of its least profitable units.

In the end, Build Corp was sold to a major Japanese concern, and the future headaches of the China business now all belonged to that company instead.

CHAPTER 14

Take the Long Way Home

You never realize how much a place has imprinted itself on you until you travel away from it. It was summer, and I had to fly to the United States. My main reason was business, but then I also took the trip as an opportunity to visit family and friends. In Arizona on my way to visit my friend Michael, I found myself at an intersection, and looking up at a traffic light, I thought, *There's a factory in Guangdong that makes those things.* I had left China, but it was with me still.

My friend Michael and his wife kept four dogs that ran in a pack around their ranch home. As I walked through the door, they jumped up on me. Looking at a fancy collar on one of the dogs, I was reminded of another factory owner in Guangzhou, one who had a thriving business making pet clothing for the export market.

Michael and I had known each other since high school, some 25 years ago. We sat in his living room, and everything seemed different to me now. My friend was still my friend, but his home looked more like a showcase of products quite likely made in China. The clock on the wall looked like the sort that was made in China, as did a ceramic vase on a table next to the sofa. Who knew what items in this home had come from China—the majority? They had recently purchased an entertainment center. I looked at it wondering how many would fit in a 40-foot container.

On these infrequent visits, we rarely spoke about my life in China, but Michael had a newfound interest. The U.S. economy was shaky, and China was growing strong. He had no idea what it was like in the Far East, and he admitted that he was curious. China was not a source of enthusiasm for his wife, however.

"We keep seeing China on the news these days," she said as though she wished the media would cover other topics instead. China sounded far off, and knowing that I lived there did not exactly put me in her favor.

The conversation shifted. We talked about other things—what some mutual acquaintances were up to and a recent home improvement project of theirs.

Michael went into the kitchen to get drinks, and his wife, Elizabeth, perhaps felt obliged to talk about China. She had always said that she did not understand why I lived there. Now, she said she wanted to ask me something.

"Do they *really* eat dogs?"

"I haven't," I said.

"You don't, but *they* do." It was a comment meant as an excuse for not exploring a topic.

The media was, in part, to blame for confounding Americans and for turning them off on the subject of China. On the one hand, news outlets depicted the country as a capitalist nation, but then those same media organizations pounded away at the idea of China as a Communist stalwart.

There were too many contradictory images: The economy was on fire, implying an imminent threat to America's lead in the global economy, but then the place was still also portrayed as poor and pitiable. China was mysterious and exotic, a land of history and culture; but at the same time, it was shown to be an industrial wasteland. Americans were confused; they didn't know whether to imagine pandas and pagodas or environmental decay and pollution.

China's government was totalitarian and overbearing, and yet the media also reported that the Chinese people were among the most contented in the world. Had the Communist Party succeeded in building its "harmonious society," or were its citizens suffering from a mass-scale Stockholm syndrome? Not sure what to think, Americans like Elizabeth steered clear of the subject altogether.

Michael was more curious than his wife about China. To him, the economy's rapid economic growth sounded impressive, though maybe a bit frightening, also. China was growing so fast. Surely the country would, in his words, "take over the world."

"China's really growing, isn't it?" he asked.

"It's all right," I said. The growth was certainly there, but just as the Chinese did not blather on about how fast the place was changing, neither did I feel any need to do so. What the manufacturing sector was doing was certainly impressive, but China also had its shortcomings.

At one time, China had a reputation for innovation, having invented paper, gunpowder, and the compass; but in more recent centuries, that spark of discovery was replaced by an instinct for copying—not just technologies but also entire business models. This replaced habit had enabled the country to play catch-up in recent years, but the model was surely not sustainable. No economy could ever win the race by merely catching the wind off another's sail, and China had big ambitions for itself. It was looking not only to lessen the gap between itself and the world, but also to reach parity and surpass industrialized economies like the United States and Japan.

And then there were all of the other issues, too many to go into in one sitting. The business sector had serious ethical challenges; problems with quality control were merely one sign. Michael considered my comments and wanted something less elliptical. Working in the manufacturing sector surely must have provided me with some sense of what was going on, generally, and if I did not believe in the boom, then what did I believe about China, exactly?

Michael was my friend; he didn't want me to run out statistics. He wanted an impression, some kind of final word. He wanted to know where I stood on things and hoped that I would make the sort of comment that we could tuck away and later recall in a future conversation.

"You think that China is going to crash," Michael said, trying to put words in my mouth.

"I didn't say *that*."

He kept pressing the point, playing with some of the ideas that I had been bouncing around. As far as he was concerned, it had to be just as others insisted—that China would either rise like a balloon or sink like a stone in a pond. He took my criticisms as a suggestion that I predicted the latter.

"The rise and fall of China," he said, trying to play with a common theme.

"More like the rise and *stall*," I said.

There were many reasons for me to be in the United States this time; one was to attend a trade show. I was also there to meet with a few U.S. companies that were exploring their options in China.

One stop brought me to the town of Waterbury, Connecticut, to a manufacturer of metal components. Having arrived at their offices on the early side, I was asked to sit in a small conference room and wait.

I noticed a picture hanging on the wall. It was an old black-and-white photograph taken sometime in the late nineteenth century. The plant workers stood in front of the factory, which made buckles. The men were all dressed in suits, and the women in the photo wore billowy, light-colored dresses. Everyone wore a hat I noticed, and for good measure, they had even brought the company horse into the shot.

This company had been one of New England's preeminent man-ufacturers. A couple of corporate mergers and a century and a half later, the business was a subsidiary of a publicly traded company, and they were scrambling to put together their plan for competing against cheaper parts being made in China by their competitors. Their so-lution, which was not a bad one at all, was to make use of the same low-cost labor.

Not all of the companies that I visited turned into clients, and I kept this in mind whenever traveling afar and on my own nickel. This particular company was looking for general advice only. Mostly, they wanted to know where they might get it wrong if they went to China. They had me do most of the talking, while everyone else took notes.

Heading out of town after our meeting, I passed other factories, and one in particular looked much like the buckle company that I had just left. From the road, I could not tell what this one produced, and I wondered: *What if I stopped at this factory as I had in China?*

There was enough time in my day, and knowing that I might never be this way again, I decided to turn off on the small state road into their parking lot.

"I'm sorry, who are you?" the company's receptionist asked me.

After explaining that I had just been to a manufacturer up the road, she considered me carefully and pressed me for further details. "I work in China," I said, and at this one word—"China"—she squared her shoulders, making herself look like a barroom bouncer.

She said that without an appointment, I couldn't meet with anyone. She was not rude, but curt, and I was embarrassed. *Whatever was I thinking to drop in on a company like that? Where did I think I was—Foshan or someplace?*

Apologizing for the interruption, I prepared a quick retreat. Perhaps realizing that she had been short with me, the receptionist softened and just before I turned to leave, she leaned toward me as if she were going to tell me a secret. "You know," she said, now sounding sweet, "China's actually our competition."

Getting into my rented car and pulling out of the parking lot, I realized that I never found out what the company manufactured. And then I thought: *What a ridiculous thing to say,* "China's our competition." If their company was facing hard times because of China, all the more reason to meet and discuss the opportunities. The buckle company had competitors overseas, and its answer was to try and make the place work for them, also. *Who ever managed to beat their competitors by running away from them?*

It was a missed opportunity, that was all. On the road to New York, I thought about the ancient Greeks who had a custom of never turning away travelers. If you found a stranger on your doorstep, you were expected to take the person in, feed him, and allow the person the opportunity to rest. And under no circumstances would a host ever allow such a guest to leave without gifts. One reason for the custom was practical. Long-distance travelers who turned up often carried information from afar. This unique custom was how the ancient Greeks got their news.

How many times had I dropped in on a Chinese company and been treated not as a stranger, but as such an honored guest? Manufacturers that did not know or expect me would take me in and treat me kindly, and I was not allowed to leave without carrying away gifts (in their case, some of the factory's production samples were forced onto me). While it sometimes felt like I was being used, at least you could respect these industrialists for their forthrightness and savvy.

Maybe it was just my changed perspective from having lived in China for so long, but it seemed that Chinese companies were more aggressive in engaging the broader world. In the United States, the growing trend was to ignore a rival when a better strategy might have been to take the threat of competition as a welcome challenge. There was something about China's economic rise in any event that was causing American companies to lose confidence.

■ ■ ■

After a full day meeting with Bernie and his Johnson Carter partners near Broadway in Manhattan, I spent my final two days in Philadelphia. I had friends to catch up with there, and it was also a chance to visit a city that I had come to know well during my graduate school days.

Summer was the best time to visit, and tourists from around the country filled the streets. Visiting the area around Independence Hall, I noticed a number of changes. A new building for the Liberty Bell had been constructed, along with a spacious visitor's center. Sitting on a corner nearby, I spotted an odd figure, a lone protester.

It was the first time I had ever noticed a protester in this part of the city, and even more unusual was that the woman's microphone was blaring an announcement in Mandarin. I went closer and noticed that she was protesting on behalf of Falun Gong, the religion in China that was considered a cult by the government and was outlawed as a result.

At the other end of the lawn, I spotted two men, also Chinese, whose knockoff Ray-Ban sunglasses and striped slacks gave them away as possibly being from northern China. I got close enough to hear them speaking in a familiar foreign language, and I said "*Ni hao*," just as I might in China. They were glad to talk with me because neither of them spoke English, and I was even more pleased, since it was my first real chance in two weeks to speak in Mandarin.

Chinese were a generally chatty people, and I was also comforted to reprise my role as *laowai*—the foreigner who lives in China.

Seeing them reminded me of China. I not only missed the place, but also my work. My time in export manufacturing was difficult and even frustrating, but still, I did enjoy it. "Find a wall that you can bang your head against," went the words of one well-known artist, "and if you accomplish nothing more than making a small crack in that wall, at least you can say—'*that's* my wall.'" I didn't know how much of an impact I was having on the manufacturing sector, but I was used to a certain feeling.

I asked the two Chinese that I met about their impressions of America, and they gave me the common complaint about how the Chinese food in the United States is so bad as to be inedible.

"What about a cheesesteak?" I asked. We were, after all, in Philadelphia. As bad as they thought their next Chinese meal was going to be, they said that they preferred to stick with what they already knew. They did want recommendations for sightseeing, though.

Benjamin Franklin's grave was worth a look I told them, and I explained why: because American tourists threw coins onto his grave. Chinese, who have a great reverence for savings and an abhorrence for waste, had a hard time believing that real money was left on anyone's tombstone.

One of them asked if I meant fake paper money, the sort burned in an offering to Buddha. No, I assured them, it was cash.

"Why would they do that?"

I tried to explain the irony in it all—for the man who had famously (and in vain, apparently) taught Americans the value of saving by suggesting that a "penny saved is a penny earned," tourists from around the country emptied their pockets of spare change, chucking it away.

I sent the pair west, while I headed south, stopping in a small pizza shop in South Philly. Signs on the walls advised customers against asking for such things as plastic utensils, Parmesan cheese, access to a bathroom, or free water. On the wall along with these numerous warnings was one sign that summed up the shop's overall attitude toward customer service: "The Answer is No! No! No!"

It was something else that would have been lost on most Chinese visitors, and like Ben Franklin's coin-strewn grave, I found the notices in the pizza shop funny but sad.

The man who rang me up at the register had tattoos. One caught my eye. It was a Chinese character printed in dark blue ink, and it covered half the left side of his neck. It happened to be a character that I recognized—*Jiao*, which could mean education, or it could be used as a verb, as in "to teach."

I asked whether he was a teacher, and I had to point at my own neck for him to get the reference. "Nah," he said, "it was a mistake. I told the guy that I wanted the symbol for 'hope.'"

In addition to economic troubles, Philadelphia had for the longest time been fighting a major crime wave, and one thing that the city seemed in short supply of was hope.

When reporting on violent crime, city newspapers referenced over 400 murders in the previous year, most of them attributed to handguns. China did not suffer from crime to any extent near that; and as a foreigner living in China, I always felt especially safe.

Wrapping up my visit to Philadelphia, I saw a T-shirt in a shop window. It had been designed to look like a baseball jersey. The shirt read: *Killadelphia*. Living in China, I never saw such things. The Chinese did not have violent crime to such an extent, and they certainly had not got to the point where they made commercial humor out of it.

After two weeks in the United States, I was more than ready to get back to China. While boarding my flight at JFK Airport, I noticed that the majority of passengers on my flight were Asian, and I already felt closer to my destination.

The man next to me was delighted that we could speak in Mandarin, and he asked me: "Where are you heading?"

"*Wo yao huiguo,*" I told him in a manner that was meant to be tongue-in-cheek.

The man's face twisted into a sour expression, and he told me that I could not use those words.

He had taken exception to my use of the word "huiguo," a verb made up of two characters: *hui* meant "to return," and *guo* meant "country." Put together, the two characters suggested a return to one's homeland. I was effectively declaring domicile; I was calling China my home.

"It is not a suitable phrase for you," he said, sounding authoritative and certain. "You are a foreigner. You should simply say that you are *traveling to* China."

He was trying to sound polite, but it felt like a slap in the face all the same. "But I live in China," I said, trying to correct this notion that I was a mere traveler. "I *live* in Guangzhou."

I thought that by naming the city, it would help, and it occurred to me to show him the keychain in my pocket, if only to make a further point. All of the keys that I had opened doors in South China. I had almost no physical ties to the United States. And if I didn't live somewhere in America, where had I been all these years?

The man squinted, pretending to give some thought to my point of clarification, but he was resolute. "While that may be the case . . ." he said, leaving his final words hanging in the air. He was harsh, yet

I recognized the attitude as an oddly familiar one. There were many others in China who shared the same chilly attitude regarding their foreign guests, and it was a reminder to me that while I no longer had a home in the United States, China was holding me at arm's length.

There was a parable from ancient China referred to as "Handan xuebu." It was a story about a man who learned of a people in a distant province that had a special way of walking. The man determined that he would go to this other place and learn their gait, which seemed so much more sophisticated than that of his own ancestors.

He spent all of his money and invested a great deal of time to get it right, but he was never quite able to pull it off. He never learned to master the new way of walking, and in the process of trying to learn, he subsequently forgot the way that he used to walk. In the parable, as a result of his folly, the man was forced to crawl his way home.

It was the story of many long-term expatriates in China, those Old China Hands, as they were once called. While never fully integrated into their adopted country, they were no longer quite at home in the places from which they came either.

The man on the airplane stared at the back of the seat in front of him, his mouth pursed tight. Having thought of more that I would like to say, I wanted to reopen the conversation, but there was no point in it; he was done.

My return to China was bittersweet. While I reached for my seat belt, the man next to me slipped his forearm onto the armrest between us—and there it remained for the entire 12-hour flight. Sitting with my arms folded all the way to East Asia, I wondered: *How long would I have to live in China before I would be allowed to call the place home?*

CHAPTER 15

Lucky Diamonds

Saul Plotnick was another new client looking for assistance in China. He was in diamonds and his company was one of the select few that purchased rough stones directly from De Beers, the world's largest diamond cartel. It was a family business, he explained, one that had revenues in excess of $1 billion.

"So, what do you know about the diamond industry?" he asked me.

The truth was, not much. I mentioned that I had recently read an article about an Uzbek billionaire who was giving De Beers a run for its money. He was glad that I mentioned the man.

"Who, Lev Leviev? We put him in business!" We sat in his hotel room in Shenzhen, and over a coffee table, he opened a portfolio of laminated pages—advertisements that showed where his company's diamonds were sold. Escada, one of Europe's leading fashion houses, was a client, and so was one of America's largest discount wholesale clubs, those membership chains where a customer could purchase frozen shrimp in bulk along with automobile tires.

He was one of two brothers who ran the company that had been started by their father; the family name was that of the company, as well.

Our meeting turned into a history lesson, with Saul explaining how his family had gotten into the diamond business. As a young man, his late father had been sent from South Africa with an assortment of stones for markets in Europe and asked to discover what prices they might fetch there.

Saul spoke of the senior Plotnick not so much in the manner of a son recalling a deceased father, but in the way that one talks about a legendary public figure. He told me that his father would have done just as well in any industry—it just so happened that he found himself in diamonds.

His father's innate sense of pricing was what had been their key to success. The reverence with which he spoke of the family patriarch made me think that he might actually be a legend in the diamond industry.

We traveled by van and met other family members who were directly involved in the business. We were joined by Saul's wife, his brother, and his nephew. They were from Belgium, but spoke multiple languages and rotated among them quickly, as if playing a game. The family was Jewish, devoutly observant. The men dressed in dark suits and wore *kippas*.

Bouncing down the highway on our way to visit a diamond-polishing factory near the town of Zhongshan, it was as though we were in an Old World caravan, the sort that my own ancestors had probably taken on their way to settling in Romania and Poland hundreds of years ago. I listened as the conversations switched from French to English to Yiddish to what I figured to be Flemish. So many languages, and not one of them the tongue of the land in which they were hoping to make their way.

On the return trip from a second diamond factory, Saul told me about his plan: he was going to sell diamonds in China. He sounded confident, as if the only question had really been his family's will to enter the market. There were some obstacles, one being that the Chinese government would only allow local manufacturers to make direct sales. But that was the point of visiting these diamond-polishing facilities. His company would set up partnerships that would give them a backdoor entrance into the market.

For a moment, I thought Saul might ask me what I thought about his plan to sell diamonds in China, and I was relieved when he didn't. The bigger issue, I thought, would be finding the demand. Chinese women did not consider a diamond ring any necessary part of a marriage proposal, and while gems held a special place in eastern cultures, diamonds were not nearly as significant as gold, jade, or silver.

The idea of a diamond offered at engagement was an invented tradition anyway, and in its marketing materials for the United States, De Beers proposed that men budget two months' salary for an engagement ring. This proposed metric was particularly meaningless in an economy where average workers were earning just a little more than $100 each month. Another obstacle was that Chinese were not in the habit of making payments for jewelry.

The plan as Saul saw it was to replicate what had worked for the company in other parts of the world. In the United States, they had done well by moving large volumes of diamonds through the warehouse clubs. Through these channels, Plotnick had specialized in selling imperfect diamonds to middle-class Americans, who didn't care about occlusions or other imperfections as much as they did about the size of the diamond or saving money.

China was a market full of opportunity, but it was a different sort of place. I suggested that China was different, but my comment was not one that Saul wanted to hear. He was set on developing business opportunities in China, in part because his company had no choice.

De Beers was a cartel that had once controlled price almost exclusively by holding back supply from the marketplace. A global management-consulting firm had done work for De Beers and concluded that it needed to work the other side of the equation by increasing demand, as well.

The cartel took the consultants' advice and then used the primary means for moving diamonds that it had—sightholders—to take on the task. This was really how the Plotnick Group had come to be in China without any idea of how it would address some of the rather large market issues. Though not a marketing company, Plotnick had to show the De Beers group that it was doing whatever it could to boost global demand.

I knew others who worked in the diamond industry. It also suffered from the kind of quality manipulation that was prevalent in manufacturing. Chinese diamond cutters were, I understood, in the habit of cutting diamonds in an asymmetrical fashion so as to get a slightly larger gem out of the rough diamond. After this was done, a jeweler could then get a fake certificate authenticating the diamond as being of a higher quality.

My standard position on all new ventures in China was that they had to be looked at with a healthy dose of cynicism. In passing, I mentioned to Saul that I personally would not jump into any China business without learning more about how the game was played.

"Pshhht!" Saul said when he heard this. He dismissed any comment advising caution as irrelevant.

"Other sightholders are already in China," the nephew pointed out. "Do you know Dalumi?"

"That's the name of your competitor?" I asked. "Dalumi?"

I smiled without meaning to, and the nephew wanted to know why. "Dalu" was how people referred to Mainland China, I told him. And the character for uncooked rice just happened to be "mi." Uncooked rice granules were not exactly the image you wanted to put into a consumer's head when trying to sell rare gems, and if I spotted the joke, then the Chinese marketplace surely would pick up on it.

Saul's nephew was pleased that I had found something laughable about their competitor. And he was fascinated by the idea of translated names.

"What does our name mean in Chinese?" he asked.

By itself, it meant nothing, I told him, and then I tried to explain that it was just a coincidence that his competitor's name sounded silly.

"Plotnick has to mean something. It probably means something really good," he insisted. "I bet it's lucky."

He had an excitable look in his eyes, and I thought of D. H. Lawrence's "Rocking-Horse Winner" and the little boy who rode wildly on his hobbyhorse. But Western names did not always mean something in Chinese. To translate a family name, I was going to have to think first about matching up all of the syllable sounds. There was no "plot" syllable in Mandarin. It would have to be "pu-la-te" or "pa-lu-tuo"—three separate characters each. I was getting a headache just thinking about the number of permutations. I told him that I would need time to put together some options.

He insisted, though, that I deliver the translation immediately, expecting that the result would be a pleasant one.

Foreigners of all kinds were attracted to the allure of what seemed to be a magical culture. To see this ultra-Orthodox Jewish man getting caught up in the country's "fortune-cookie mystique" was too much for me, though, and this kind of fetishism reminded me of the pizza shop worker in Philadelphia, the one who had in error tattooed the Chinese character "education" on his neck.

Jews and Chinese had much in common, including an interest in education that went back thousands of years. There was one tradition whose seminal text began with the verse, "To study and at times to go over what one has studied, is this not the greatest pleasure?" It sounded as if it was something right out of *The Talmud,* the ancient Jewish text, but was actually from *The Analects of Confucius.*

And, out of this tradition for study came a reverence for the written word that extended to the superstitious.

In World War II, when China provided sanctuary to an estimated 30,000 Jewish refugees, those who were told of the possibility that they might go to Shanghai needed no encouragement after hearing the city's name. The "hai" in Shanghai sounded like the Hebrew word "chai"—which means life. This one word had powerful connotations; it was the two-letter symbol that some Jews wore on necklaces, and it also appeared in "L'chaim," the toast offered when glasses were raised—"to life."

Chinese were just as superstitious when it came to naming, and it was said that those Chinese who immigrated to Canada and settled in the British Columbia city of Richmond did so because to them the city's name sounded like "rich man."

After a visit to Shanghai's diamond bourse where Saul tried to secure the largest office space inside the exchange, we went to visit jewelry stores in the city's commercial district.

Saul went straight to a showcase in one store and pointed to three diamond rings. He asked to inspect them. Looking at the diamonds through his jeweler's loop, he made a face. There was something that he did not like about them. It was not that the diamonds were bad; quite the opposite, he said that they were *too* nice. Each diamond was clear in color and free of any flaws. He muttered and said that it was not what he had expected.

China's luxury market was a paradox. Though living in a developing country, Mainland Chinese either purchased at the top end of the market or else they chose not to buy at all.

Chinese preferred to postpone major purchases until they had accumulated a more substantial amount of wealth, and their pattern of saving was at least partially influenced by great instances of poverty in Chinese history.

Researchers have recorded over 1,800 major famines in China (going back to the first century BC). Starvation has a way of changing behaviors, and one of the most certain ways that an individual could lose scarce resources was to advertise that he had them.

During a famine, someone who thought a relative was hiding a small cache of grain might literally kick down the front door and search the home. In Mainland China, even though things had improved greatly since the Cultural Revolution, the tendency was still to hide accumulated wealth, at least until some tipping point had been reached and it mattered less who learned the extent of such wealth.

They spent only after considerable wealth had been accumulated for another reason having to do with face. Chinese postponed major purchases so that they could do things in a more enviable manner. To buy luxury goods that involved compromise or economization sent the wrong message.

Walking through the street on the way back to the van, our small group was approached by three elderly women. One woman held out a number of watches for me to inspect.

"What is it? What do they want?" Saul asked.

"Rolex watches," I said.

He was interested in the watches, to my surprise. His company was one of the very largest diamond wholesalers in the world. If there was anyone who needed a counterfeit watch less, it was Saul.

This was nothing unusual, though. Foreigners on business were invariably interested in counterfeit products. They liked them for their novelty, because they were sometimes hard to come by, and because purchasing them involved the sport of haggling over price.

"Ask how much they want," he said.

The woman nearest to me named her price, and there was a brief moment of back-and-forth until she settled at 100 renminbi. It was about $12 at the going exchange rate. It was a low price, even for a fake.

Saul kept walking and thought about it.

"Tell her that I will take three—for 50 renminbi each."

The women looked not just old, but frail. They labored just to keep up with us as we walked at a pace set by Saul. The price they offered was already extremely cheap, and I told Saul so.

He shot me a look and said, "If they can't do 50, tell them to forget it." I held my tongue, but was quite certain that they would hold out for more.

Hearing the counteroffer, the women pulled long faces and then they fell behind as we walked on. In an effort to save myself from embarrassment, I offered to take three watches for myself. Maybe they could make up for the low price through volume.

As he climbed into the van, Saul looked at me with a raised eyebrow, as if to say, *What's it going to be?* The women saw this and exchanged quick glances.

After climbing into the van, I was just about to close the door when the old women said they would make the trade. Watches and money quickly exchanged hands, the van door closed, and we were again on our way.

Saul looked at his watches and crowed.

"You see?" he said. "I *told* you that I was going to get 50—and I *got* the 50."

It was the first time I had seen fake watches sold so cheaply, and by the time our plane landed in Hong Kong, I had an idea why they were sold at such a low price. The minute hand on one watch fell off, and then I realized that all three of mine were broken. I said nothing about my watches, but suspected that everyone else got the same deal.

Our last stop during our trip together was to be an industry trade show in Hong Kong. Saul wanted me to attend a couple of meetings with prospective partners who were also going to be at the show. He also wanted to be sure that we set aside time to discuss the possibility of working with him beyond this one project.

The company had on display behind thick Plexiglas a pair of stunning diamonds—one, a flawless clear stone; the other, a perfect yellow diamond. These were not shards to be lost in the shag carpeting, but showcase gems that were nearly palm sized.

They had the intended effect on the public. Show attendees came by the booth and gawked, and something about the way visitors became slack jawed made me think the stones might not be real. When one woman, a tall redhead, stopped and looked dispassionately at the display, I asked her if she thought they were.

"They're real all right," she said, surprised that I would be working at the exhibition but did not seem to know the difference. She then explained how you could tell. It had to do with how the light refracted from the diamonds. I thanked her for the easy lesson, and I asked her what she was doing at the show.

She was from Dallas, Texas, but worked primarily out of Africa. Her business had her joining safaris there, and she sought out a particular kind of high-end adventure, one that put her in the company of big-game hunters who were spectacularly wealthy.

On these hunting trips, she wore jewelry she had designed herself. Looking at just the necklace she wore, I could imagine her decked out in a safari outfit with jewels dangling about her neck, ears, and wrists, while holding an elephant gun.

Most of the participants on these adventures were married men who, by the end of their trips, felt rather guilty about spending $100,000 on a safari and returning home empty-handed. More often than not, she said, someone from the hunting party would ask her to have something made for his wife back home.

"I have the piece made up while we're all still in Africa and have it sent by FedEx. If the timing is just right, the package arrives just as he's walking through the door."

She said that she was in the business of saving marriages. It was a fascinating career that she had made for herself, I thought—the opportunity to work abroad, while meeting new people.

"You heard about what happened at the show?" she asked.

That morning, a gang of con artists from South America had walked away with a small case of diamonds stolen from a Belgian diamond merchant. Two of the criminal group had posed as a married couple, while another pair pretended to be wholesalers. With the merchant's attention diverted, a fifth went into the booth and lifted the diamonds. Everyone was talking about the case, and the gang was said to have walked away with over a million dollars worth of diamonds.

Allowing someone else to take my place in the Plotnick exhibit, I went to where the robbery had taken place with my new friend. Hong Kong police officers were hovering about, while a number of curiosity seekers looked on. The Belgian who had been robbed was slumped in a chair, looking particularly devastated.

"Surely, the guy has insurance," I said.

"Of course, he does. He will probably even inflate the value of whatever was taken, but that doesn't make up for it."

"How's that?"

"People are superstitious, and it's a commodity product. When you can get your diamonds from anyone, why buy them from someone who has such bad luck?"

The theft cast a shadow over the exhibition, with exhibitors alternatively trading gossip and trying to pretend that they did not want to know anything about what had just happened.

That afternoon, Saul said that he wanted me to meet with one of his prospective partners, a diamond dealer from Hong Kong. My impression of most Hong Kong business merchants was positive, and I had actually liked another that Saul introduced me to, but this prospect did not seem right.

Privately, I told Saul that I did not have a good feeling about him. The fellow reminded me of those shady dealers that the *South China Morning Post* was often reporting on—the ones who gave kickbacks to tour group leaders who brought tourists through their shops.

For a moment, he looked thoughtful, as if he might actually be considering my comments, but then he brushed them off as irrelevant.

Saul thought that I might be able to help his company, but in some other capacity. He wanted an office set up, and he wanted to start developing business in South China. While he wanted to talk details, his brother had objections. The two of them spoke about me while I was within earshot.

"He has no diamond experience," Saul's brother said. The brother lifted a jeweler's loupe that hung from a lanyard on his neck to make his point.

Saul later told me not to worry about his brother's objections. All of this business about reading a diamond, he said, was not so difficult. He gave me some promotional material from a nearby booth. It was a catalog from the Gemological Institute of America. One of their courses, he said, would help fill in any knowledge gaps.

"How long is the course?" I asked.

"Maybe a week," he said.

"Only one week?"

It didn't sound like a very long time at all. I told Saul that his brother might want to consider that it took a great deal more time to learn Chinese, and that I had been working in China for a number of years.

Whatever difficulties the company would face, they certainly would have more to do with understanding the marketplace than the product. China was not such an easy nut to crack, I suggested.

As with other clients, I advised caution, as well as a clearer understanding of the challenges ahead. No matter what their strategy for China was going to be, I suggested that they find someone who was strong in handling China affairs. If I was not a suitable person to work with them for the long term, then I would help them find someone who was.

The trip was winding down, and we were in a taxi on the way to the airport in Hong Kong. Saul took the time to offer his take on China and his assessment on my own outlook.

"You worry too much," he said. "This one you should watch out for, and that one . . ." parodying my earlier remarks. "You know, if I worried as much as you did about business, I wouldn't *have* any business!"

Believing that he was onto something, he continued making his point. "You have to work with what you've got. Not everyone in business is honest—fine! I have one customer who is always cheating me on the karat weights. He always says the diamonds weigh a little less than they actually do. So what, I get a good price for the diamonds."

Someone else I knew had made a similar point about business— that it didn't matter if a person was dishonest, just so long as you got what you wanted out of the deal.

Hong Kong's neon skyline could just barely be seen in the distance as we drove down the highway. It was late. Saul continued to lecture me in the dark.

"There's a supermarket I know in Italy," he said. "They put little things by the cash register—so that the customers have something to steal while they're waiting in line. It's good for business."

Some of what Saul said amused me; now, I was laughing. This was one of the reasons I worked with these colorful characters. Never mind the entertainment value, these were lessons you didn't get in business school. This notion of a company knowingly putting out things to be stolen was a riot, though I didn't like the rest of the implication—that I was in some way naive.

Saul seemed to be giving me a kind of brush off, but then he surprised me by asking how much I would charge to help him with the company's business in China. His criticisms had been a set up. He was knocking me, like a prospective car buyer pointing out dents in a fender.

The airport loomed into view, and he pressed me for a number. "*Nu, tachlis,*" he said. He wanted me to get right to the point, but there was none.

What I brought to the table was formal business training and a background in China. His brother had already made it clear that things like language skills and on-the-ground experience didn't count. What they wanted was someone who could count occlusions through a jeweler's loop—even if the skill only took a week to pick up.

The Plotnicks flew back to Europe, and it was the last time we ever spoke. Saul and his brother hired someone else. I heard from a friend that the new hire was an Israeli who had once worked in diamonds. He had been a diamond polisher some years earlier in Eastern Europe; it was his only real qualification. He had lived in China for a couple years, but he didn't speak any Chinese, and even his English was said to be lacking.

The new hire helped Plotnick by setting up an office in Shenzhen, the city just across the border from Hong Kong, but nothing moved. Demand was weaker than the brothers had figured, and they had not anticipated how strong competition was, either. The diamond polisher they had hired was apparently unable to develop any business for the company. He was, they said, not up to the job.

Foreign companies often brought in expatriates who were not capable of operating inside of China. Unable to speak the language, they could not order lunch for themselves. And, unless they had a business card in their hand, they couldn't get across town in a taxi, either. If a fire broke out in their office building, they needed to find a translator to explain why everyone was running around.

The story did not end well for either the diamond polisher or for the Plotnicks. Unable to make things happen, the fellow they hired grew frustrated in his job. After more than a year of failing to make any progress with the business, one day he went to the office that he had set up for the company, cleared out the diamonds that were kept in the safe there, and skipped town.

Interpol eventually caught up with the diamond polisher somewhere in Central America—but without the $5 million worth of diamonds that was initially claimed to have been stolen. He was sent to prison and served a lengthy sentence, and the incident made international headlines. It was one of those stories floating around South China, and it also made the rounds in the diamond industry, which specialized in this sort of gossip.

For years to come, whenever "China" and "diamonds" came up in the same industry conversation, so did this one company's name—not as an example of how things should be done in China, but as a cautionary tale.

CHAPTER 16

Trophy Trash

My latest client, Frank, was from New Jersey, an Italian–American in "waste management." And just when it was all starting to sound like something from an episode of *The Sopranos,* someone at the company quietly told me that they had hired a new chief of operations, an ivy leaguer whose father used to be one of New York's leading labor figures—one with reputed mob ties.

So it was true—*everyone* was coming to China.

Waste Corp was a trash hauler in the traditional sense. It had routes in residential parts of New Jersey as well as commercial accounts in New York City. In addition to picking up garbage, the company also collected recyclable paper.

The company had set up a venture with a partner in Jiangmen, a town just a couple hours south of Guangzhou. Frank had even put $1 million of his own money into the project, but after operating for a year, the business still remained a mystery to him.

But everything at the venture was fine, he insisted.

Before the joint venture was conceived, Waste Corp sold its recyclable papers to brokers on the East Coast, who then sold the paper to Hong Kong agents, who in turn sold it to companies inside China. The idea behind the venture was to sell the paper to the paper mills directly. The partner, Winston, was running the venture, and the plan was to split all profits evenly between the two sides.

I pulled into the plant and found Winston near a large expanse of concrete. He was supervising a crew that was spreading several truckloads of recycled newspapers.

"We sort better than in America," Winston said, as the workers busied themselves with picking through the papers. What Winston meant was that the joint venture facility could do it cheaper. Workers were paid by the ton, and most were averaging about $80 per month. It was even less than what factories paid.

At Waste Corp's plant in New Jersey, workers pulled out only the most obvious pieces of foreign material as the recyclables moved along a fast conveyor belt on their way to be baled. America's lowest wage earners—illegal immigrants—were earning more than 25 times what workers at the South China facility averaged.

China needed great volumes of raw materials like paper fiber, and it also happened to be in a position to sort the product efficiently. Even so, it surprised me to hear from Winston that most of the paper recycled in the United States was making its way to China.

It was an interesting business, and I wondered how the government viewed all of it. Winston said that the Chinese government liked the idea of cheap recycled paper fibers. At the same time, the country did not want to become a dump for the world.

About 1 percent of the venture's wastepaper recyclables were allowed to consist of proper garbage—the not-so-empty milk carton, the inevitable half-eaten ham sandwich. Although workers were sorting newsprint, it actually smelled more like trash.

While Winston went through more basics of the business, I watched as a group of workers, mostly women, crouched down between large piles of paper.

"At least they get meals and a place to sleep."

"They get a place to sleep," Winston said.

In most factories across South China, workers got both room and board. For meals, Winston was forcing the workers to visit a shop that he ran on the premises, a kiosk of sorts that sold things like crackers and instant noodles. The workers had no choice but to spend their money in the company canteen because alternatives were too far away, and in this way, Winston was also recycling paychecks.

Wastepaper recycling was very much a hands-on business. Selling the paper in China required negotiations with savvy buyers. Winston explained the reason why careful sorting was important. If just one piece of low-grade paper was seen poking out of a pile of otherwise high-quality recyclables, a buyer could argue that more of the low-value stuff was buried within the lot—and in that case, the buyer would make the case that the paper belonged to a cheaper grade.

Careful sorting helped to maximize value. Its greatest benefit was that it removed doubt. Waste Corp expected Winston to break up the wastepaper into a half dozen different categories. Curiously, though, he recorded more than 30 different sorting categories, and this information was not passed on to Frank.

Some of the many separate categories that Winston created included one for books that had their bindings cut off, and in the back of the facility there was a collection of old wiring and other electronic waste. Why Winston was not reporting these other categories seemed suspicious, but it was not anything that officers in New Jersey cared much about. They were more interested in what was happening with the most valuable papers they were shipping to China—the office papers that were collected in New York.

Waste Corp's biggest accounts included commercial office towers in Manhattan, and many of these buildings housed Wall Street firms that cast off great volumes of recycled office paper.

Paper fibers could only be recycled a few times before they broke down to fiber lengths too small to use. Americans were great about sending their used papers abroad, but for themselves they used more virgin pulp paper fibers—the good stuff—at the very beginning of its usability cycle. For this reason, U.S. office papers were priced higher than similar papers from other parts of the world.

Winston was not selling the office papers that he was collecting; he was stockpiling them instead. He took me to a warehouse where the office papers were kept. From a distance, the bundles looked like large bales of cotton, though they each weighed over a ton.

Trying to get an idea of why the paper might be so highly prized, I asked what it could be recycled into. Winston explained that it could be turned into printer paper for the China market, or anything else that required a quality, bleached fiber, including toilet paper.

I had a number of friends who worked on Wall Street, and I wondered whether any of them knew where all of their deskwork eventually ended up.

Standing near the office papers, it was easy to see what the papers were and where they were coming from. Poking out from the bales I spotted term sheets, prospectuses, and financial reports. E-mail records also made their way into the warehouse, and surprisingly, none of the papers that were stored had been shredded. Looking closer, I recognized the names of specific financial firms, and even individual names could be lifted from the sheets.

On the side of one bale, I spotted a beige-colored piece of plastic. It was one of those magnetized badges that were used to open security doors, and it had belonged to an employee of an investment bank.

I pried it loose from between some papers and had a look. It indicated a title: Vice President. I wondered under what circumstances the badge had been thrown away and into the wrong recycling bin. Was it about a promotion, or was tossing this piece of plastic into the paper bin some last act of defiance on the way out? What other stories were among all of those papers, I wondered.

Classmates from business school were at these firms. I mentioned this to Winston, telling him that if I had not made the decision to come back to China, I might have pursued a similar track. Instead of working to create the mountain of paperwork, though, I was on the other end of the process—considering it, watching it get sorted.

Winston seemed to have an idea that these were not just any papers, and one clue was in his office.

On each worker's desk was a "tombstone" made of Lucite—one of those awards that bankers receive for their having worked on a deal, such as an initial public offering or a corporate merger. These symbols of merit had made their way into the paper recycling bins of financial firms in the same way that the plastic badge had.

I picked one of them up. It was shaped like a tall pyramid, with a sharp point at the top. I noted that etched onto the clear material were the names of several blue-chip institutions; Goldman Sachs and Merrill Lynch were two of the names I recognized. Having once represented a career achievement for some business executive, it was now trophy trash, a different kind of prize for someone here in South China.

There was a lot of hidden value in the wastepaper recycling business, and it seemed that Winston had his eye on whatever worth he could find. He was engaged in undetermined activities, and it was hard to gather what his intentions were.

In one corner of the warehouse, I spotted a recycling category that did not make it onto any documentation. It was a large pile of envelopes. They included both dyed and bleached papers; some had plastic windows, others did not. The only thing that the papers had in common that I could determine was a mailing address. Every single one of them in the pile, though coming from various sources, had a U.S. address. The letters had all been sent from large corporations—credit card companies and insurance companies mostly.

Could Winston be collecting papers in the hope of selling them to someone interested in creating a mailing list? It seemed so unlikely, but I had seen entrepreneurial locals work harder to find even smaller amounts of potential value. Just in case it might matter, I took a photo and sent it to Waste Corp.

One of the biggest mysteries about the venture was why Winston was stockpiling so many office papers. He insisted that he could not find a buyer, but this surely could not have been the real reason. There were many paper mills in South China, and demand was strong amid rising commodity prices.

Winston was sitting on literally thousands of tons of papers from Wall Street at the venture. The printed records from the world's largest financial firms; surely someone in China would have been willing to pay for a peek before they were sent for recycling. If not, at least the cache was something Winston could show off to government officials. This was how it went in South China. Winston could use the papers to suggest that he was *connected* and that he was an important person to do business with, or to know. Even if it had been too time consuming to mine information from thousand of tons of paper, the *hint* of value—the internal communiqués of Wall Street firms, after all—would have been enough.

Waste Corp was not charged with guarding the secrets of its customers. The more pressing problem at hand was figuring out why the venture couldn't turn a profit. At first, Winston would not make available economic information, including market data for wastepaper, and I had to contact several paper brokers on my own to understand that operators in China were tight lipped about the real prices that buyers were paying.

The wastepaper recycling business was known to be profitable, and yet this one venture was just barely breaking even. Winston was claiming that he could get no more for a shipment of paper than a broker would pay in New York. It made no sense.

While still working on the shampoo and other projects, I was now at the recycling facility almost every week, trying to figure out the business. Frank made it clear that he liked and trusted Winston, but the more time I spent with the local partner, the more I suspected that Waste Corp was being taken for a ride.

"Winston is like family to me," Frank had said. When I met Frank in China before the project began, he told me about how Winston had been to his house in New Jersey and how they had all gone fishing on his boat. This partnership was supposedly Frank's secret weapon in the industry, and so whenever something at the business seemed unusual, Frank came up with excuses. He was protective of his partners.

The new head of operations, David, the one whose father had those alleged mob connections, warned me that if I was going to suggest wrongdoing, I had to have proof. It was not that he doubted me, but he was conservative. And he knew that Frank was inclined to give Winston the benefit of the doubt.

"There is a difference between malfeasance and misfeasance," he lectured. In other words, there might be something wrong at the venture, but it could just be a matter of mismanagement.

Winston might need guidance. Just because a venture didn't turn a profit did not imply criminal-type behavior. At least the business was not losing money, David noted.

■ ■ ■

It took several weeks to get financial records from Winston. He said at first that he did not have any, and then he said that he kept them, but that the figures were all meaningless.

What I really wanted to get a hold of were the records of transactions between Winston and the wastepaper buyers in China, but he said that these were never properly recorded. The reason he gave was that he feared an audit by local government officials. Frank trusted him to document revenues in a general way, and Winston kept the rounded-off figures of all major transactions in his head.

Waste Corp was expecting data from me, and because Winston would not provide much of it, I tried to collect what information I could about pricing from the marketplace.

I found a domestic company that provided market data, and from this source I learned that going rates for paper were much higher than what the joint venture was reporting back to New Jersey. The most interesting piece of news that came my way was that office papers were selling for well over $400 per ton, more than double the $195 that Winston was claiming buyers were offering him for the same papers.

If it were true, then Winston was taking in papers and claiming breakeven, while he was in the meantime selling all of what he took in for an incredible markup.

David suggested that it was not enough information. I would need to see a transaction myself in order for anyone to take seriously the possibility that fraud was taking place.

The very same week that I had this conversation with David, Winston said that he wanted me to meet someone. He asked me into his office and introduced me to a young woman. She was a wastepaper buyer, he said.

Winston took a seat at one end of a long coffee table, and the woman sat at the other. I was directed to sit in a chair opposite the empty sofa; and with a notepad in my hand, I was left to take notes.

Winston and the young woman began discussing a contract for wastepaper. They were negotiating the price on some cardboard and newsprint.

"How much are you paying?" Winston asked in a plain tone.

"We cannot pay much at the moment," the woman said. "The market price is weak, as you know."

"I know. What is your best price?" Winston asked.

Their dialogue was wooden. The young woman quoted some prices, and Winston nodded. There was a lull in their exchange, and the two of them giggled.

How strange, I thought, and then I realized that they must be friends; and that this negotiation was like a show put on for my benefit. Winston and this young woman were like two kids at play rehearsal. In flubbing their lines, they could not help but laugh.

Winston, of course, knew that I was obligated to report back what I had seen in this "negotiation," and I think that he was laughing at himself in part because he was genuinely amused by what he had put together.

Wastepaper was a cash business anyway, and Winston had already told me how he met with buyers late at night, often over drinks. Whatever happened between buyers and sellers, it happened behind closed doors. In any event, the prices that he and the woman mentioned did not match the news that I was getting about market rates for wastepaper inside China.

When Winston finally handed over the financial documents that he had, they were as meaningless as promised. There were, though, some rather accurate records for the sorting operation itself. There were no dollar values assigned to sales, but at least I had a record of the kinds of papers that were sorted along with their weights.

With manufactured goods, every product in a production run was more or less the same. In the soap and shampoo business, we knew, for example, that one pallet of Watermelon Fresh body wash was going to be identical to another. Not the same with wastepaper recycling, where each shipment was unique. Variability left room for a lot of game playing, but at the same time when the broader business was taken into account, the business was actually knowable.

Commercial office buildings tended to generate a consistent volume of office recyclables, just as residential neighborhoods put the same volume of newspapers on their curbs from one week to another. The business should have shown rather consistent trends, but Winston was painting a different picture of the venture with the sorting numbers.

Figures that he recorded showed, for example, that trash content was rising over time. When I relayed that piece of news back to Waste Corp, Frank suggested that it might have just been that his workers in New Jersey were being less careful. He said that he was going to ask his workers to do a better job of picking through and removing trash content.

The joint venture was supposed to subtract a small value from any water that evaporated in the wastepaper over time, and related losses due to water content were on the rise. When asked why he thought the papers from New Jersey were experiencing increasing levels of water weight, Winston suggested that the papers were picking up moisture as they crossed the Pacific Ocean. However unlikely an excuse, he could not explain how this phenomenon was trending up over time.

If there was a real smoking gun, though, it was the recorded weights of the paper types that Winston said he had. When the venture was just getting started, office papers accounted for 70 percent of all wastepaper taken in by the joint venture. Over a period of one year, the proportion fell every month until Winston was claiming that the higher-value papers made up only 30 percent of shipments.

The business was continually said to be at breakeven, though the figures related to the business looked increasingly worse. It was almost as if the business was at a risk of showing a profit and that Winston had to work harder over time to prevent the possibility of repatriating funds. Maybe it was greed, or maybe it was his way of testing limits, seeing just how much he could get away with. Or, maybe the issue of keeping the business at breakeven was a matter of strategy.

Winston's plan had apparently been to introduce a large number of small distortions, knowing that his partners would not be able to catch him on all of the minor nibbles. If his partners called him to task on the paper mix, then he still had the fudge on water content or trash content to rely on. The same thing was being done in manufacturing. Factories manipulated quality on a large number of variables, taking small gains out of each; if they were caught in one area, they still had the advantage of others.

It seemed at first a little unusual to me. By running so many schemes at once, Winston was increasing his chances of getting caught doing something dishonest. In an environment where everyone is expected to do the right thing, the smallest indiscretion is a sign of moral failing, but China was a low-trust environment. Local players operated on the presumption that everyone was engaging in some level of game playing, that others would expect a degree of inappropriate activity.

By spreading the shenanigans around, an operator could make related wrongdoing appear less damaging. No auditor could ever be so diligent as to catch every maneuver, which meant that profit lost on one shortcut could still leave other sources of margin. Maybe Winston also figured that if he got caught on any one of his small schemes it wouldn't matter because separately none was significant enough to cause the breakup of the partnership.

■ ■ ■

There was an old joke that used to make the rounds: "What's the definition of a *50-50 joint venture* in China?"

Punch line: "It's an investment vehicle where the foreign partner loses 50 percent of his money in the first year and the other 50 percent in the second."

If it was funny, it was only because it really used to be like that in China. Foreigners came in with large sums of cash and left without it soon enough. At some point along the way, local operators came to understand that this practice was bad for the economy in general, and the word was put out that fraud of this sort was not to be tolerated. Those who cheated foreigners were not prosecuted necessarily; the behavior simply stopped on its own.

Outright fraud cases had gone and were replaced with a more sophisticated model. Rather than an entire investment vanishing into thin air, foreigners who came in with capital found that their businesses went nowhere special. The money was not lost exactly, but then there was little or no profit. It was a con all the same, but one that was more subtle.

Foreigners doing business in China were inclined to say that they were doing well, even when they were not. I knew this from working with many clients whose secrets I shared. Like a gambler, they exaggerated their wins and had selective amnesia about losing streaks. And they justified their adventures in any way they could so that they could at least say they had broken even.

It was what Frank was doing. He knew that the business was not a success, but at the same time, he wouldn't admit that it was a failure. The venture at least gave him bragging rights back in New York and New Jersey. While the joint venture did not generate profit, he could tell everyone how wonderfully well things were going for him in the Far East. The result of such a pattern of behavior was that even more foreign companies were jumping onto the bandwagon. "If those guys can do it, then so can we," the competition would say to itself.

Winston was a hustler who knew the value of a slow bleed. He had not run away with Frank's investment. He kept the money in play so that he could reap even more. The margin that Waste Corp realized on its office papers was close to zero, but sources that I found suggested triple-digit returns. With the way that Winston had arranged the deal, Waste Corp saw none of this potential profit.

■ ■ ■

Winston took me out to lunch, and I mentioned my concerns for the venture to him. By now, he was aware that I knew more about what was really going on, but it seemed that he felt untouchable. His case was too hard to prove. The most damaging claim that could be made was that he was selling paper for below-market rates; and because the transactions were all done privately and in cash, I would never be able to say that he sold the paper at one price and reported another.

At lunch, Winston pointed out to me that Waste Corp's core business was profitable. "You shouldn't worry about Frank," he said. I wasn't, but the joint venture was not doing well.

"The business isn't profitable," I said.

Winston said, "Maybe you can help with that."

He then made a proposal. In all the time I had been in China, I had never been offered a bribe. Winston's offer was as close as anyone ever came. He said that he would like to bring me in, after I was through working with Waste Corp.

"What would you need me for?" I asked. I was already looking forward to getting out of the wastepaper business.

"I would like to do another joint venture," he said.

"Another one?"

His plan was to start a separate business that would handle just plastics, but this made no sense. The wastepaper venture was already taking in a small amount of plastic, and the facility had plenty of space.

If I were willing to help talk Frank into making another investment, he said, he could pay me well, and then he named a figure that was precisely double what Waste Corp was paying me for the current project. The message was clear: make sure that the status quo remains, and there will be further opportunities to earn fees. Of course, this raised a question. If the venture was not realizing a profit, where was Winston coming up with money to toss around?

It was time to wrap up my project with Waste Corp, and I had to decide what kind of information to deliver. I had an idea of what kind of good-news report Frank wanted to receive, but my role as I saw it had little to do with helping foreign companies delude themselves. All of that trash coming in from Wall Street reminded me too much of career opportunities that I had given up. I had come to China to help foreigners get to the truth; it had never occurred to me that some of them might not want to know it.

In the world of private investigations, there were husbands who had their wives followed, not to catch them doing something wrong but to remove the specter of doubt. Frank wanted me to prove that Winston was *not* cheating him out of any money. He wanted me to tell him that everything was all right.

In the end, I shrugged it off. I put together the kind of report I thought I would have wanted to receive if I were in New York and wanted a clearer picture of what was happening in South China. It included the sorts of graphs and spreadsheets that Waste Corp was looking for, but it also pointed to unethical conduct on Winston's part. It was, I thought, a visually appealing report, and I was proud of the final result.

In our last conference call together, just after he received the report, Frank asked me who the hell I thought I was. Did I not understand that Winston was like family to him? He did not reference the report in any way, and I wondered whether he had only been given the quick interpretation by someone who worked for him. In any case, he was upset, and when he hung up, he did it without saying goodbye.

My fees were paid, which was a nice surprise given the manner in which my report was received; though for the same reason, I never expected to hear from anyone at the company again. The decision to show them what was really going on was probably the right one, but it was also a guarantee that there would be no follow-on project work. I wasn't worried; I had my work at the soap and shampoo factory to keep me busy, and there were other projects as well.

For the longest time, I imagined that everyone at Waste Corp carried on with business as usual. Frank's company kept supplying paper at a price that would continue to enrich Winston, and no one would wish to complain or be made the wiser. About a year after the project ended, out of sheer curiosity, I picked up a phone and called Waste Corp.

One of the managers answered the phone and told me what had happened shortly after I submitted my report. Frank decided to pull the plug on the venture just like that; and somehow, he had managed to get back his original $1 million investment. If Winston had given that kind of money back without any trouble at all, then surely he had made much more than that amount over the course of the venture and wanted everything to end quietly and without fuss.

It took me longer to get curious about what happened to Winston, and I worried about getting in touch. A few more months later, though, I rang him from my place in Guangzhou, and I told him that I wanted to see him. If there were any hard feelings on his part, he did not reveal them.

One reason I wanted to see Winston was that I wanted to know if his experiences with Waste Corp had changed him in any way. He had killed the goose that laid golden eggs. I wondered, *did he have any regrets?*

He gave me a tour of his new facility, a rather modest operation; and rather quickly into our meeting, he asked if I knew anyone who might be able to send him recyclable materials from the United States. He had no partner in this new venture and was having difficulty finding supply for his business. I told him that I did not know anyone but that I would keep a look out.

It was as if his relationship with Waste Corp had been completely forgotten. There was not even a lingering hint of reminiscence on his part. And Winston seemed like the exact same person, though he may have been a bit desperate. If there was any sign at all of a lesson learned, it was probably on his business card. It was yellow and purple, and at the top in bold letters was his new company name: *Integrity International Trading, Limited.*

CHAPTER 17

"You Heard Me Wrong"

With importers coming from all around the world, dining options expanded in the city of Guangzhou. Russians came and opened their own restaurants, as did the Italians and French, as well as many who came from various corners of the Middle East. Many of these foreign restaurateurs were also importers, and they often outfitted their establishments with items they had manufactured in China for themselves. Some even turned their places of business into a kind of showroom, an example of their sourcing capabilities.

For many Americans who claimed that they liked the idea of eating authentic Chinese food in China, the novelty quickly wore off and they soon enough sought fare that was more familiar. Typically, after just a few times out to a local restaurant, importers wanted to know about alternatives. Doug was my newest client, and he was already asking about options on his first day in China. I told him about a new restaurant in town that was operated by a Turk who had done his best to replicate an Istanbul experience by building a brick oven and having his Chinese staff dress in traditional Turkish costumes.

At the restaurant, Doug took out several magnets from a bag and placed them on the table. His company manufactured architectural hardware, and the items that he showed me—catches—went on the inside of cabinet doors. It was one of his company's most popular items, and they sold in the millions. Made in Michigan, these magnets were in homes across North America.

"We need the samples to look exactly like this," he told me.

Picking up one of the magnets, I noted that they seemed to be made of aluminum. Doug confirmed that they were. I turned one of the catches over in my hand. On the back, stamped into the metal, was a marker: MADE IN USA.

"You want this country of origin mark removed?" I asked.

He looked at the magnets on the table and blinked twice.

"Right," he said. "We better leave that off."

His father had started the company decades ago to manufacture engineered hardware items, and I knew through our previous conversations how apprehensive Doug was about bringing the magnet business over to China. It was one of the main products that his company still produced in its Michigan plant.

We spoke generally about changes in manufacturing, and even though he was soon going to stop producing a major product line, Doug surprised me by suggesting that he was not concerned about changes in his industry.

"We're in a relationship business," he said.

Importers said this sort of thing all the time, and I knew what it meant—that Doug's company was having a tough time competing on price. This line about relationships was what his company's sales agents told its customers when it looked as though they were about to bolt for a competitor. "But you can't leave us," they would insist. "We have a *relationship*." At some point along the way, U.S. companies began to care less about these personal connections, though, just as they began to care less about whether a product was made in the United States.

I asked Doug whether his customers would miss the mark on the magnet casings. He showed only the slightest hint of cynicism and shook his head. His customers wanted a low price, he said. "They want quality, too. Don't get me wrong. It has to be made well."

American consumers had once preferred to see the MADE IN USA tag, but there had been another shift in the marketplace. Somewhere along the line, made in China began to sound like a bargain. Other importers noted the phenomenon. When an importer told a retail buyer that an item was quoted at 65¢ and made in the USA, the buyer figured it could be purchased somewhere else cheaper. When the same product was quoted at 65¢ and was said to have been made in China the buyer figured it could not be found for any less.

Doug said that his plan was to move some of his company's manufacturing to China, and the motivation was to realize some minor cost savings. I asked whether his Michigan plant could make components as cheaply as it could be done in China. He said that it probably could not.

"You'll be moving all of your manufacturing to China then?" I asked.

"No, we can't do that," he said, looking uncomfortable. "I mean, we can't just make *nothing*. We still have equipment."

This was not exactly what they were teaching in business school. Investment in plant and equipment was a sunk cost. If you could manufacture an item outside of your plant for less, then that is what you did.

Doug said he was concerned about how it might look if he got out of manufacturing altogether. "If we didn't make anything," he said, "then we would just be brokers."

For many years, his company competed directly with distributors that brought components in from overseas. These other companies owned no equipment; they made nothing.

American manufacturers belittled these other players, explaining to their customers that these other companies were mere middlemen. Increasingly, though, U.S. manufacturers were supplementing their own domestically manufactured product lines with items made abroad. The more they outsourced, the more they looked like hypocrites.

There was another reason why some manufacturers were reluctant to let go of their manufacturing operations altogether, and it had to do with the company valuation. Manufacturing assets helped increase the value placed on the business. An importer that just brokered parts was not seen as owning anything but a customer list and some tenuous supplier relationships.

I asked Doug if he had any concerns about his workers in all of this. Manufacturing the magnets might put a few people out of work. Doug was defensive on the point.

"There's more than manufacturing jobs at stake here," he said. Doing what was economically right for the company was a more important priority. He also had employees in sales and warehousing, and there was general office staff to think of, also. "We might lose a few manufacturing jobs, but we'll make up for it."

My interest in discussing the fate of his manufacturing workers seemed to agitate Doug.

"Have you ever actually *worked* with union people?" he asked me.

I told him that I had not.

"Our guys work four 10-hour shifts each week. Every weekend for our guys is a three-day holiday. Well, every so often, we need a few of the guys to come in on a Friday to help with a delivery."

Doug leaned forward while telling the rest of this story about his union workforce. It clearly touched a nerve with him.

"One week, Mark, my manager goes to the back to pick a couple guys for the Friday shift. They all want to work on Fridays, you see, because of the overtime pay."

"So, my manager goes into the shop and picks a couple guys. Two minutes later, another worker shows up in his office and bangs on the door. This guy says to Mark, 'How come you didn't pick me for overtime?' So Mark says to the guy: 'I would have picked you, but when I walked by your station, you were *asleep*.'"

Doug shook his head thinking about it and started to crack a smile.

"You know what this union guy says to my manager? He says, 'Yeah, I was asleep. You still should have picked me, *asshole*!'"

He laughed out loud at the thought of his manager suffering that kind of abuse, while still not able to get over how his Michigan workers felt so entitled.

Working with importers, I didn't get the sense that they were going out of their way to move jobs offshore, and Doug probably wished that he had never needed to come to China. Pricing pressure had something to do with it; and to some extent, changing customer expectations played a role as well. The poor attitude of unionized workers did not seem to motivate as much as it relieved some of the attendant guilt.

I told Doug that I understood the idea behind free trade, but that I still felt sorry for some of the workers in the States. "When these guys were kids, their parents told them to finish everything on their plates because there were children starving in China. Now, look at them. They are all grown up and are being told that if they don't pick up the pace, there's someone in China who will do the job for them."

The first factory Doug and I visited was a manufacturer of drawer pulls, the metal handles installed on kitchen cabinets and desk drawers. The company representative that I spoke with said that he was a manufacturer, but during our factory tour, he seemed less than familiar with the plant. Doug picked up on this as well.

Chinese manufacturers had no problem working through agents. If an agent insisted on earning a certain percentage or amount, the factory simply raised its prices enough to offset the payment to the agent. Importers preferred not to work with agents for this very reason— because their involvement tended to inflate costs.

In theory, agents were supposed to shop around and find the best deal for the customer. In reality, they sent business to friends or relatives. Because relationships were involved, whenever there was a quality problem—and there often was—the agent was likely to back the manufacturer by saying "the factory says that it is not their fault."

Even worse was when the manufacturer and the agent did not share a personal connection. Whenever there was a problem, the factory owner and the agent would argue over who was going to shoulder the responsibility to fix the problem; and while they fought, the importer was left to wonder what could be causing so many delays.

The agent system benefited manufacturers, though, so they would allow agents to do whatever was necessary in order to catch the order. Agents understood that importers wanted to believe that they were going direct, and so manufacturers allowed agents to represent themselves as the owners of these factories.

In China, so many were faking it, and an importer had to work hard to draw back the curtain to see what was really going on in any given operation. It might have been more polite to accept everything at face value, but what if something bad happened? An importer had to know who was pulling the strings; he had to know who was ultimately responsible.

There was one fellow, a middle-aged, paunchy man, who had been presented as the manager of the plant, and he answered more of our questions than anyone else. When Doug mentioned purchase volumes, I noticed that it was this "manager" whose eyes lit up the brightest.

Out on the factory floor, the man who claimed to be the factory owner was walking with the "manager."

Doug and I walked a few paces behind them, and after a while I called out: *"Laoban!"* This was the generic term used to refer to any factory boss.

When the man posing as the manager turned around, we got a quick sense of who actually owned the place, and when the man who was just an agent realized that he missed his cue, he confessed to his actual role in the deal. In the West, when a ruse was uncovered, embarrassment was often cause for one party or another to blow up the deal; in China, it accompanied only a small acknowledgment in a change of situational power.

One of our next factory visits was to a company that made stainless steel tubing, the kind you find in closets and bathroom showers. Doug called it a "commodity product" and said that he was working on thin margins. We already had an order that was ready to go and were traveling to the factory only to make sure that everything was in order before finalizing the deal.

The plant was the general size and shape of a football field, and although it was large, it was in fact not much more than a metal shed. Inside were several long machines that produced endless lengths of steel tubing. At one end of the factory, rolls of flat steel were fed into a process; the flat metal was curved into a circular shape, and after that, the loop was automatically closed with a welded seal. Workers waited at the end as the pipe was sent down the line, cutting it and laying the tubing down in neat piles.

After inspecting the plant, we went into the main office to sign a manufacturing agreement. Doug looked over the invoice.

"Wait a minute," Doug said. "It says here 1.99 renminbi."

"That's not right. We already confirmed 1.9," I said.

The factory had quoted 1.9 renminbi per foot, which was roughly 25¢ at the current exchange. When I asked the factory owner what had happened, he scratched his scalp, tilted his head, and suggested it must have been a mistake on my part.

"Ni ting cuo le," he said. "You heard me wrong. 'One-point-*nine*,' you know, sounds very much like 'one-point-*nine-nine*.'"

But we had been quoted on other products to one-tenth of a renminbi, I pointed out.

One renminbi was worth a little more than a dime, and a tenth of a unit was equal to about a penny. Doug said that he also could not see the logic in quoting to the tenth of a penny.

"If they wanted to quote 1.99, why didn't they just call it 'two'?"

"I am pretty sure we were quoted one-point-nine."

"That's what I have in my notes," Doug said. He laughed at the absurdity of the discussion we were having. The difference between 1.9 and 1.99 was almost 5 percent though, and it was a problem. His anticipated gross profit had been closer to 10 percent.

While I worried about Doug, I could not help but be impressed by what this industrialist had done. Nearly half of the expected margin had been wiped out with just a single turn of phrase—*you heard me wrong*.

"Hey, look at this," Doug said. He was inspecting the invoice further. The factory had offered the lengths in meters. "I told them we needed everything in feet."

Ten-foot lengths that had been ordered were listed as being three meters long.

"We always measure in meters," said the factory boss.

"But you quoted us in feet."

"Only because you wanted to be quoted in feet."

"But the invoice is in meters."

"Because we must use the metric measurement."

This also made no sense, and I protested. The factory boss defended himself by saying that 10 feet was just about three meters anyway.

"*Chabuduo,*" he said. "The lengths are nearly the same."

I didn't have to reach for a calculator to know on which side of *chabuduo* we would end up. The difference between the two measurements would represent another 1.5 percent loss in margin.

When I pointed this out, the factory man tilted his head the other way this time and scratched at his scalp some more.

Doug had been counting on 10 percent and that was a gross figure. We were down to only 3.5 percent profit now and had not yet taken into account inland transportation and other expenses. At the current price, it was unlikely that there would be any profit at all for Doug's company.

The visit was a complete waste of time, Doug said, once we were in a taxi. My only defense was that I could not have seen any of it coming. We had contacted a number of suppliers. This one had seemed just as good as any other, and the pricing was favorable. My client said it was all right in the end, but I was bothered by the way things had turned out for him.

Cross-cultural negotiations were supposed to be about creating understanding and mutual respect. International trade was tough enough, what with inherent language barriers and great distances between buyers and sellers. I was feeling embarrassed, not so much for myself as much as for the way Doug had been treated. He was new at the China game and a lot nicer than other importers I had worked with; certainly, I thought, he deserved better than this.

Some described Chinese business style as "soft," though I never knew what to make of such commentary. Factory owners were aggressive more than anything else, and perhaps even a bit cruel. This one factory owner had encouraged his prospective customer to board a plane in the United States and fly all the way to China. Once the investment in time and money had been made, the factory took advantage.

On the way to our next stop, Doug said that he would probably end up giving the factory the order anyway. He had an important customer back home that was already counting on the shipment of tubing. Even if he made no money at all on the order, there was some value, he said, in keeping his customer satisfied.

Why didn't Chinese manufacturers take the same approach with their own customers, and why were they eternally focused on short-term gambits? Chinese business leaders were continually preaching how they valued relationships, and yet it was more often foreigners who understood what it really meant.

CHAPTER 18

"Price Go Up!"

Bernie didn't like coming to China, so he said. Though he was president of his own company, he was at his best a salesman. His time was better spent meeting with customers in the United States. Visiting with a prospect for a couple of days, Bernie explained, he could close a deal that could keep King Chemical busy for many weeks.

The trips to China were an interruption, but they were unavoidable. This time, Bernie was coming in to solve problems that we were having with pricing. The factory had been attempting to push through a number of last-minute price increases, and the problem was so serious that it threatened the viability of the entire business.

In the manufacturer's conference room, Bernie placed a large file case on the oval-shaped table. He dropped a pile of papers onto the desk and took some sheets from the top—it was a set of financials prepared by his company's accountant.

"First, I want her to see this," he said, turning the papers so that they faced Sister. "I want her to see how much money we've lost so far."

He pushed the financials across the table, pointing to a figure at the bottom of one page that was in parentheses. Bernie and his partners had apparently suffered losses of nearly $2 million.

Bernie was quick to point out that while the loss was substantial, he still had faith in the business. Johnson Carter was about to turn a corner, and he was speaking with a growing number of new, large accounts. These were major retailers, he said, and they were all very excited about doing business with his company. But if Johnson Carter could not catch these orders because of pricing problems, then the orders could not be sent to King Chemical.

"We can make so much money together," he said. "But first, we have to understand each other. We have to recognize that what affects one company affects the other."

Bernie went on to describe some of the companies he was speaking with. They included Wal-Mart, Colgate-Palmolive, several drugstore chains, and all of the top dollar store companies in the United States. I knew that this was really happening because I was occasionally asked to speak with company representatives on behalf of Johnson Carter.

"Within two years," Bernie said, "we will be producing at volumes that'll rival the largest manufacturers of health and beauty care products in the world."

With the way things were going, it did seem possible.

Sister nodded as Bernie spoke. While she appeared to agree with him, she was distracted. She glanced over at the financials, and just as Bernie finished his small speech, she reached out and touched the pages. She could not have understood the words there, nor did she have the financial training to understand the figures.

The financials were printed on crisp, white stock paper, and what seemed to attract her was the general look of the documents. Though the work was undoubtedly from a template—probably done with accounting software—it was professional.

King Chemical didn't keep accurate records that might alert managers, employees, or local government officials about how profitable their business was. The company was doing millions of dollars worth of volume, but its accounting was still either scratched off in pencil or kept in Sister's head.

Bernie's talk had been a prelude, a philosophical setup for a discussion that he wanted to have about pricing. Specifically, he was troubled by how the factory moved to raise prices only after he had negotiated Johnson Carter pricing with its customers.

It took several months for Bernie to secure an order with a major retailer. Styles and quantities had to be determined, and labels were often custom made. In some cases, customers wanted formulations adjusted. Decisions were made by committee, and prices were always agreed to in advance of any green light for a production run. Bernie was sure to confirm prices with the factory before confirming his own pricing with his customers, but then right after Johnson Carter received its order from the retailer—often just days before he planned to wire transfer funds to China—the factory would notify Bernie of a slight price increase.

Because large retailers made decisions by committee, it was next to impossible to make any changes once an order had been firmed up. Retailers expected that commitments made would be honored, so Johnson Carter was not likely to go back to the retailer just a week or two after all of the paperwork had been signed and risk upsetting the business relationship.

Of course, Sister denied that she was dealing in tactics; she claimed they had no choice. "Price go up!" she said, sounding urgent. It was one of the few phrases that she took the time to learn how to say in English, and she repeated it often.

Bernie said that he could appreciate the claim about rising prices, but how could the factory give notice of a price increase only after Johnson Carter had confirmed pricing with King Chemical and initiated the order with the retailer?

Increasing prices at the last moment was about moving profit margin from the importer to the manufacturer, and Bernie was not buying Sister's excuses in part because he had been the victim of eleventh hour attempts rather often. Every time Johnson Carter placed a particularly large order, the factory made the same move. It waited until just after the orders were secured, and only then did it announce the increase.

Bernie was frustrated in trying to fix the pricing problem. He had a number of substantial orders that could not be processed because of the last-minute price move. He said that he would not go back to the retailer to ask for a price increase, and he could not suffer the losses himself.

After a long day of negotiations at King Chemical, Bernie promised that it would be the end of the business relationship. He gave the standard line that Americans give when jerked around. "Don't they understand if they screw me like this, I'm never coming back?"

Threats were of no use in our case. The factory had managed to increase prices on a number of items on Bernie's last visit, and he had similarly complained. He had raised his voice then and threatened that he would never return. Not only did he come back, but he brought even more orders with him this time.

What frustrated Bernie was that he had counted on a certain profit margin, but King Chemical had managed to cut right into that expected income. Bernie had done his part by going out and developing business. Having done this, he was now being told that his share would be diminished.

In certain parts of China, there were fishermen who trained birds to catch fish. They tied the necks of the cormorant, a bird which looked a bit like a pelican, with a piece of string so that it could not swallow the fish that it caught from the river. Just as soon as the bird had a fish in its bill, the fisherman yanked it back with a rope attached to its foot.

These fishermen could be seen in action on the Li River near the town of Yangshuo. What struck me most about the thing when I saw it was the bird's incredible optimism. It didn't realize that it was a sucker, and no matter how many times it was sent out into the water, this gullible bird had its quarry taken away.

Watching King Chemical's last-minute pricing tactics, I came to understand: Johnson Carter was the bird; the factory was the fisherman.

Bernie flew around the United States and signed up new clients, customers who would enable him to send millions of dollars worth of business to China. He created a margin for himself, and just as soon as he was about to enjoy the fruits of his labor, the factory came and took them away—well, as much as it could manage anyway.

The fishermen, of course, allowed the bird to eat some of what it caught—typically just the smallest fish that passed through its constricted neck—because the bird had to survive in order to keep catching fish. In a similar way, King Chemical did not take away so much of Johnson Carter's margin that the importer was washed out of the game. The factory had to know just how much it needed to give away to capture the business and how much it could take back through short-term maneuvering.

The phenomenon of last-minute price increases was not a new one. Chinese manufacturers have actually been at it for quite some time. One of the first journalists to enter China following Chairman Mao's revolution was an Australian newspaperwoman named Lisa Hobbs. She arrived in 1965, and among other places spent a good deal of time at the Canton Fair. In her book, *I Saw Red China,* she described what the Chinese government did to importers in those days:

> Typical of the way in which business is conducted is the fact that on April 14, one day before the Canton Fair opened, the Chinese Government sent telegrams to every foreign buyer in the world with whom they did business and announced a flat price increase of 20 percent on all product over last year's price.

■ ■ ■

There was little that Bernie could do, really. Long disagreements over price increases led only to production delays, which affected Johnson Carter more than King Chemical.

King Chemical didn't much care whether it delivered the goods in March or in May. Like many other Chinese manufacturers, the company had access to cheap capital, and it also had less need to get any particular deal done. Johnson Carter was like most other American firms. Cash flow was tight, and Bernie was under a great deal of pressure to make his company profitable.

There were short-term financial needs, and then the retailers were all placing additional pressure on Johnson Carter. Just like many importers did, Bernie realized that it was better to get some revenue in the door than to lose business. Other importers were in the same situation, which was why short-term pricing schemes of this nature were played throughout South China.

Factories that raised prices at the last moment never admitted to running a gambit, just as they never would claim that the issue was about wanting to earn more. Manufacturers insisted they earned no profit (even though it was obvious that they were expanding rapidly).

When they went for a price increase, they blamed impassive market forces over which they had no control.

"Price go up!" was the resounding chorus heard across the manufacturing sector, and factory owners said that it was out of their control, that it had to do with the cost of raw materials.

The problem with the argument was that commodity prices moved down, as well as up, but this was not the picture that these manufacturers painted.

Whenever commodities prices rose sharply, they cried: "Price go up!" When prices slackened, though, they fell silent.

And the sudden commodity price increases were not nearly as urgent as some made them seem. Many of the manufacturers kept a stock of key raw materials, meaning that they had supply from when prices were lower. This did not prevent them from trying to gain more profit on the news of a price increase on raw materials.

If they did not have their own private stockpiles, manufacturers often held contracts that guaranteed a certain price for a period of time.

"The price of plastic has gone up $200," Sister said.

Bernie asked how much the factory was paying on a per-ton basis, but Sister would not say. Chinese manufacturers did not like to provide detailed market information, though they were glad to announce the increased amounts. They would not indicate, for example, what the price had been or what the new price was at that very moment. They would hint only at a change.

They would only say: "Price go up!"

It was like asking someone for the price of unleaded gasoline and being told that it had gone up 25¢. The news of an increase was not useful without the rest of the information.

Bernie wanted to be put in touch with suppliers who sold key raw materials to the factory. He wanted to learn about pricing in general, and he wanted to track trends. All he was asking for was basic market information.

King Chemical refused to make any related introductions, and they refused to help Johnson Carter figure out how much, or in what way, prices were actually moving.

When I managed to find some market data, from a company that tracked commodity trends, the factory insisted that the figures provided did not apply in their case. Sister did not offer to look over the information that we had, but she was happy to repeat: "Price go up!"

On one level, you couldn't blame the factory owners. Their own subsuppliers were subjecting them to similar price games, and their own domestic contracts were not always honored. Westerners were really just being pulled, willy-nilly, into a game that went on in the local market.

Still, factory owners took advantage where they could.

On one project I was involved with—we were making precision component parts—the rising price of copper posed a challenge. The market price for the metal was said to have doubled, and the factory used this piece of news to double its price to my client.

It sounded logical enough, except that the manufacturer had conveniently forgotten that the metal was just a part of the total cost. Copper metal made up maybe 50 percent of the total price that we paid. By doubling its price to us from $2.50 to $5.00 on the one item, the factory covered the increasing cost of copper (from $1.25 to $2.50), but then it also watched its profit margin rise. Assuming a 20 percent margin, it went from earning 50¢ to $1.00.

Chinese manufacturers were good at finding the opportunity in a crisis, and while the pinch from rising material costs was genuine, these manufacturers figured: Why let a good excuse go to waste? They liked to play thick, and they pretended not to understand their own businesses.

When a textile importer asked for better buttons for his China-manufactured shirts, the factory mentioned that it had buttons that cost 5¢ each. When the invoice was printed, the new price reflected a nickel increase for each button. The factory had forgotten to subtract the cost of the older, cheaper buttons that had been replaced. The importer who told me this story said that when the fact was pointed out, his supplier simply went: "Huh?" as if he had no clue what was being suggested.

Chinese factory owners looked for small excuses as a way of gaining minor advantages. However when there were real, substantive changes in the marketplace, these same factories found the will to keep their prices firm.

The United States had been pressuring China to appreciate its currency, and China finally announced in 2004 that it would revise the currency peg, under which the U.S. dollar equaled 8.26 renminbi. In connection with the revision, the U.S. dollar would be devalued by about 3 percent against the renminbi.

Every factory that I was working with then pointed to the major news announcement and sent out a notice saying that their prices would be increased by 3 percent. You had to believe them that it was necessary—it was in the news, after all. In this way, they got a small gain out of the importer's bottom line.

Oddly enough, though, when the Chinese currency was devalued by a much greater percentage—10 percent and then even more—the very same manufacturers said that we should not worry about the impact of further changes. When importers were ready to bolt, manufacturers cried: "Don't go anywhere—we'll hold prices steady."

Chinese suppliers could work magic when it came to keeping their prices cost competitive, and yet they had a strong affinity for the small nibble, and it was these small bites that frustrated importers more than anything.

■ ■ ■

Made in China was billed as a deflationary force for the American economy. At least this was the claim that many economists made. Chinese manufacturers were keeping our cost of living down by offering to make products for less. Sitting in pricing negotiations with Chinese manufacturers, you got a slightly different idea of who was doing the work to hold down prices.

Manufacturers might have offered low prices as an incentive to bring in big pieces of business, but over time they worked on ratcheting up their prices—and they were extremely savvy about how they did it.

If there was anyone who was really working to keep costs down for the American consumer, it was the fellow who was arguing with the manufacturer that he needed prices to be held low. If there was any real deflationary hero, it was not the manufacturer, but the importer.

One of the reasons that prices were on the rise had to do with how importers were losing at the negotiation table. One of the reasons that this was happening was because manufacturers played the game better—they were more formidable negotiators.

I sat with Bernie in one negotiation as he tried to work out pricing with the factory. He had one retailer that wanted prices for some new bottles that were about double the size of some existing Johnson Carter products.

The factory prepared a quote for these larger bottles that came as a surprise to Bernie. On a bottle that was double the size, the factory quoted nearly triple the original price. It was the exact opposite of what every supermarket shopper already knew—that as package size increased, so did the value.

"I can't take these prices to my customers," Bernie said.

"We are doing our very best," Sister said.

"But how do you explain these prices?" Bernie shook his head, knowing that he would have to explain the logic to the buyer at a retail chain. Trying to make sense of the pricing scheme, he asked how much it would cost if instead of doubling the size of the bottles, we shrank them in half.

He wanted just to get a picture of Sister's methodology. She calculated the price and said that, for a bottle that was half the size, the price would remain the same as the original size. Bernie threw up his hands in frustration looking as though he might walk out of the room.

"How can it be the *same* price?" he asked.

Bernie figured that maybe the issue might be volume. He said that production volumes were going to increase if he could get the pricing worked out. How would Johnson Carter's prices be affected with triple the volume of business? Sister said that such an increase would make no difference to her company whatsoever.

"Ask her what if we increase volume 10 times?"

"Pricing would be about the same," Sister said.

"How can there be no difference? Ten times!"

Chinese factories were not in the habit of offering discounts for volume. Chinese raw materials were purchased at market rates that did not differ much based on volume, and the factory owner claimed to be producing at cost. Dropping the price suddenly, on the hope of slightly larger volume, would punch a hole in Sister's story about manufacturing goods for next to no profit.

After days of back and forth, Bernie was frustrated. As he did every visit, he somehow thought that negotiations with King Chemical would go faster and more smoothly. Like other importers, he figured he would fly in, get his business done, and then quickly be on his way back home.

Sister had a different idea. She was determined to keep everyone at the negotiating table for a much longer time and used some of her pricing games as a means of collecting information. When Bernie reacted angrily at one product pricing model and then less frustrated with another, it gave Sister a rather good idea of where Johnson Carter's margins were tight and where they enjoyed more profit.

Chinese factory owners did well in negotiations, despite language barriers. They relied more on emotion and on their instincts. Sister did not need English in order to conduct business; she could see just how well she was doing by looking at Bernie's expressive face.

Bernie was an excellent salesman, but even he fell victim to some of the more obvious manufacturers' tactics. When Sister suggested a price increase for one product type or another, she picked up on his visible panic. Prices were all over the place, in part because Sister was pressing different buttons, assessing Bernie's varied reactions.

Factory owners conducted themselves in such a way that increased, rather than minimized, the frustration of the importer, which seemed strangely counterproductive. After all, it cost money to find and keep a customer. And yet importers who did business in China reported having this same experience.

In other sectors, companies went out of their way to reward customers for remaining loyal. This was the logic behind every frequent-flier program. Rather than reward customers, factory owners punished them. It was as if these importers were participating in a *reverse* frequent-flier program; the longer an importer stayed with its supplier, the worse the deal became.

Chinese manufacturers understood the benefit of offering enticements to get a business relationship going (often at extreme prejudice to initial profitability), but after some interval, the factory jeopardized goodwill in order to fund its return.

Supplier relationships were almost never better than they were at the very beginning. Manufacturers intentionally degraded the quality of their product, and at the same time, they found small ways in which to ratchet up prices in the short term. Business relationships were supposed to improve over time, but these manufacturing relationships only got worse.

■ ■ ■

At one point in the pricing talks—on our fourth straight day—it seemed for a moment that Johnson Carter and King Chemical were close to agreeing on a number of key issues. Regarding one order, the manufacturer suggested that it would match price targets, with an exception on only a few products.

The next day, Sister came back and said that she could not do it. It was the timing that upset Bernie the most, and he was visibly angry. Sister remained calm and said that she understood. She thought that maybe it was time to consider dissolving the partnership altogether. "We can still be friends, of course," she said.

Bernie could not believe that it was happening to him. It was one thing that prices were going up. Now, the factory was suggesting that he leave and go to another supplier. It happened all the time in negotiations. At a critical point in the talks, the factory took the entire deal off the table.

The news seemed to have been delivered to Bernie at precisely the most inopportune time, done in a way that would maximize his frustration. Sister had allowed Bernie to believe that progress was being made, and just as he was looking forward to concluding some parts of the negotiations, just as he was made to think that things were on track, she delivered the sucker punch.

South China manufacturers actually went out of their way to make an importer lose his cool. It was also a tactic, a technique used in the negotiation. Professional interrogators did the same thing by placing a suspect under emotional pressure. It was the easiest way to know that the information collected was to any extent reliable.

Chinese had an idiom, *Hun shui mo yu*: you muddied the waters first, and only then did you feel around for the fish. When an importer was clear minded, it was easier for him to evade. When the importer was emotionally confused, it was easier to read his intentions.

Unaware of what was being done to him, Bernie tried to put things back on track. He tried to convince Sister that she was short-sighted, that there was a better way to go about building a business between the two companies.

"Why can't they just see the bigger picture?" he asked. "If they would just stick to our plan, we could build *such* a business."

Working between the two groups, I could see their different perspectives. One major disconnect was the time horizon. Bernie was thinking about the next several years. King Chemical, on the other hand, seemed focused on only the very next purchase order.

Bernie's view was that the factory's short-term maneuverings were adversely affecting the long-term viability of the business partnership. While that may have been the case, it was not possible to say that the factory's approach was inferior. The factory's methods worked rather well, actually.

If export manufacturing were like a game of football, then the factory was concentrating its efforts on short, running plays. Chinese manufacturers were just trying to cover the 10 yards necessary to get to a first down. They were in it for the long haul, but their strategy was to get there by advancing in small, incremental distances.

Bernie was frustrated if only because he was thinking of a mutual strategy that was more dramatic in scope. He was looked for a grander, coordinated effort, one that had a long-range focus. He was interested in the poetic, downfield pass.

Claiming that the factory's methods were wrong would have been a mistake. The game could be won just as well—as King Chemical, and indeed, China itself was proving—by advancing down the field just a few yards at a time.

China was an agrarian culture. For thousands of years, its farmers struggled through floods, droughts, and resulting famines. R. H. Tawney, a British historian, said that the life of the peasants was so precarious that it was lived as if they were up to their necks in water, that the slightest ripple would drown millions. Chinese farmers learned to make use of every inch of land, while looking over their shoulders to pick up whatever new agricultural tricks they could in order to increase output.

Mark Elvin, another historian, had a theory about why China never found its way to an industrial revolution. He suggested that farmers were so good at finding small ways to increase efficiency through tinkering and that success with short fixes dulled the impetus to build machines that could replace human labor. He called it the "advantage of backwardness."

What is surprising is how little has changed, even as the country has moved from agriculture to a focus in export manufacturing. Factory owners were just as focused on life at the margin. While they worried less about natural disasters, they behaved as though they were struggling just to get through the season.

Certain behaviors that made little sense to an American importer—like last-minute pricing maneuvers and the clever manipulation of product quality—would have made more than enough sense to a nineteenth century Chinese peasant or to someone who labored his life away some 2,000 years ago.

Some of the Chinese I have known recognize this cultural inclination as a shortcoming. On occasion, you would hear someone chiding another about being "*shu mu cun guang*"—like the mouse that can see only one inch ahead of itself.

What had kept the nation from creating its own industrial revolution was more than likely this enduring cultural trait—an endemic myopia—and knowing that they suffered from it was what led common folk to welcome the larger and more direct role that government played in their lives.

In the microcosm of the factory, this myopia was keenly felt. Workers awaited instruction from above for even the smallest task assignment or objective. They seemed incapable, or perhaps unwilling, to coordinate among themselves, to see beyond their immediate circumstance.

■ ■ ■

On the last day of our meetings with the factory, Bernie said that he was at the end of his rope. He did not want to change suppliers because of the time it would take to get an alternate up to speed. There was another reason that he had not wished to quit the relationship—and it had to do with how King Chemical knew too much about his business.

The promise of continued orders had kept the factory from engaging in broader, unscrupulous acts. Once the manufacturing relationship ended, who knew how the factory might respond. King Chemical might approach Johnson Carter's largest customers and try to take them away, or maybe the factory would court some of the importer's competitors. Johnson Carter was growing fast enough that others would want to know how Bernie had done it.

King Chemical had access to all aspects of the product line. It had the molds for bottles as well as the label designs and the formulations. Since quitting the business would potentially create losses for King Chemical, they would likely be motivated to fill the income gap in some way.

One thing Bernie worried about was that King Chemical would counterfeit his product line. If it did so, Johnson Carter would be in no position to learn about such activities once the relationship was dissolved. Johnson Carter leaving the relationship might change motivations in ways that we didn't even understand.

Bernie said that he felt that the factory left him with no choice. Quality was a continued question mark, and the pricing games were now too much to bear. We had to find another supplier, he said. A new supplier might be just as bad as the current one, which was another argument against leaving, but at this point it was a chance worth taking.

After our last pricing meeting with the factory, Bernie pulled me aside. He told me that it was time to chase down another opportunity. "Be discreet. Make a few appointments. Show them the catalog."

Bernie flew back to the United States, and I lined up a couple of initial meetings. The first manufacturer was a surprising disappointment. The factory owner told me that he knew all about Johnson Carter. Just looking at the catalog and seeing the company name, he knew that we were tied with King Chemical. He knew what we manufactured, and he added that he was friends with Sister, as well.

Like many other sectors, the health and beauty care industry was one that existed in a tight network. Some manufacturers in the industry were even related to one another. Others shared an educational background, having graduated from the same chemistry programs at the same universities in South China. Others shared a kinship that was based in part on membership in the Communist Party. And then some had suppliers in common.

China's tight networks were a part of its advantage. They were one of the reasons that manufacturers were able to get things done so quickly. Factories were connected not just to subsupplier networks, but also to other manufacturers. They shared information, contacts, and resources. But these networks were also a threat—to importers. While it remained illegal for companies to collude, it was difficult to monitor such activities from abroad.

Critics of globalization talk about how we have outsourced our values by allowing overseas firms to make products under conditions that Americans would never allow at home. One of the other things that we gave up with global trade would inevitably be the opportunity to prevent marketplace collusion.

Sister found out about my visit almost immediately after the meeting was finished. It actually pleased her to know that I had been to see one of her competitors, and she seemed to enjoy that the news had traveled back to her so quickly and that we were having little luck in finding an alternate supplier.

In pricing negotiations, Bernie had hinted on occasion that he might take his business elsewhere. When he made these veiled threats, Sister was inclined to soften her position in response. Now that Johnson Carter had actually taken action and the plan had *backfired*, our bluff was called, leaving Sister in an even better negotiating position.

Another manufacturer might have become upset if its sole foreign customer was thinking of leaving, but Sister was, on the contrary, quite friendly toward me.

She mentioned that she wanted to travel to the United States, and she asked me if I would get Bernie to write her an invitation letter, the sort that she could use to secure a visa from the U.S. Consulate in South China. She wanted to visit relatives and also, she said, she wanted to travel to Las Vegas.

Specifically, she mentioned wanting to go to Cosmoprof, the world's largest health and beauty care trade show. She said that she would be looking for "ideas" there, but the opportunity to visit would have opened up the chance for her company to exhibit, as well.

Obtaining a visa to visit the United States was a challenge for many Mainland Chinese, and while they were certainly as welcome to visit and to immigrate as anyone else, the issue of travel to the United States was one that some importers considered. Visitor visas were not meant to be a competitive advantage in business, but they most certainly were for Chinese manufacturers.

One of Bernie's concerns was that Sister would begin flying to the United States on a regular basis, that she would manage to meet with his own customers or possibly with his competitors. Once foreign nationals were granted their first visa to visit the United States, subsequent visas were typically easier to obtain. Bernie insisted that he would eventually get around to writing Sister an invitation letter, but he never would.

CHAPTER 19

You Wouldn't
Want to Be There

From my work in China manufacturing, I was already familiar with how old equipment made its way to the developing world. In one printing factory in South China, I saw an old Heidelberg press that had come in secondhand from Germany. At another factory, one that made pantyhose, I remembered some dingy-looking textile machinery that had been imported from Italy. The equipment at both of these plants looked outmoded, and I thought: *China is where old machines come to die.*

And, so, when Maria asked me in the spring to take her to a carnival that had come to town, I had to object. I had driven past and seen it myself. The carnival had the sort of rides that tossed passengers around and upside down. There was English lettering on some of them. These were rides that looked like they had previously worked in a state fair. I tried to imagine how they had come all the way to China, and I wondered about their mechanical worthiness.

No, I told Maria, the carnival was not for me. She protested, and so I explained my fears.

"Well, maybe *these* rides were made in China," she offered.

"*That's* supposed to be a comfort?"

She pouted and was unrelenting. I next told her about a time that I had been to another park up north in the city of Dalian. I had been traveling with a friend, and we discovered an amusement park—the permanent kind—and made our way over to a big Ferris wheel there. It was late in the season, with almost no one else in the park. We were the only passengers on the tall ride.

When we had been lifted to the top, the operator cut the motor for the wheel, and the car we were in rocked back and forth. The park was quiet, except for a great squeaking noise coming from the cars. They had not been properly oiled in ages, if ever.

Trapped in the stopped car, I had the chance to look at the metal all around us. So much of the metalwork in China was done on the spot in a jerry-rigged fashion, and I could see that this had been an especially poor welding job.

When the operator started the wheel and stopped it again suddenly, the entire ride shook, and for a moment I was certain that something would come loose and that my friend and I would fall out. What should have been one of the most gentle rides ended up being a spine-chilling experience—especially because it was MADE IN CHINA.

It has been said that the price one pays for pursuing a profession is the intimate knowledge of its ugly side. Perhaps that is all that it was. In any case, my work in China manufacturing gave me another perspective, causing me to see many things differently.

One day, Maria mentioned that something seemed to be wrong in the spare bedroom of my high-rise apartment. There was a smell, she said, and she suspected the furniture. Chinese furniture makers were in the habit of using formaldehyde, a regulated substance, in their manufacturing processes. Maria wanted to know if I had ever had the room tested with a formaldehyde kit to see if the furniture was emitting related fumes.

"A formaldehyde kit? Where in the world would I get a formaldehyde kit?" I asked.

It sounded scientific, like something found in a laboratory. Maria mentioned that the kits were sold everywhere and that I might get one at a supermarket or hardware store. It was true. The kits were not at all hard to find, and many families in China tested their own furniture. I wondered whether other economies in the world made formaldehyde kits so widely available.

Manufacturing literacy was high in China, and locals knew how products were made. Formaldehyde in furniture was a common concern, just as tainted baby formula powder had been. Chinese consumers had a natural mistrust of local industrialists that was not exactly misplaced.

With all of the problems we were facing at the soap and shampoo factory, I found myself losing faith in all sorts of products manufactured in China. I was soon careful to purchase health and beauty care products that were not made by local companies, but by large, multinational corporations—but then I realized that the body wash I had been using, while it was made by a reputable, global company, was actually manufactured in a plant located in South China.

Even if headquarters were in the United States, this company's manufacturing assets were in China. The staff was all local, and I knew these production managers well. They subscribed to the same philosophies that Sister at King Chemical had; they believed that what a consumer didn't know couldn't harm him.

I found myself using less body wash, eventually relying on hot water for my showers. When no one seemed to notice the difference, I stopped using the wash altogether. And then I stopped using soap, as well. This was not a conscious decision, but in the back of my mind, I had begun to think: *Why take any chances?*

Working in manufacturing had caused me to lose faith. When clients came to China, we spent long days and nights together. At one point, I began asking importers if they had doubts of their own. Even before product recalls made global headlines, importers that I worked with admitted that they saw uncertainty with China-made goods. They did what they could, but shrugged off any real sense of worry. They had to earn a living, after all, and, as one importer reminded me, "every business comes with risk."

Back in the United States, a debate was stirring. Economists who supported free trade without qualification were making the case that bilateral trade with China was helping Americans to save money. The often-quoted statistic held that each U.S. family was saving $300 per year through outsourcing to China. Even if these savings were real, they seemed small and did not take into account certain risk factors, which were unquantifiable. How much was it worth to know that the products you purchased were lead or melamine free?

When the quality crisis hit in earnest, some argued that shoddy products were nothing new. America had gone through the very same thing in the nineteenth century. It was what every developing economy must endure, and the problems would be sorted out in time. When politicians pushed for free trade with China, though, none of them had ever suggested that the American public would be involved in any sort of trade-off. If anyone had joked about how sending manufacturing orders to China came with a jump back to 1849—a time that predated consumer safety protection—for only modest savings, most consumers would have been against it.

After the crisis in toys hit in 2007, I received a note from executives at Toys "R" Us who had read an article I wrote on quality fade that year. They wanted to talk generally about the challenges facing China manufacturing, and one senior executive wanted assurances that what China was going through was no different than what Japan had faced in the 1950s when it had a reputation for manufacturing low-quality goods.

China's case in the 2000s differed from Japan in the 1950s, or the United States in the nineteenth century. One of the reasons was the type and extent of quality manipulation that was common in China.

There was a degree of quality cheapening that was the result of mere *corner cutting*—which involved skimping on raw materials or taking shortcuts in the production process. But you also had serious game playing that went on between a manufacturer and an importer, instances where manufacturers were manipulating quality levels in such a way that their customers could not tell at all what had been done to the product. The phrase "corner cutting" was too benign when the manipulation of quality involved changing the product so that the manufacturer could succeed in bypassing quality assurance tests set up by third-party laboratories.

Never have so many manufacturers in an economy tried to "slip one past the inspectors," and never has any economy had so many foreign agents on the ground in order to preempt disaster.

My role in China was to facilitate trade between China and the United States; I was a go-between, but after working for many years in the manufacturing sector, I had doubts. Manufacturers were simply much better at playing cat-and-mouse games. China watchers were suggesting that quality would improve in time, and that as the country developed, there would be fewer problems. My own experiences suggested the opposite—that things were getting worse, if only be-cause factory owners were picking up more tricks as they went along. And importers who placed increasingly larger orders in China did not help matters, but gave factory owners courage and the sense that they could push limits.

I increasingly expressed my views to importers that I worked with. It was all but impossible to prevent quality manipulation schemes, I would point out; the factory could not be beaten. I had become cyn-ical. While working in China manufacturing, I sometimes suggested to clients that they not bring some products to China. I was aware that by making such suggestions, I was turning into a hypocrite, like the butcher who whispered to his customers that they ought to consider the value of a vegetarian diet.

While continuing to work in the industry, I began to make notes. And I tried to justify my staying in the quality game by thinking that maybe American consumers were better off having someone like me on the job, someone who actually cared. Seriously, though, who was I kidding? Manufacturers I worked with got away with whatever they wanted, and importers did not have the leverage to pressure their suppliers to behave in an ethical fashion.

Some said that the answer to China's quality challenge was to test more of its products. The problem with this solution—at least in health and beauty care—was that it was too expensive. For many product categories, Johnson Carter earned not even 10¢ per bottle. If there were 20,000 pieces in a 40-foot container, the importer might earn only $2,000 in profit, and then the laboratory wanted to charge more than $200 for each separate test that it might run. Testing just one bottle for the presence of five different toxic substances could run more than a thousand dollars.

Johnson Carter's solution was to put the ball in its customers' court. If the retailer wanted to test for the presence of certain forbidden chemicals, it was welcome to do so. We would send the bottles off to the laboratory to have the tests run, and then the retailer would be billed at a later point.

These retailers did the math and realized that they couldn't test very much of the product and still earn a profit. Anyway, what were they going to test? The laboratory had to be told what it was testing, and that was the problem—if the factory did introduce an inappropriate substance, we would need to know what that substance was in order to run the screen.

In the end, retailers decided to take importers at their word, and importers had no choice but to do the same with manufacturers—take their word that they were creating a product that was effective and not harmful. It might have worked, except unilateral changes made by manufacturers to products—without warning—suggested risks that were incalculable.

Checking the product one morning, I noticed that our cherry-scented liquid soap smelled strange. It was the first time that I had noticed it. The product smelled like cherry all right, but it was a medicinal kind—someone had switched the fragrances, and the cherry scent we had was now closer to the kind you might find in a throat lozenge.

Sister insisted that they were using the same fragrance, but a week later I got confirmation from the New York office that the cherry scent did not match samples that had been sent to them from the manufacturer. Bernie worried that quality fragrances had been swapped out for inferior ones or for ones that we did not care for anyway. There was a cultural issue involving fragrances. What smelled nice to Chinese consumers did not necessarily smell the same to those in the United States.

I suggested that we take the entire product line to an international supplier of fragrances. Having a reputable foreign supplier deliver fragrances, instead of a local supplier that we could not control, was really the only way to assure that the factory would not take small savings and ruin the product. We knew of just such a fragrance supplier in Hong Kong, and so I made plans to visit them.

There were few things more refreshing than an excursion to Hong Kong. Guangzhou was an old Chinese city, and it had a crumbled look to it. The tones were all muted grays. Hong Kong was a world-class city, one that, at least in the commercial parts of town, was always crisp looking by comparison.

But the people of Hong Kong did not necessarily believe themselves lucky, and they often complained about pollution. As for us in Guangzhou, we got so little direct sunlight that their complaints across the border seemed laughable. At least in Hong Kong you could see your own shadow walking down the street. The factories in Mainland

China produced so much particulate matter that the skies were dark. If the sun appeared at all, it shone weak and enfeebled, like a tiger in a Chinese zoo—defanged and declawed.

Guangzhou was not entirely backwards. There were signs that the place was coming along. A surprising number of luxury brands could be found in the city, as well as other examples of extravagance toward the top end of the purchasing range. There were German car dealerships like Mercedes Benz and BMW, and there were surprisingly large displays for brands such as Bentley, Rolls Royce, and Ferrari.

This did not mean that you could get whatever you needed in town, though. There was no good English bookstore, and you were hard pressed to find a shop that made a decent loaf of bread. This was one of the things on my mind as the train pulled into Hong Kong—a simple sandwich, one with slices of avocado. Though there were plenty of fruits and vegetables available in Guangzhou, avocados were nowhere to be found. The lack of availability of certain fruits in South China presented a real challenge at King Chemical.

Perhaps even more surprising, shoes were also in short supply in the region. The majority of shoes that the United States imported were coming from China, and yet there was hardly any selection in South China—and the factories and trading companies were just a stone's throw from where I lived.

On the train, pulling in across the border, cell phones began to jingle. It was the sound of Hong Kong phone companies picking up the cross-border roaming signal; the ringing sound was like a welcome to the former British colony. Rushing off the train along with others who were equally excited to have arrived, I went to pick up a pair of black leather China-made shoes and grabbed my lunch—a chicken sandwich with avocado, and I thought: *first-time visitors to East Asia who visited both Guangzhou and this global capital might easily confuse where the boom was taking place.*

I had just enough time to meet an old friend in the financial district before heading off to the fragrance supplier. On a crowded pedestrian platform in Central, the main business district, I spotted my friend, who worked in finance, analyzing and assessing companies in Mainland China.

"How is Guangzhou?" he asked me.

"You mean how is *China*," I said.

It was an old joke between us. For him, I was the friend who lived just over the border in that rough-and-tumble world. For me, he was that friend who lived a more relaxed life in surroundings that were comfortable.

In response to the slight ribbing, my friend was quick to let me know that he had plans to move to China. "My company might post me to Beijing, actually," he said. The year before, it had been that his company might move him to Shanghai, but the relocation never transpired, and he continued to report on China from Hong Kong.

"Why not Guangzhou?" I asked, just to see the quick flash of horror on his face. Beijing and Shanghai were two options; anything else for a finance professional was out of the question.

At the mention of Guangzhou, he straightened his tie and ran a hand through his curly hair. "I'll move to China," he said, "when the timing is right."

And that was the issue, really—the timing of it all. China was still seen as underdeveloped. Health care and education were inadequate. And then there was all that business about wanting to find English books, a decent pair of shoes, and avocados. The pollution was also a common complaint, but it was only going to be getting worse in the years to come, which suggested that it was not only a matter of waiting another couple of years.

Jim Rogers, the global investor, had recently made headlines when he sold his Manhattan town home for $15 million and announced that he was moving his family to China. He said that he wanted to leave the United States because the focus of the global economy was shifting to Mainland China. Rogers was a vocal booster for China's real estate sector, and it appeared for a moment that he was personally going to take advantage.

Flying around China, Rogers considered a number of different cities to live in, including Shanghai, Dalian, and Qingdao, but in the end the "China bull" settled with his family in Singapore. It was a nice, safe place, an efficiently run city, but much like Hong Kong—it was not exactly China.

Financial analysts who reported on the Mainland Chinese economy from the hermetically sealed environments of Hong Kong and

Singapore were upbeat on China. Sure they were! They didn't have to suffer the constant reminders of how difficult the environment was.

Finance professionals who talked up China didn't mind the opacity of the place. They minded having to report on the enigmatic economy while living inside it. They didn't mind the occasional trip into Mainland China, but they were sure to make their visits brief. Somehow amid the economic boom, it did not strike anyone as particularly odd or comic. China was apparently *the* place to be—it was just that you didn't actually want to be there.

■ ■ ■

I took my suitcase of soap and shampoo samples and wheeled it down the hall toward the offices of the fragrance supplier. Just outside the door, I spotted the Frenchman, Yves, with whom I had an appointment. The look on my face must have given away my first impression of him.

"You are surprised that I smoke," he said and then went into an unsolicited explanation of why so many perfumers smoked. "After working with the fragrances for too long, the nose needs a break," he said.

Inside his office, he brought me to a showcase that housed many products using the company's fragrances. There were some global brands there that I recognized.

He took me on a small tour of their offices, which included a walk through the warehouse. As soon as we entered, Yves excused himself and went looking among the steel drums for something.

A round-faced Hong Kong man stood at a table, mixing chemicals, sniffling as though he had a cold. I asked if he was feeling well.

"I'm always like this," he said.

"From the fragrances?" I asked.

He looked surprised, as though I might have hit on something. "You know," he said. "Come to think of it, I once took a two-week holiday, and my sinuses cleared up."

I asked if he ever thought of quitting, but he said that he needed the job. In all the time that I had been working in Mainland China, I thought, I had never run into a factory worker who complained.

The showroom at the fragrance company doubled as an office. Yves brought me back to the showroom and asked that I open my case and place my samples on the table. I was to hand him the bottles without showing him the labels. He did not want any visual cue. I took out the cherry-scented liquid soap and handed him the bottle.

He held it up to his nose and paused.

"Cherry," he said. He noticed the medicinal quality and said that his company could provide a better fragrance.

"Hand me another. Something not so easy this time."

Instead of a fruit-scented variety, I reached for one called Herbal Fresh.

Yves brought it to his face while closing his eyes and this time lifted his nose slightly in the direction of the ceiling. He took in a deep breath. Our formulations were meant for discount stores, and yet he handled the product like it was vintage wine.

"Almond," he pronounced and placed the bottle on the table.

I took up the sample and had a sniff for myself.

"You're right," I said.

"Of course I am," he said with a wry smile.

The next sample I handled him was labeled Aloe Vera. He spent less time on this one.

"It's also almond," he said.

"Also almond? Are you sure?"

He looked at me and cocked an eyebrow. I handed him more samples, and he gave the same response—"almond"—to a number of other styles. For an as yet unknown reason, almost half of our samples were made up of this mysterious almond scent. Someone at the factory must have made a substitution, I realized.

"We have a problem here," I told Sister on the phone.

Hong Kong was supposed to be a part of China, but the phone call was an international one. The connection was terrible, and Sister could not hear me.

"What?" she said.

"The fragrances. They are all almond."

"I can't hear you."

"Why did you switch the fragrances?"

"What?"

I gave up on complete sentences and shouted the word for almond into the phone: "*Xinren!*" The one word made it through, and Sister at once launched into a denial.

"*Meiyou! Meiyou!*"

When I got back to the factory the next day, she was no longer in the denying mood. She admitted the fragrance switch and said that she thought the almond scent was nicer. "Didn't you think so?" she asked.

My opinion was beside the point, I told her, just as her own didn't matter. Johnson Carter's customer placed its order and had already received a sample set. It approved the order based on what we sent them, and the customer had an expectation of what it was going to receive.

With all that we had been through with King Chemical, Sister still didn't get it. The nature of the customer relationship itself was something that eluded her. She made unilateral decisions on the product, instead of having a discussion first. The way she figured things, it was easier to beg for forgiveness after the fact than to ask for permission in advance.

We had millions of bottles on their way to the United States. Those who were in charge of buying at the retailers didn't like surprises, and if they discovered that we made changes without their prior approval, we were finished. For whatever reason, Sister could not or would not understand that.

For every single major quality fiasco—the sort that would make the papers—there were probably hundreds of smaller disasters that never got any publicity at all. Some importer's collapsing cardboard boxes, the flimsiest of plastic bottles, or the generic scent of almond that was placed in random bottles—these instances of quality manipulation were not ever going to make the news, though perhaps they also should have. The lives of consumers would not be affected, but they would have been telling examples of the challenges that importers faced. Perhaps knowing about these instances would have made the more serious cases of quality failure less of a surprise.

Part of the problem in understanding the quality situation in China was in the way the media reported on it. They dealt with instances as isolated cases, or at worst, as problems facing a specific industry. When toys were found to have lead paint in them, it was suddenly a "toy industry problem." When melamine turned up in dairy products, it was described as a "dairy industry problem." The issues were more universal than that; they were "China problems."

Anyone who worked in Chinese manufacturing for a number of years and over a broad number of product categories could have predicted the quality crisis. Chinese factories across a broad number of sectors were in the habit of ignoring the requests of their foreign customers and thought nothing of changing specifications without notice. It was easy to see where a habit like this would lead.

A common phrase heard around manufacturing companies was: "*Anquan Diyi*"—Safety First. One supplier joked with me that these companies were taking as their motto, instead: "*Zhuanqian Diyi*"—Make Money First.

Some blamed the Communist Party for this attitude. The one-party government does what it wants, when it wants. And while there are advantages to ruling without restraint or controversy, such a system limits predictability, and it has left Chinese entrepreneurs keenly aware that they are subject to the whims of officials who may or may not know which policy is best.

Knowing that entrepreneurs may be focused on the short-term, industry observers have suggested that the manufacturing sector's moral gap might be solved through increasing third-party inspections. But there were too many problems with such a fix. The first was that importers had to know what they were looking for in the first place. Unscrupulous industrialists were not going to tell importers where to look.

Some suggested that the answer to quality problems was to pay the factories more for their merchandise. One problem with that solution was that price competition was severe; paying higher prices would push Johnson Carter out of business. The other issue was the assumption that money would solve the problem. Suppliers that acted unscrupulously at 30¢ per unit were not likely to behave differently at 36¢ a unit. The factory owner that believed herself clever enough to substitute ingredients without asking permission could not be counted on to do the right thing just because the price of the product had been increased by a few pennies.

Chinese manufacturing had serious issues, and these were not very well understood while looking at them from a great distance.

CHAPTER 20

Of Course, You Would Think So

"I recognize you," the taxi driver said.

"You must be mistaken," I told him. Just as foreigners often thought that many Chinese looked alike, Chinese were in the habit of confusing one Westerner for another.

"No," he insisted. "I have picked you up before."

The driver held up three fingers, saying that it was his third time running into me. When he named the shampoo factory as one previous destination, I figured that he had me pegged.

I had been picked up in both Guangzhou and Shantou by taxi drivers who told me that it was their second time running into me, but this was my first triple.

Finding it quite a coincidence, I mentioned it to some Chinese friends who were visibly put off by it, offended even. It didn't matter if you ran into the same people all the time—and I did—you weren't supposed to intimate that China was small, or quaint. China could not be anything but enormous. It might be a small world, but the Middle Kingdom was supposed to be unknowably large, and the Chinese took great pride in their numbers.

It was interesting how foreign economists doubted nearly every single statistic produced by the Chinese government, and yet no one

ever challenged the population figures directly. It was a data point left
out of discussions, as if it were a strict taboo.

The longer I lived in China, though, the smaller it seemed, and the
more I had to wonder whether the government's reported population
figures weren't plumped up a bit. If it had been done only by accident,
you could at least imagine how it might have occurred.

The administrator of some small district was asked to count heads.
When he reported his final figure to superiors, they came back and
suggested that a margin of error be added. There were, after all, migrant laborers all across the country who arrived and worked without
authorization. Their numbers were probably added in many districts
without ever being subtracted in another location. And then there
were other unknowns, like the homeless and those reported millions
said still to be living in caves. And, of course, under China's one-
child policy, many families failed to report childbirths. Officials had
to compensate for all sorts of factors.

After the estimated figure was tallied and passed up to the county
level, it was adjusted upwards, again, for similar reasons—just to be on
the safe side—and then it happened again at the provincial and national
levels. At each stage, some officials in charge thought it prudent to
add to the final figure. This was China, after all. No one would ever
doubt a larger figure, naturally.

China had a motive, of course, for inflating its population statistic.
For hundreds of years, the government has been selling the promise
of a large consumer market to foreign investors. Conservative estimates helped no cause, and in China political concerns always took
precedence over the truth.

The best part about census estimates, however, was not what happened inside China, but what went on abroad. In just about any year,
no matter what figure the government reported, financial analysts,
journalists, and other researchers were all willing to stake their professional reputations on the officially reported figure being on the
low side.

"China itself doesn't know how many Chinese there are," they
would say. When China was claiming that it officially had a population
of 1.3 billion, foreigners who had "done the research" came back
with a figure rounded up to 1.5 billion. And these people were never
criticized or asked to produce their methodology—in part because

there were too many who wanted to believe a higher number. Who needed any "friend of China" when you had these sort of enablers around?

Westerners who visited China for the first time had no problem coming away with the impression that China was enormous. They popped into cities like Shanghai, Beijing, and Guangzhou, and they imagined a similar urban density cast out over a landmass the size of the United States. They guessed that China was uniformly populous, without stepping away from these coastal, dense urban centers. They did not understand how the interior of China was unlivable, that mountainous regions and other geographic barriers did not lend themselves to agricultural or even residential development.

They also failed to take into account cultural differences in urban planning. Chinese did not have the same desire as Americans for elbowroom but instead had a preference for *renao*—the hustle and bustle associated with urban living.

American urban planning was characterized by suburban sprawl. One neighborhood blended into another. In China, where they built with density in mind, you could drive from downtown Shanghai and, within half an hour, find yourself amid open fields with few signs of actual life. Even in the Chinese countryside, villagers preferred to live in relatively tight quarters, with one residence jammed up against the other.

Foreigners who have written on China tend toward Poloesque hyperbole, talking up the size of anything—"Oh, the scale!"—and relying on bloated Chinese government statistics as a means for eliciting an emotional response from reading audiences. Relating to population figures, specifically, they have been inclined to use language commonly reserved for astrophysicists attempting to describe the size of the Milky Way. Their intent has been to instill a sense of grandeur and awe. Why these observers did not report the same on India—a country that visually appeared more crowded—was curious.

China was supposed to be unimaginably big, but for those who lived in China for longer periods, the place shrank over time. For me, the phenomenon was not only related to taxi drivers; I also bumped into people—other Westerners, especially—that I knew, in airports, restaurants, on trains, and on the streets. Part of it was perception. Foreigners who were on the ground tended to know of one another.

Their communities were more tight-knit, and they were more visible. The Chinese who lived in China at least, those who held positions in government and industry, were also more likely to know one another. The perception of China as a small place had something to do with demographics. There were many who had very little, and then there were the principal players in the economy. China could seem at times like *Ben-Hur*, the 1950s Hollywood epic production; there was literally a cast of thousands, but only a small handful got billing.

Shantou was a city of a supposed 5 million people, which was the number of people that lived in Philadelphia, San Francisco, or Washington, D.C. And yet, all of the foreigners who stayed in Shantou turned up at one of only three hotels in the city.

And so it was, perhaps, not all that surprising that I would come down to the lobby one morning and see a group of Westerners and think that they might actually be some fairly important persons. Business travelers tended to arrive solo, or in pairs. This was a group of about 10, and as there were hardly ever any tourists in this eastern part of the province, I asked a front desk clerk who they were.

"Darts players," he said, "from England."

Darts players from England? How random, I thought.

They stood near a large, potted plant in the center of the lobby. I walked over to them and introduced myself. One of them, a man in a black T-shirt, shook my hand and told me that they had all flown in for a tournament.

"It's tonight," he said. "You should definitely come."

I was familiar with the arena where they would be playing. It was on the way to the factory from the hotel. I knew little about the game, though, and as an American I had a hard time imagining that it was any kind of serious sport. What was darts if not a game of chance? The board even looked like a roulette wheel, with its black and red spaces set about a circle.

Chalking this up to a learning opportunity, I decided that I would go. That night at the stadium, I sat next to a middle-aged Chinese man who asked if I was with the British team. I told him that I had just come as a spectator, and the doubt on his face made me realize that I was the only foreigner in the stands.

"Are you with the event?" I asked him.

"No," he said. "I am a factory."

That was how factory owners said it—*wo shi gongchang.* They did not run a factory or own a factory. They *were* the factory.

He admitted not knowing much about darts, but his factory was a supplier of sporting goods, and he supplied a product to a trading company that sold darts. He was a smaller player in the world of export manufacturing, he said, and like many manufacturers he had some kind of idea that this was a chance to develop more products for the domestic economy.

Manufacturers in many sectors were focused on exports, while they secretly hoped for domestic demand to catch on. You saw this in many unusual places. For example, in an area where there was a large concentration of factories making Christmas decorations, you found festive displays in the hotels nearby. It didn't matter what the product was. If it worked outside China, manufacturers wanted to make a go of it in China, as well. It was neither westernization, nor modernization—it was simply a matter of business.

"The Chinese team is here," the man next to me said.

For someone not very interested in the game, he was paying attention.

The event had not been set up as an exhibition, but as a match between nationalities. It was the British players against a team of Chinese. It seemed like an unlikely setup, given that darts was a popular sport in England and almost nonexistent in China. The only time I had ever seen the game played in China was in some expatriate bar, and even then, the board and darts were in bad condition.

The players started, and I found the rules easy enough to pick up. Players got three darts at each turn, and the objective was to reach 501 points as quickly as possible. All of the sections on the board had a different point value from 1 to 20, with spaces inside each section worth double and triple points.

In order to get to 501 points as quickly as possible, players focused efforts on a small space within the 20-point wedge that brought "triple 20."

The players from England turned out to be surprisingly skillful, and one player in particular seemed to surpass them all. He was the man I had met in the lobby earlier that day. His name was Phil Taylor, and while I would not find out about this until later, he was actually the dart-throwing world champion.

Taylor's preeminence was suggested by an emcee flown in for the event who referred to him by his nickname, "The Power," without a hint of irony.

The audience watched as Taylor went to the line and threw his first three darts. Each dart went right to the triple 20. It was not just that they landed in this small space, but even the way it was done was impressive. His first dart landed to the left of the tiny space, and the second dart flew straight over to the right side of it. His third dart came in on a slightly higher trajectory, so that its fins could land on top of the darts on either side.

It represented an incredible level of skill, and making the performance even more interesting was how he played without any fuss, or hesitation. When he finished placing all three darts in the triple 20, he turned around and gave a sheepish grin as if he could not believe his luck.

The crowd clapped, but not too loudly and not for very long.

Taylor's Chinese opponent went to the line, looking less confident. He glanced at his feet to make sure they were not crossing the line, and then made several false starts before finally throwing his darts. Out of three darts, none made it to the triple 20.

The crowd applauded politely for him.

Taylor was a surprisingly large man, and after lumbering up to the line, he put another three darts into the triple 20. And, just as before, he placed one on the left in the minuscule space, another to the right, and he floated the third in from above. It did not take any prior knowledge of darts to understand that he was a virtuoso. Watching his performance I felt like someone who has no idea about golf observing Tiger Woods as his introduction to the game.

Taylor was an oddity in the world of darts. Throwing a perfect game could be done in nine darts. The "nine-dart finish" was so rare that the cash prize offered for pulling it off on television was in excess of a half-million dollars. In his career, Taylor had thrown more nine-darters than any other player in history.

When Taylor managed to nail another three darts to the triple-20 spot, I must have gasped involuntarily, because the man next to me was clearly bothered.

"Our players have not prepared well," he said.

It was a strange comment to make, because it seemed to be beside the point. I understood the idea about cheering for your own team, and I understood also about rooting for the underdog. Taylor's performance called for some of those other motivations to be set aside, I thought.

"Don't you think he is quite good?" I asked.

"Of course, you would think so," he chuckled.

This display of jingoism made little sense. Taylor was such a remarkable player that ignoring his display of skill was a shame. And anyway, it seemed to be the reason why we were all in the arena. The exhibition was meant to inspire a new generation of players, but somehow it got turned into something else. Chinese had a tremendous respect for achievement, and yet no one showed the least bit of interest. They did not cheer Taylor; quite the opposite, the stadium was filled with a palpable resentment. They were looking to their local players, and they were hoping for some kind of miracle.

Taylor was scoring points, but he was losing the crowd. He must have sensed it, because on the very next round, he missed the triple 20 with all three darts, and by a margin that was too wide to have been a mistake. He was dialing back his game.

I found the poor play to be a disappointment, but the crowd did not share my opinion. They perked up and viewed the flub round as an opening, a chance for the local player to catch up and beat Taylor.

On his next turn at the board, the Chinese player measured his throw carefully, bending his arm at the elbow and flexing it back and forth. He squinted hard and leaned forward more, but under this new sort of pressure—the thought of overtaking the great master—he folded. One of his darts bounced off the board and landed on the floor, causing the audience to let out a collective groan.

The referee was about to call the score when Taylor raised his hand in a gesture that signaled a pause. Taylor then walked over to the board and collected all three darts of his opponent, and with both hands he shoved the darts directly into the triple-20 spot.

It was a cringe-worthy gesture. The local team was playing so badly that it needed the sympathy of the team that was trouncing it. The game itself had been turned into a sham now, Taylor's pity making the Chinese side's defeat so much more of an embarrassment. But apparently, the crowd saw it in a different light.

The referee shouted the score. "One hundred eighty!"

Hearing this, the announcement of a perfect round, the audience went wild and broke out in an uproarious applause. It was far louder than anything we had heard that night, and I was taken aback, lost in bewilderment. It was a fictitious score, so what were they cheering exactly—the local player, as if he had actually scored 180 points? Even if counted on the scoreboard, it was an illegitimate accomplishment. Could it be, I wondered, that they were cheering Taylor and his gesture instead?

The man next to me laughed, and he looked at me now in an approving way. *You foreigners are all right,* he seemed to be saying. If we had not been sitting so close together and in such uncomfortable chairs, I thought that he might have actually hugged me. The man pointed to the board and laughed aloud, and I detected in him—and in the crowd—a fantastic relief, as if everyone had been saved from some great humiliation.

It was important for the game to be won, and it mattered less how the score was achieved. Appearance over substance was a cultural theme in China; it quite likely weighed on the reporting of population statistics. The Chinese had a deep, nationalistic need to feel superior in every way possible. Justification was a driving force in China, one that influenced behaviors in the manufacturing sector as well.

CHAPTER 21

The New Factory

Chinese manufacturers were in the habit of saying that business wasn't good even when it was, but it was not that difficult to tell who was thriving. All you had to do was ask how long they took off for the Chinese New Year. Officially, the holiday lasted one week. After realizing some degree of success, though, manufacturers closed for longer periods of time.

Struggling manufacturers didn't dare jeopardize the production schedules of their importers for fear that they would upset key business relationships. Once the manufacturer had achieved some degree of success, though—after it had put cash in the bank and had a backup plan—it worried less about inconveniencing customers.

Factory owners blamed circumstances beyond their control, like the weather, and many of the factories that I worked with started to announce two- and three-week holidays. Then I got notice from one company in the automotive sector; just weeks before the Chinese New Year, it announced to all customers that it would be taking off an entire month. Business for some was that good in the middle of the economic boom.

King Chemical was growing, and while the owners had previously taken off just one week, this year they announced that they would be shutting down for two and a half weeks. We had all just returned from the long break, and Bernie was back in town again. It was a routine visit, one in which we would discuss pricing and more new orders.

Sitting in the front seat of the car, Bernie scanned the rolling landscape. He noticed everything that was new. Saying that he was pleasantly surprised by all of the development, he sounded like a duke surveying his distant landholdings. Importers who came to South China to do business sent large sums of cash. While they watched the place develop, they could not help but entertain the idea that they somehow had something to do with all of the growth.

We rode on and passed the turn in the road that would have taken us north to the shampoo factory. Bernie pointed out that we were off course and asked what was happening.

"I want to show Bernie something," Sister said.

"What does she want to show me?"

"I don't know."

"Well, ask her!"

Bernie had always said that he didn't like surprises. He liked to know what was happening and when, and he had planned out his first day of meetings rather carefully. I asked Sister what she had in mind, and she said that she wanted to show Bernie their new plant.

"They want to show you a new factory."

"What new factory?"

"I don't know."

"He doesn't know!"

Bernie was fidgeting, and the car now seemed too small. In the trunk, he had a case full of purchase orders. Time was already going to be tight that afternoon, and this surprise meant that nothing would get done on his first day. The news of a new plant was too significant to push aside, though, and we waited to see what Sister was talking about.

We turned onto a narrow road and into a parking lot. This new facility seemed much bigger than the original one; it looked to be more than double in size and was also a good deal more modern. Construction was not yet complete, but even at a glance it appeared as though something big was going to happen in the space.

Sister gave us a tour of the new factory. In the back, they had installed a number of shiny, stainless steel mixing tanks. New conveyor belts had been installed in the packaging station. Over at the side of the plant, we were taken to see a new water purification system.

Bernie turned to me, purple faced. When he was angry, his jowls shook. "How could you not know about all this?" he asked.

People at the factory were not obligated to say anything about any expansion plans; and while they had mentioned nothing to me, they had obviously not spoken about it to Bernie either. The more we were shown, the more aggravated he became.

"This makes no sense," he said. "They don't have enough orders to keep one factory busy, and now they build another one. Ask them why they built this factory, ask them."

Trucks could not move very easily in and out of the other location, Sister said. Bernie said that was not a good reason to build a new plant. "The trucks moved in and out of the old factory just fine. They loaded up the containers, didn't they?" A blueprint of the new factory was brought over and shown, and Sister detailed how the new factory had better symmetry. Some consultant from Shanghai had advised on the architecture of the plant and declared that this new one would also have better *fengshui,* all but guaranteeing a more auspicious future for the business.

Bernie didn't like the idea of a new factory. It was not just that it was an unexpected change. It could spell any number of different directions for the business relationship.

Bernie paced back and forth on the factory floor, bothered by the thought of it all. King Chemical had been his diamond in the rough, but this new place was a polished gem.

"At least I know why prices have been going up so fast," Bernie said.

We walked to the front of the factory, where we had come in from, and Bernie tried to work out what this meant for his business. While he paced and his mental gears clicked away, Sister stood off to the side and waited patiently. Sensing his concern, she told Bernie that he shouldn't worry.

"Why should I worry?" he said, his tone laced with sarcasm.

"Tell Bernie that we are still partners."

This patronizing comment incensed him, and he threw his hands up in the air. "Some partners! How can we *possibly* be partners when they don't say anything about a new factory?" When he spoke now, spittle flew from his mouth.

For someone who hated surprises, the new factory was a big one for him to get his head around. In the car, he asked me if I thought any of this was about Wal-Mart. Bernie said that he had flown to Bentonville, Arkansas, to meet with Wal-Mart representatives, and executives with their private label product had already been to visit. I had taken them on a tour myself, and they were scheduled to return again. Could King Chemical have built this entire new factory in preparation for their return? It seemed unlikely, but it also presented another problem. How could Bernie claim to be a partner and then surprise the Wal-Mart people with the news of a new factory? What King Chemical had done to Johnson Carter, Bernie could not do to Wal-Mart. American retailers didn't understand this sort of behavior—hiding information and springing big news for the sake of effect.

Bernie mentioned Wal-Mart. Sister responded by hinting that there was nothing to worry about—she would have the new factory up and running by the time the Wal-Mart people came back for their second visit. Hearing Sister put it that way, Bernie went bug-eyed. He changed the subject and asked how much it cost to build the new plant.

"Why?" Sister asked. "Would you like to invest?"

Bernie did a double take. Was this what the new factory was all about, a lure for investors? That could spell even more trouble for Johnson Carter. If King Chemical were to enter into a partnership with an American importer, then Johnson Carter might find that it was placing its orders with a direct competitor. It might mean the end of everything.

Bernie said that he was interested to learn more about any investment opportunities, and so yes, he wanted to know how much the new factory had cost. Sister paused while going through the mental math, as if she did not already know how much. Taking into account everything, she said, the factory cost around $2 million.

"Then it cost half that," Bernie said. In an aside to me, he suggested that the factory had probably inflated the value in a double-up-and-halve gambit. They would double the estimated cost and then get a company to come in for half. In effect, the new partner would end up paying the entire tab for the plant.

Sister said that, while they were interested in partnership opportunities, it had not been their reason for building the factory. They simply thought that it would help them increase business.

I had a question of my own to ask Sister.

Assuming that no partners were going to come in, how long did they expect it would take to pay back the initial investment? Sister said that they were looking at a payback of probably three years. In the United States, investments in plant and equipment were amortized over decades. Sister's short-term time horizon was more than likely going to place pricing pressure on Johnson Carter products, more so than if Sister had expected to pay off the new factory over a longer period of time. There was no particular need for extra capacity, which meant that if new customers did not soon come to the factory, the financial pressure on Johnson Carter would be great.

Chinese manufacturers liked to build shiny, new factories, if only because importers liked to see a more polished operation. Bigger importing companies, the corporate sort, were risk averse. Facilities that sparkled provided a ready-made excuse: if things ever went wrong with the supplier relationship, the importing agent could say, "who would have figured?"

Importers were always saying things like, "The factory was so clean that you could eat off the floor." They didn't understand that it was a show put on for their benefit, so that they could feel more comfortable. They also did not have a sense of how these better-looking factories raised costs.

Manufacturers that had no instinct for marketing somehow still figured out that a dog-and-pony show could widen their margins. And if that was not ironic enough, the trick was pulled on companies that completely understood that marketing was just a facade. Retailers knew well the art of throwing 10¢ more into packaging so that they could justify a retail price that was 35¢ higher. It was the same thing the factory accomplished by manufacturing products in a prettier space. Western companies insisted on low prices, but they would trade up for some sparkle.

The world had never seen anything quite like it. Chinese manufacturers built new plants, not because they needed the capacity, but so that these plants might serve as an advertisement—like some kind of billboard sign. China's banking sector enabled the phenomenon, so that industrialists could build first and worry about catching the business later.

A new factory had what real estate agents call "curb appeal." Prospective customers came and concluded that the prettier operation was also the better one. A smooth-looking operation did not mean that there would be no quality issues, though; because every single problem we faced at the original plant could just as easily occur in the new one. It wasn't as if an entirely new crew was going to be running the new factory. The plant manager who spat on the floor at the original factory would probably be doing the same thing at the new one, and workers who placed dirty fingers in otherwise sterile bottles were not suddenly going to stop the practice simply because they were working in a space with higher ceilings or because the new factory was a little brighter. In this new plant, I would still be chasing after workers to wash their hands.

It was still the same business relationship; it was the same set of shortcomings. Manufacturers kept secrets from their customers; they manipulated quality levels. They made unilateral decisions regarding product specifications. They had a blatant disregard for shared business interests, as well as for consumer safety. The new factory solved none of these issues; it only served to raise costs.

■ ■ ■

Sister was very proud of the new factory. For her, it signaled an arrival. It took a number of years, but the nature of the relationship was about to change. The construction of this new factory was the most obvious sign of the imminent reversal.

The rest of the day we tried to discuss business, but it was no use. Sister was stubborn on many points throughout the negotiations. Bernie wanted to go over an amended agreement, and there were issues related to price that needed discussing. Throughout it all, Sister heard Bernie, but she appeared disinterested. She sat with her arms folded, as if she had already made enough points that day. Sister wanted Bernie to know that she no longer needed his business.

Bernie eventually said that he wanted to call it a day. He wanted to be taken back to the hotel. He appeared disappointed and possibly preoccupied. The new factory had been too much to process. He had been blindsided by it.

On the ride back to the hotel, Bernie vented. He complained that he had helped establish King Factory in the first place. All that business about how the factory wasn't earning any profit, he didn't believe it. While he was losing money, it seemed that the factory was putting cash aside. Even if the new factory had been built with the help of partners or a cheap loan, Bernie felt that it still could not have happened without his help—and he felt that there should have been at least some gratitude for all that he had done. The factory would soon have customers willing to pay more, and Bernie was going to end up competing with them for the factory's time. And if other higher-paying customers came into the picture, Johnson Carter was less likely to get favorable pricing. Already, we were begging the factory to get orders into production, and it was likely to become even more difficult.

In China, it was nearly axiomatic that new and inexperienced factories were easier to work with than established, successful ones. Factory owners fussed and fawned over their customers at the beginning of the relationship, but once they broke out, their attitude changed. When they needed the business, it was one thing; after they had reached some of their goals, they seemed to care less. Despite all of the lip service that Chinese manufacturers gave about the value of relationships, there was no guiding principle in these arrangements, except the principle of situational leverage.

The entire business about fawning over foreign customers to gain their business was just strategy. Once factory owners achieved success, they wanted all of the privileges that came with improved status. Chinese factory owners worked hard. They put away savings and waited patiently. They portrayed themselves as poor and suffering for as long as necessary, but they looked forward to the day when they could drop the act.

But King Chemical did still need Johnson Carter's business, and this paradox was something that characterized much of the export manufacturing sector. Factory owners on the one hand gained an advantage by portraying themselves as struggling. On the other hand, they wanted respect; they wanted to let everyone—including their customers—know that they had arrived.

The two instincts worked at cross-purposes, though, and factory owners swung between the two positions in a pendulum-like fashion.

One moment they cried about how they couldn't make it; the next, they were suggesting that importers get down on their knees and thank them for the opportunity to manufacture goods in their production facilities.

China itself was involved in a similar contradictory pattern; while the nation wanted to become a major global player, there was still too much to be gained by insisting that they were just barely getting by. They wanted to be feared and respected, but at the same time they saw the advantage in being pitied.

Much of the prickly nationalism that was occasionally witnessed in China was the result of a related pattern. Tired of holding their breath, large swaths of the population cried loudly that their time had come. China as a nation had arrived. After coming to their senses and realizing such vocal expressions went against the longer-term aim of a much bigger arrival, the nationalist hordes quieted once more, their virulent expression of nationalism slipping back down into the undercurrent.

■ ■ ■

The next morning, Bernie was a different man. He was no longer upset, but rather cheery. With Bernie, you could never tell if these shifts were merely mood swings or if he was managing impressions.

"Tell them that I love the new factory," he said. Both Sister and A-Min smiled at hearing this. One of the benefits of building the new factory, so it seemed, was to give King Chemical leverage. Sister and her husband wanted Bernie to know that they no longer needed Johnson Carter. They could use the factory to attract other business. The reality was that there *were* no new customers, though, and they had invested heavily in the new plant. They needed new orders more than ever.

Bernie said that he had good news. He had made some earlier hints about a large piece of business, and now he wished to discuss the matter.

Everyone was seated and waiting for Bernie to begin the meeting. He ignored everyone in the room—Sister, her husband, me, and a worker from the office. Bernie shuffled through his papers appearing lost, like an absent-minded professor looking for his lecture notes.

"Ah!" he said. "Here it is. ... "

He dropped a thick folder on the table. He opened it and began turning up pages in a yellow legal pad. Occasionally, he shot a cautious look toward Sister and A–Min, as if he might be contemplating holding back something. While we all waited, Sister and A–Min watched Bernie closely from the edge of their seats.

Bernie turned to me and said, "Tell them, first of all, that I love the new factory. I think it's a great idea that they built it." I translated this, and there was some polite nodding at the table followed by a long pause. "Now, tell them that I have something very important to discuss with them."

Sister and A–Min waited patiently for what Bernie had to say.

"I want you to tell them that we're going to do telephone numbers."

"Telephone numbers?"

"That's right."

I didn't quite understand.

"Just tell them, just like that—*telephone numbers.*"

He looked excited, as though what he was saying would be taken as fantastic news. I had to guess at what Bernie actually meant, though. It seemed like a piece of newly discovered jargon for him.

"You are talking about volume? Orders are going to be in the seven digits, something like that?"

"Just tell them what I said. We're going to do *telephone numbers.*"

Telephone numbers in the United States had seven digits, but landline numbers at the factory had eight. Even if I could translate the phrase, the idea was not exactly the same. Instead of talking about a volume in the seven digits, it would suggest volume in the eight-digit range. I explained this to Bernie.

"Even better! Tell them! Telephone numbers!"

Sister and her husband watched the exchange between Bernie and me. All that they could tell was that Bernie looked excited, and that I appeared confused. And whatever Bernie wanted to tell them, I seemed reluctant to let them in on it.

Bernie had large orders, I explained, and they were going to be much larger than anything the factory had seen to date. Most of the time, we placed orders for hundreds of thousands of dollars worth of product at any given time. The order sizes were about to step up, and Bernie was hinting that the order sizes would be for millions of pieces—possibly tens of millions of pieces—in one go.

Smiles broke out around the room. Sister and A-Min were overjoyed in a way I had never seen. Their plan had worked, so it seemed. No sooner had they built their new factory than orders came in. It was just as every friend of theirs in manufacturing told them it would be.

These orders that would be placed at the factory, Bernie said, were going to be enormous. He would detail them soon enough, but they were almost certainly going to transform King Chemical.

Sister and her husband looked as though they had just won the lottery.

No sooner had the news sunk than Bernie turned serious.

The room became quiet as everyone waited for Bernie to speak.

"Now," he said. "My next question is very important."

I looked at Bernie, waiting for the rest of whatever he wanted translated.

"Go ahead," he said. "Please translate what I just said, that my next question is important."

Sister and A-Min heard this, and they nodded slowly. Good news was supposed to come with some kind of catch. Bernie was now probably going to use his new order as an attempt to push for further discounts or for some special terms.

Bernie raised a hand in the air to ensure that he had everyone's attention.

"Now," Bernie said. "What I need to know is, can they handle the volume?"

When they heard this concern of Bernie's, more smiles broke out, and A-Min began to laugh.

"No problem," he said in English.

Bernie appreciated the gesture, but he already knew that there was a problem. The factory was not set up to produce that much merchandise in such a short time. We could not make enough bottles fast enough, and while we could have increased the bottle-making capacity by creating new molds, we didn't have time for that either.

The factory's solution was to begin producing bottles immediately. Typically, the factory would have insisted on waiting for a deposit, but the news this time was too good, and there was no time to spare.

Bernie flew back to the United States, and he promised to transfer the funds as soon as possible, but the money for the deposit never arrived in China.

By the time the factory got the idea that these supposed million-dollar orders were not coming, it had already produced hundreds of thousands of bottles. They were labeled and stacked in an extra warehouse. It always seemed just a matter of a few more days before the money for them would come, but in the meantime the factory processed orders for other Johnson Carter customers. Since the other orders had their own labels and sometimes their own kinds of bottles, the bottles in the warehouse could not be used.

Sister came to me, sounding nicer than usual, and she asked for my help.

"Please speak with Bernie," she begged.

The deal was one that was made between her factory and Johnson Carter. This, she understood.

"But we have so many bottles in our warehouse," she said. She sounded almost tearful. Whenever I tried to mention the large number of bottles in the warehouse, Bernie always brought up something else to discuss, another piece of business that we were also working to process.

"Don't worry about those bottles," he said. "We're going to take them—eventually."

But he never did. The bottles sat in the warehouse for months.

Whenever he had problems with the factory on pricing, Bernie brought up the issue of the bottles in the warehouse. Bernie told Sister that if the factory stuck with the prices as they were initially agreed on, he would do his best to take the bottles out of the warehouse.

Bernie was going to help, but only if the factory cooperated in other areas.

It all seemed too convenient for Johnson Carter that the factory was sitting on a large volume of product that had no use anywhere else. Sister was upset about the bottles, but she was furious that they were being used in preventing her from making certain moves.

"He was supposed to take the bottles anyway," Sister said. "Bernie can't use that against us!"

But he did. And he did it well.

Around the time that this was going on, I met an American importer of furniture and home decorations. We were trading stories, and I happened to mention this one. He had supplier relationships set up all around China, and he had more experience than I did. He recognized the gambit almost immediately and said that Bernie must be a pro.

"The guys in my company call it 'getting the factory knocked up.'"

It was a crude analogy, but it described the situation pretty well. Any factory that was pregnant with raw materials that only one particular importer could use would not stray too far from that customer. Pulling the plug on the supplier relationship would now come at a cost; there would be resulting losses to the factory.

China manufacturing operated in a world where principles were in short supply, and the court systems could not be counted on to keep operators honest. In such an environment, just about the only thing that anyone could do was look for a bit of leverage. Stuffing your supplier with excess inventory was one solution. It was temporary, though, and the factory was not likely to fall for it often. It was just a matter of time before the factory repositioned itself and, once again, had the upper hand.

CHAPTER 22

Profit Zero

E merging markets are difficult places in which to do business, and South China may be among the most difficult of all. For those who wonder how they would fare at this game, I propose a scenario.

Imagine yourself landing at the Guangzhou airport late one night. You get to the curb and find a taxi driver who says he is willing to take you to your hotel for $20. It's a reasonable rate, but then the driver stops the car once you have left the airport.

You are in the middle of nowhere—no streetlights or other signs of life—and there are almost no other cars on the road. The cabbie informs you that he cannot possibly take you into town for only $20—but for $30, now, he would be more than happy to.

If you do not wish to pay the extra $10, he won't hold it against you. He will allow you to get out of the taxi where he has stopped without charging you the fare for driving you from the airport to this darkened, roadside void (because he's not a bad person, you see).

It's a multiple-choice question. What do you do?

A: Pay the additional amount the driver wants and let him take you to the hotel for $30.

B: Get out of the car and find another ride.

C: Tell the driver that you will agree to his conditions, but when you arrive at the final destination, explain that he acted in an unethical manner and pay him only the original $20.

Those who answered A—give the driver the extra money he wants—are true humanitarians, with perhaps a soft spot for bankruptcy lawyers. Ten dollars is not a lot of money in the grand scheme of things, but in percentage terms it's substantial. An importer who allows a manufacturer to swallow profitability in a last-minute pricing scheme will lose business. Last-minute price increases are a gun to the head, and anyone who gives in easily to such tactics will, sooner or later, find themselves out of business.

Now, if you answered B—get out and find another ride—you are in even more trouble. There is no one on the roads at this late hour, and whoever does pass by is not going to stop for a strange figure standing in the dark. In contract manufacturing, it can take a substantial amount of time to get a new relationship started. Getting out of the car with the hope that you will catch another ride is like telling the factory to take a hike, that you'll be taking your business elsewhere—except that there is nowhere else to go.

Your manufacturing orders need to be sent to the retailer within two or three weeks. You don't have the four to six months that it takes to set up a new supplier relationship. By the time you find a new supplier and get them up to speed, your customers have left you for the competition. In other words, you're out of business.

No, you're smarter than that. You're not falling for either A or B, and you probably believe that anyone who behaves in such a poor, unethical manner deserves to have the same thing done to him. Let's play by their rules, you're thinking; when in Rome, and all that.

Answers A and B are for China novices, you say. You went with the third option, C, telling the driver that you'll agree to a higher price. But, then, when you get to the hotel, you hand him a $20 and tell him that's all he deserves (and that he ought to be ashamed of himself).

What you have forgotten is that the taxi driver wants that last $10 a lot more than you do. He also believes that he deserves that extra 50 percent—if only because he had been so clever in the first place. Proving to him that he is not so smart registers with the driver as a loss of face, and he will hold out until the police are involved for the principle, as well as for the money.

The "polite discussion" you have at a police station lasts until 4 AM, or until you give in. The taxi driver doesn't mind the extra inconvenience, because for him it is not an unforeseen annoyance but simply a part of the job. Before he ever laid eyes on you, he planned to find a customer—preferably an unsuspecting foreigner—negotiate a price, drive halfway down the road, and then renegotiate.

Many deals that initially seem too good to be true in China, like a low price, often end in tears and disappointment.

■ ■ ■

In the wake of so many product recalls of China-made goods, many people rushed to the defense of Chinese manufacturers, saying that low prices were to blame and that importers had pressured manufacturers into making products for next to no profit.

This claim—that manufacturers were pitiable and that they had been forced—did not square with my own observations in China. For years, I watched as manufacturers willingly entered into deals where profit seemed low, but at the same time these manufacturers grew wealthy.

Factory owners cried poor but then they built fantastic capacity expansions and were personally transformed by sudden wealth. China was in the middle of the greatest economic boom in world history, as anyone knew; and while it might have been argued that some factories were prospering while others were losing their shirts, this did not seem to provide a full explanation for what was happening. Working in China manufacturing, I began to ask questions.

Why would a Chinese manufacturer willingly make a product for a dollar and sell it for only a dollar? Chinese manufacturers did not have the same concerns for covering their fixed costs as their counterparts in capitalist countries had. Could it be that this was all part of a long-term strategy and that "profit zero" was economically efficient?

■ ■ ■

One day I was standing at the front gate of King Chemical when I saw something unusual. One of the factory's trucks that was about to leave the plant appeared loaded with empty Johnson Carter bottles. Plastic bottles were typically brought into the site from a supplier, but they never left empty. These were bottles for our bubble bath line. It was one of the bottles that the factory actually produced by itself (in a small building at the edge of the property), and because the factory also filled them on the premises, it made no sense that the bottles should be going anywhere. Catching the driver on his way out, I asked where he was heading.

"To the other factory," he said. "The one by town hall."

This happened a few months before the episode involving the new, shiny factory. At that time, we were aware of no other operation, and Bernie had been concerned. "I need you to *find* that other factory," he said, "but don't tell anyone you're looking for it."

Hiring a car, I drove around the area that the driver had indicated. He had referred to a government building that was not in the city of Shantou, but in a smaller municipality closer to King Chemical. After two days of searching, I found the place in a block of buildings along a polluted irrigation canal.

It was hardly what you would call a factory, though: just a tiny building with a few workers inside. They were labeling plastic bottles by hand, with Johnson Carter labels. The odd thing about the makeshift operation was that they were preparing bottles for bubble bath, and at that time we didn't have a standing order for the product.

"What do you think they are doing there?" Bernie asked, although he already had an idea. We had been working with an agent out of Australia who sold health and beauty care products in the Middle East and throughout Southeast Asia. He had placed a few orders (several containers' worth), including, coincidentally, an unusually large volume of the bubble bath. The Aussie sent us a few orders and then vanished. Bernie tied the two events together and figured that the agent had contacted the factory directly and was ordering Johnson Carter product behind his back. Bernie was cut out of the picture, and by trading in bootlegged versions of Johnson Carter merchandise, the agent and the factory both earned slightly more for themselves.

Counterfeiting was a huge problem in China, and one of its most pervasive forms involved the manufacturer selling surplus product to unauthorized agents. For Chinese manufacturers that sold product to their primary customers for close to cost, contraband operations of this sort were an important profit center.

Sister immediately learned about my visit, of course, and was only awaiting Bernie's response. I asked him whether he wanted me to confront King Chemical about the makeshift labeling operation. Bernie surprised me by saying that he wanted the matter left alone. He didn't want to pursue it. There was no point in upsetting the factory, he said, for the profit that could be earned on just a couple of containers. Johnson Carter was shipping out hundreds of containers; to raise a fuss with the factory on such a small matter would only place Johnson Carter's broader business at risk.

American importers who conducted large volumes of business shared this attitude when it came to counterfeiting in China. Just so long as these backdoor operations did not directly interfere with an importer's core business, a small amount of such illicit activity was actually tolerable.

Johnson Carter had more business than it could handle in the United States, Bernie explained. He barely had the time to fly to China. Trying to catch and manage accounts in such far-flung markets as Dubai or Manila made no sense. "If it means so much to the factory," he said, "that they have to go and sneak around like that, let them have it."

Bernie's idea was to let the factory carry on with whatever sideline businesses they might have created. The biggest challenge was keeping prices low. If the factory was able to generate additional income through a bit of bootlegging, then the manufacturer could consider the opportunity created as one of the many benefits of working with a company like Johnson Carter.

■ ■ ■

Chinese manufacturers did not only counterfeit big-brand products. They were also involved in the counterfeiting of their customers' products, even when those products were not very well known. They copied because it was easy, or in many cases, because they were not as good at creating their own new concepts. Chinese exporters were good at manufacturing merchandise, but they lacked a marketing instinct—which was paradoxical, given their skill at stagecraft and their ability to manage impressions.

It was easy to forgive manufacturers their lack of marketing savvy, but it was more difficult to overlook the wide gap that remained in product design. China manufactured so much of what the world purchased, and yet it did not do original design. It was somewhat telling that, even at the height of the export boom, China did not have a single school of product design worth mentioning. Finding it difficult to catch design talent, manufacturers continued to rely on their customers to tell them how a product should be made.

What manufacturers lacked in originality, they made up for in their ability to copy. They were masters of mimicry, and factory owners would simply insist: "We only need your product sample." No matter whether it was a winter coat, a toaster oven, or a lamp, manufacturers could be counted on not only to reverse-engineer the product with great precision, but also to replicate it with great speed.

The ability to take an initial sample and duplicate it was the real magic that brought so many importers to China in the first place. International trade was a game that required short lead times. This was especially true in industry sectors where style and seasonal change was involved. Garments, shoes, toys, accessories, home furnishings, and even hardware—these were all sectors that were heavily influenced by frequent, often seasonal, changes in design. For companies that originated changes in product design, the goal was to move a product quickly from the drawing board to production. For the large number of importers that operated as copycats, there was a similar rush to get behind these trendsetters and to move faster than their competitors in getting their products to market.

■ ■ ■

Americans somehow imagined that Chinese factories existed to manufacture merchandise only for the United States, but this was not the view from China at all.

From China, the world appeared divided into two parts. One half of the world was made up of countries where intellectual property rights enjoyed wide protection. Because patents and trademarks were honored, there was, not coincidentally, a great deal of investment going on in the area of product design and marketing. Order sizes in this *first market*—which included the United States and Canada, as well as a number of Western European countries—tended to be larger. Chinese manufacturers favored importers from these economies, not so much because of their volume, but more for what they could lend in the way of design and marketing. Manufacturers gave considerable discounts in order to entice the first-market importers to place orders in China.

The other half of the world was made up of secondary economies where intellectual property was not well protected. In this *second market,* investment in product design was low. China still wished to do business with this other half of the world because, while its volumes were low and it did not provide much in the way of design, it tended to pay higher prices for goods out of China.

One of the features that characterized China's export market in the first decade of the twenty-first century was the way in which it took advantage of being at the very center of the globalization phenomenon. China was at a crossroads of international trade, and importers were arriving, not just from places like the United States, but also from Latin America and the Middle East—economies where trademark and copyright were not observed. Manufacturers that produced products using unique, original designs provided by importers realized that they were perfectly positioned to take advantage of the situation by moving designs from one part of the world to the other, while earning a premium in the process. This was not customer segmentation, but an arbitrage opportunity.

The United States was one of the wealthiest economies in the world, and yet Americans paid less for their products than consumers did elsewhere. It was, in fact, one of the great ironies of the global economy. Products that retailed in the United States for only $1 in a dollar store could be found in the developing world selling for $2 and $3, and it was one reason why tourists from poorer economies took their trips to the United States as shopping sprees.

Many of the manufacturers with whom I worked realized about half their revenue from just one or two customers from this first market. These customers were either from the United States or Canada, or they were large customers from leading economies such as Japan, Germany, or France. The balance of their business was made up of anywhere from 50 to 100 smaller importers from the second market. First-market importers might generate no profit at all, and a manufacturer's entire bottom line could, instead, derive solely from second-market customers.

An example in counterfeiting illustrates how some manufacturers took advantage of the arbitrage opportunity in an outright sense: A manufacturer accepts an order for 500,000 pieces from a first-market importer that produces a unique design. Rather than merely fill the order, the supplier keeps the machines running and its people working until it produces a total of 700,000 pieces. The original customer gets his order for a half-million pieces, and then the factory sells the surplus of 200,000 pieces at a considerable markup.

For manufacturers willing to engage in an illicit practice of this kind, it made sense to agree to produce the original order at close to cost. The margin that could be earned on surplus product in some categories easily exceeded 100 to 200 percent, and trying to earn a modest 10 percent profit on the original order might mean losing out to a competitor who would bid lower.

Intense competition was a major driving force in China, and any manufacturer that actually attempted to work out a profit margin for itself on an original order might find a competitor pricing the initial order at cost or sometimes below cost. The uniqueness of the product was what mattered most, and it had everything to do with how aggressively some factories quoted. Some of the smarter importers I have met, those who actually understood how the game worked in China, went out of their way to suggest that their product was unique—in other words, that they had something that might be counterfeited and sold through other channels.

In any event, Chinese manufacturers who complained that they were not earning a profit for themselves were not always telling the entire story.

■ ■ ■

Chinese manufacturers had other reasons for being in business, and they operated in a world where economic principles differed. One aspect that made manufacturing different in China was the symbiotic relationship formed between the export manufacturing sector and government.

Throughout the 1980s and into the 1990s, when the planned economy failed to create enough jobs to attain full employment, the Communist Party looked to private industry to put people to work. Entrepreneurs who could offer jobs garnered a degree of political clout with government officials. In the 2000s, manufacturers were encouraged with a different political emphasis—bringing in foreign currency. Chinese companies that were not able to earn much of a profit were still able to earn political influence, and it was with these motivations in mind that manufacturers found themselves entering into deals.

Johnson Carter might have had something to do with changing King Chemical's political standing. I understood this the day that Sister showed me a picture of her husband meeting with Communist Party officials. In China, political connections were more important; money was ephemeral, but *guanxi* was everlasting.

Chinese industrialists did not mind manufacturing merchandise for no profit, just so long as doing so created an opportunity in some other way. I was working on a furniture project when the owner of one factory explained that, even though times were tough, he had just built a new facility for $5 million. Before construction on the new facility was complete, he had a new property valuation performed, which came in closer to $10 million. The company owner said he was going to the bank to borrow the difference, and then he planned to take this extra cash and put it into various investments; he was going to invest in residential real estate.

Because they felt that they had something to gain, King Chemical offered to produce products for Johnson Carter for close to cost. And while the health and beauty care industry was not heavily influenced by fashion, there were still trends, and many new products originated in the first market. Johnson Carter was aware of new changes as they happened, because it was working closely with major retail chains. The samples that Johnson Carter sent to King Chemical went right to the factory showroom as examples of the factory's capabilities. New customers were shown these samples and asked if they would like to purchase them, or some modified version.

Chinese manufacturers did not need to steal the intellectual property of their customers to gain an advantage. Sometimes, all that was needed was access to the general idea of a new product or product line. Johnson Carter introduced all kinds of new products, including tea tree oil, body sprays, and body butter. When Johnson Carter asked King Chemical to produce a kind of antibacterial soap, the factory had to ask for details about the process. In business, information is power. Once the factory had the knowledge about how to make a particular product, it could then tell prospective buyers that it had this new capability. Johnson Carter helped push King Chemical to the head of its field by supplying it with trend information and product knowledge.

King Chemical was not involved in any real estate schemes. The company was in manufacturing for the opportunity in international trade—but even then the owners did not think of their business in such a plain, linear fashion. Chinese industrialists were characterized by their singular willingness to make major sacrifices for the hope of a benefit in the distant future, and one key strategy for manufacturers involved manufacturing goods for no profit at all.

One of the key challenges that new manufacturers faced was that importers preferred to work with suppliers that had experience. In this regard, Chinese manufacturers faced the same paradox as college graduates. Experience was needed to land a good job, but without a prior job there was no experience to be had. The factory agreed to produce merchandise at close to cost in order to prove its expertise. For the manufacturer, Johnson Carter's account was the equivalent of an unpaid internship. Once the factory learned how to make a product line that was up to export standards, the factory owners could convince other importers to take a chance with them.

King Chemical's showroom was filled with examples of products that the factory had made for Johnson Carter. Along a single wall in the showroom, Johnson Carter's modest product line appeared rather impressive, especially to those importers who came from the second market. These prospective customers did not know that Johnson Carter was a new company. An American company produced the product line and trusted this particular supplier; that was enough.

There was another reason to work with an importer for next to no profit, and that was for the opportunity to connect with the importer's customers. Business know-how did not only involve product specifications; it also involved the knowledge of who the players in the industry were. Johnson Carter was working with most of the biggest retailers in the country. This included supermarkets, drugstores, and discount chains—all of which were willing to sell soap and shampoo products made in China. The factory wanted access to these players; at the same time, retailers also got it in their heads that they could *disintermediate* or remove the importer.

When disintermediation took place, it tended to benefit the Chinese company more often. An importer who was purchasing a product at $2.25, for example, might have sold that product to a retailer for $4.40. The retailer then got the idea: *I'll go around the importer, straight* *to his supplier, and I'll pick up the same product for $2.25.* However, when the retailer went direct, it was surprised to learn that the manufacturer was not willing to sell at $2.25, but was instead trying to get the same price ($4.40) that the retailer had been paying the importer.

In the end, the factory would cut the retailer a small discount to entice the importer's customer to cut the importer out of the picture. Once the supplier and the retailer had burned their bridge, the supplier was then, of course, free to raise prices.

Johnson Carter had customers that were looking to go around it to purchase direct, but the importer held a key advantage that its customers did not; it had buying power. In the area of private label soap and shampoo products, Johnson Carter bought in larger volumes than any one of its customers. Companies that disintermediated the middleman quite often suffered, if only because they did not have as much volume. Manufacturers naturally welcomed the possibility of customers losing buying power because it gave them the chance to charge more for their products.

Manufacturers entered into business relationships where they earned no profit, knowing that they could find a profit opportunity down the road. China's nonperforming loan ratio was high, in part because lenders were passing out cheap money in support of this profit zero strategy—and it did work. Manufacturers built large facilities, and when the importers saw these factories, which looked capable and safe, they came rushing into the marketplace. It was a long-term strategy that involved patience and an inevitable reversal of fortune for the manufacturer.

While some importers were under the impression that China exported products primarily for the United States, the reality was that America took in only one-fifth of all that China made. While significant, what also had to be taken into account was that, because American companies tended to pay less for China-made products, their orders accounted for a considerably smaller proportion of profit for Chinese exporters.

American importers were important to these suppliers, not for the profit that they generated, but more because of the opportunities that they afforded.

Wal-Mart's economic significance to China is a case in point. Manufacturing products for the retail giant has rarely been a chance

for manufacturers to earn wide margins, because the company demands to purchase at the lowest prices possible. But Chinese factory
owners liked the idea of being able to say that they were a supplier
to Wal-Mart, because Wal-Mart's reputation for supplier audits was
so strong. Estimates of Wal-Mart's outsourcing volume in China were
right around $9 billion at a time when China was exporting more than
$1.2 trillion worth of goods. Wal-Mart, in other words, accounted for
less than three-quarters of one percent of all exports out of China.
The retailer's true value to the economy was in providing factories
with a reputation that they could later monetize.

Wal-Mart was moving from supplier to supplier in China, giving
new players a chance to capitalize on its reputation, and yet its purchase
volume was reported to be flat over a number of years. Wal-Mart
enjoyed the advantage of lowered prices at each new supplier, but
eventually there would be no more manufacturers willing to produce
at such a low cost for the sake of gaining a reputation. There was
value in saying that you produced for Wal-Mart, but there was nearly
as much value in saying that you had been manufacturing goods for
Wal-Mart and then told the company to take a hike.

Economies of scale did not have the same force in China as
the principle did in other markets. One reason was that commodity
prices were controlled at the national level. Raw materials sold in
large-scale quantities at almost the same price that they sold in smaller
amounts. Larger operations were more likely to be scrutinized by
government officials, which meant higher compliance costs. And then
there was the matter of manual labor still coming in cheaper, especially
when managed in an informal, local manner. These factors helped
explain why so many sectors were still fragmented, and why large
manufacturers subcontracted work out to small shops, even when
they had the capacity to do the work themselves in their shiny, new
facilities.

Johnson Carter enjoyed low prices until King Chemical took on
new customers who could pay higher prices. These smaller customers
would create volume of their own, and they set a benchmark that
the manufacturer felt Johnson Carter also had to match. It had taken
years to work out the kinks in the supplier relationship, and Johnson
Carter was less inclined to switch suppliers and start all over again.
The factory owners understood this, and it emboldened them to raise

prices further. At the end of the day, Johnson Carter would rather pay a little more than risk trying a new supplier relationship.

Commodity prices were on the rise, but what was changing even faster was the attitude of factory owners. American importers were feeling the pinch more than any other group, and this had everything to do with how manufacturers were no longer interested in giving their first-market importers a major break. Chinese manufacturers wanted the price that United States consumers were paying to be more in line with what consumers were paying elsewhere around the globe. Taking manufacturing orders to China had once appeared a bargain, but that advantage was slipping as Chinese manufacturers saw fewer reasons to give American importers such significant discounts.

Chinese manufacturers found that they did not need their first-market importers as much. After a few years of working with these importers, the bulk of know-how had been transferred. And volume from second-market importers was significant enough that the first-market importer made up an increasingly smaller percentage of revenue. All of these things added to pricing pressure.

American importers who came to China did business in a manner that was more straightforward. They bought a product for a dollar, expecting to sell it for two. Chinese suppliers, on the other hand, sold a product for a dollar when it cost them a dollar to make. They did this because they wanted to catch the customer's customer, or they were running a real estate play, or they were looking to build up important personal connections with government officials. Chinese manufacturers did not think in a linear fashion; they saw business as multidimensional. Importers were thinking checkers, while manufacturers were playing chess.

American importers who did business in China scratched their heads and asked: "How do they do it?" This was what Bernie had asked me on his first trip to China, and the answer was made clear. The deal that King Chemical offered was not much different than a no-money-down special. There was naturally a catch, but importers figured that they would somehow come out ahead—and they even felt sorry for their suppliers when they were offered these too-good-to-be-true enticements.

Importers streamed into China. They trained their suppliers and did not realize that it would end with their manufacturer in the driver's seat. Chinese suppliers practiced a kind of economic jujitsu, which entailed using an importer's own greed against itself. It was straight out of Sunzi's *The Art of War,* and it only occurred to importers much later—if it occurred to them at all—that their suppliers knew from the very start where they planned to be at the endgame.

■ ■ ■

When the United States pushed for greater levels of bilateral trade with China in the 1990s, it was under the assumption that China would become easier to work with as it rose to prosperity. If the importer-manufacturer relationship has shown anything, though, it is that the opposite is true. As Chinese manufacturers have grown bigger and wealthier, they have managed to find—and to exercise—more leverage in their relationships with foreign buyers.

The manufacturer-importer relationship can be seen as an allegory for the future of relations between the United States and China, and one of the challenges going forward will be learning how to engage China. Some leaders may feel that they have only the political past to use as a guide; but in fact, they have many microcosmic examples to take from business, and in those models can be found an appreciation for a variety of strategies and tactics.

When it comes to free trade, taking a backward step is many orders of magnitude less desirable than not moving forward toward increased levels of openness. During the Clinton Administration, when Most Favored Nation status for China was debated in Congress, there was a chance for the United States to hold out for political and economic reform in China, but the opportunity was lost.

Improved structural conditions made possible then might have more appropriately set the stage for stability going forward. Instead, American politicians and business leaders rushed headlong into greater levels of interdependency with China, a nation whose reliability is questionable.

This decision, to fling open wide the doors of trade with China— before we were ready, before China was ready, before we understood what we were getting into; an action motivated by our own greed— this decision more than anything else was the one thing related to China that was truly poorly made.

AFTERWORD

Just after *Poorly Made in China* was first published in the spring of 2009, I was invited to an hour-long radio interview on WFAE, an NPR-affiliated radio station broadcasting from Charlotte, North Carolina. At one point in the interview, the program's host, Mike Collins, asked me a question: Why had I written this book?

It had been months since I submitted the original manuscript to my publisher, and I'd only recently come back to the United States from East Asia. I wasn't accustomed to the formality of such an interview, and for whatever reason, I found myself caught off guard. Having spent the better part of two years working on the book, you'd think I would have had the answer to such a question reduced to a sound bite, but I was lost, and unable to verbalize my reason for putting pen to paper, I fumbled a response that fell flat.

Since then, I've had plenty of time to reflect on the motivations for book writing. There are many, of course, who write for money; others write in an attempt at fame. In my case, while paid an advance, it took far longer to write the book than expected, and in fact I had to draw from personal savings to finish the project. I am not a journalist, and the book was not a career move. The time spent writing was time spent away from work.

As far as fame goes, any attention that the book received caused me only anxiety. Because of the nature of this book—and particularly because of its sharp title—I worried that I might never work in China again, or that, if allowed back into the country, potential clients would see the book only as a liability. Such fears were already by then materializing in the form of cold receptions and unanswered e-mails.

After the radio interview, just outside his recording studio, Mike thanked me for coming by, and then he asked me again the same question—though this time in an off-the-record sort of way. The benefits of putting out a book like *Poorly Made in China* seemed so obviously dubious, and he was wanted to know: Why *had* I gone to the trouble?

I paused for the briefest moment and reflected. I knew what he was getting at now. With the pressure of the interview behind me, I forced a weak smile and in a private way told him, "Well, I guess *someone* had to write the book." He gave me a memorable look of disappointment and regret, telling me that he wished I had said exactly that while we were on the air.

Despite my weak interview skills, I did what I could to give the book a push in the months that followed. There were other interviews, most of them also local in nature, and the book managed to pick up a few positive reviews along the way, also from minor press. And then, about nine months after publication, the book caught a lucky break. *The Economist* and a couple of other national publications called *Poorly Made in China* one of the year's best books. It was an honor, and it helped lift the title into the limelight. And then came the critics—the informal kind, anyway.

No matter where I went, people I met were giving me their yeah-but explanations for why the book had been distinguished in that way. No one said they didn't like the book, but it was somehow suggested that it was chosen as a best-of-year book mostly because it was topical. China had been the source of so many quality scandals, and people were merely following up on a subject. "You were in the right place at the right time," I heard, the implication being that the book might not have even been noticed if there had been other books on this one topic.

Related comments made me realize something that had until then eluded me completely, that mine was the only book published that tried to make sense of China's quality challenge. How strange, I thought. In almost any news cycle, a large number of headlines on any subject will spur at least a few book titles some 12 to 18 months down the road. Here it has been over three years since China's first product scandals, quality problems out of China persist, and yet we have only one published book.

I have had no problem with the right-place-right-time comments, because it was true: I did work in manufacturing, and it gave me something to write about. These belittlers, though, made it seem that I was the only one working in China manufacturing. What about the thousands of other foreigners who worked there, as well? And what about the much larger number of Chinese—tens of millions, literally— who were also working in industry? Surely more than a few have been privy to the industry's deepest and darkest secrets.

There ought to be a sense of pride over having been alone in publishing such a book, but that's not the feeling at all. Quite the opposite: I find it disturbing that so many voices are silent. There is a sense that more people could write, but that few do because there is a general reluctance to cover China in any critical fashion. There is a presumption, perhaps not without basis, that it is unwise to write negatively on the place; China's government is authoritarian and heavy-handed, and God only knows what might happen.

Since the book came out, I have often been asked whether I've been allowed back into the country. The simple answer is that I have—and why not? I continue to work as a go-between for U.S. companies that are doing their manufacturing in China. My work as a middleman helps to facilitate the flow of U.S. dollars into an economy that benefits from such resources. The millions of dollars that I help bring into the country each year ultimately serve to further support China's Communist Party.

Make no mistake, though: China isn't throwing any parades for this author. It took my publisher many months to get customs to approve importation of the English version of this book, and we have yet to find a publisher on the mainland who is willing to acquire foreign rights to have this book translated for the local market.

Elsewhere around Asia, publishers have enthusiastically picked up foreign rights. Deals have been signed in Vietnam, India, and Indonesia. Even Hong Kong and Taiwan jumped on board with an acquisition of rights for traditional Chinese characters. But for simplified Chinese, a language version that would have served the mainland, there have been no takers.

I personally got involved with the effort to find a publisher in China, speaking with one publishing house that was introduced to me by a writer friend. There was significant initial interest in the book based on the reviews, but then the publisher got cold feet. I was told point-blank that a book such as mine would be too much of a publishing risk, because of the possibility that it might attract the wrong sort of attention.

The editor who was responsible for reviewing my book never made it past the first few pages, as far as I could tell. In a note from the editor, I was told about concerns over certain "sensitive issues" (like my use of the term *sweatshop* on page 2).

Among the tougher questions I've been asked since this book's publication is, especially on the quality front: Haven't things gotten better? It would be wonderful to say that we are out of the woods, but what do we say about a place where so much self-censorship goes on?

Asked to predict whether there will be further quality scandals out of China, I don't take a guess but instead offer my guarantee that there will be. Nothing like real progress can be made in a place where publishers fear to publish, where people fear to speak.

ACKNOWLEDGMENTS

This book was made possible with the generosity and help of many. While I take responsibility for any problems within the narrative, my deepest and heartfelt thanks go out to the following individuals who devoted their time, extended a courtesy, or were otherwise supportive of my efforts: Tom Alain, Jason Bernstein, Brooke Eplee, Anatole Faykin, Jeffrey Hurwitz, Bennett Hymer, Handol Kim, Scott Klepper, Ariel Kronman, Martin Lakin, Rachel Lakin, Jim Llewellyn, Hugo Restall, Benjamin Robertson, Marianna Salz, Steve Sher, Benjamin Schwall, Gabriella Wortmann.

The unpredictability with which the People's Republic of China responds to even the most oblique criticisms of affairs within its borders has caused many to act accordingly. There were numerous others who supported this book, but who asked that their names not be mentioned on this page, or anywhere else. These individuals included both Chinese as well as foreign nationals.

No individual should have to fear the consequences of expressing him- or herself, or of supporting those who do for that matter. Free speech ought to be a universal right, especially as discussion and debate are good for society. By choosing to remain in the shadows, my anonymous supporters have helped this book make one last but important point—that certain other things must also change before there is any hope for a world in which China plays a larger, leading role.